SAMS
Teach Yourself
Today

e-College

e-College

Applying for college, taking classes, and financing your education online

George Lorenzo

SAMS

201 West 103rd Street, Indianapolis, Indiana 46290

Sams Teach Yourself e-College Today

International Standard Book Number: 0-672-31978-0

Library of Congress Catalog Card Number: 11-105554

Printed in the United States of America

First Printing: September 2000

03 02 01 00   4 3 2 1

Trademarks

Warning and Disclaimer

Acquisitions Editor
Betsy Brown

Development Editor
Alice Martina Smith

Managing Editor
Charlotte Clapp

Project Editor
Dawn Pearson

Copy Editors
Mary Ellen Stephenson
Jason Hicks

Indexer
Eric Schroeder

Proofreaders
Kimberly Campanello
Tony Reitz

Team Coordinator
Amy Patton

Interior Designer
Gary Adair

Cover Designer
Jay Corpus

Production
Ayanna Lacey
Heather Hiatt Miller

Dedication

Dedicated to all the high school, college, and university students, faculty, and staff of the 21st Century.

Table of Contents

PART IV Going to College Without Setting Foot on Campus

Acknowledgments

Thanks go out to my wife, Gabriele, for supporting me in all my chosen endeavors. Her encouragement and sincere interest kept me on pace to meet a tight deadline.

A great big thank you to my daughter, Lisa, and my son, Salvatore. As I pounded away on my computer keyboard in my basement study, Lisa and Sal would pass by and ask what chapter I was on. They gave me an unbelievable amount of energy to complete this book on schedule.

A hearty thanks to the nice folks at Macmillan: Acquisitions Editor Betsy Brown, who gave me my first shot at a book; Development Editor Alice Martina Smith, a skilled editor who is a real pleasure to work with; and Copy Editor Mary Ellen Stephenson, a talented professional.

Finally, a big thank you goes out to Dan Carnevale at the Chronicle of Higher Education.

INTRODUCTION

Writing this book became a labor of love as I journeyed for days on end through cyberspace, finding one higher education-related Web site after another. Indeed, it's a huge e-world out there, with plenty of excellent Web sites.

I can assure you that I have searched the World Wide Web for the best sites that provide information and services for the college bound. Basically, this book will save you a lot of valuable time. I've done all the work for you. Just follow my lead, and you'll obtain all the information you need, and more, about using the Web to help you find the college or university that is right for you. One glance at the Table of Contents will give you a good idea about the wealth of information available on the Web for the college-bound student.

Unfortunately, as the Web grows, so does the amount of useless information available on the Web. As more people learn how to make Web sites, more despicable acts of computer piracy will occur, and more totally inane Web content will materialize on our computer screens. It can be difficult to separate the good from the bad. The first impression of a well-designed home page can be deceiving, and it's often not until you really get into a site's content that you learn about its true mission—to take your hard-earned money. By then, unfortunately, you have already wasted some of your valuable time. With that in mind, I have tried to show you as many Web sites as possible that exist only to give you reliable and useful information at no cost to you. Believe it or not, there are many such valuable sites in cyberspace. Yes, there is a very positive side to the World Wide Web.

A vast universe of networked knowledge awaits you every time you connect to the Web. You can take full advantage of it by seeing the Web as a valuable advisor and assistant that sits on your desktop, waiting for its e-College master.

My goal in writing this book was to make the entire higher education search process as easy as possible for you. I believe I accomplished that, and I wish you, dear reader, all the luck in the world in accomplishing your higher education goals.

Who Should Use This Book

Sams Teach Yourself e-College Today was written primarily for college-bound students who want to use the World Wide Web to assist them with finding, choosing, applying to, paying for, and taking higher education classes online at the right higher education institution.

In addition to being a handbook for college-bound students, this book is a highly useful tool for the parents of college students, who in most cases are the primary sponsors of their children's education.

Admissions and financial aid counselors at both high school and college levels, as well as other secondary or postsecondary professionals, can also use this book as a valuable tool and time-saving device that can help them help the college bound.

Finally, prospective students of all ages can use *Sams Teach Yourself e-College Today* as a catalyst to a lifetime of learning that can easily be discovered on the World Wide Web.

PART I

Using the Internet to Find the Best College For You

CHAPTER 1

Finding College and University Web Sites and Guidebooks Online

Welcome to the world of higher education on the World Wide Web. This is a large and rapidly growing online world that is easy to get lost in. It is also a very kind and helpful world full of online destinations that will help you find the right college.

In this first chapter, we will cover some of the basics of where to find college and university Web sites and how to move through them. The goal is to help you understand how to navigate these Web sites so that you can see, from the online perspective, what colleges and universities have to offer.

You will be introduced to some of the leading Web portals to higher education, and you'll see how these portals can take you through directories of college and university Web sites. By visiting these portals, you'll also see what kind of valuable services they offer for the up-and-coming college student.

While you're touring around all these Web sites, you might want to prep your computer for some of the audio and video content you'll be introduced to. In case your computer isn't already up to speed, you'll learn how to make your system multimedia friendly by downloading appropriate files from the Web.

Finally, if it's hard-copy printed matter you want, we'll show you where to go to preview the abundance of college guidebooks that can be purchased online.

What You'll Learn in This Chapter:

- ▶ The basics of college and university Web sites.
- ▶ How to use Web portals to find directories of college and university Web sites.
- ▶ What you need to view multimedia content on the Web.
- ▶ Where to find college guidebooks online.

It's Dot *edu*, not Dot *com*

All degree-granting institutions of higher learning have Web sites, but their URLs (also called domain names) are not *dot coms*. (As a reminder, URL stands for uniform resource locator and is a Web site's global address.) The URL suffix (also called the TLD for Top Level Domain) for colleges and universities worldwide is *.edu*.

All *.edu*'s Are Not Created Equal:

Just because a Web site address has an *.edu* suffix does not mean that it's a fully accredited institute of higher learning. The process of registering URLs is not completely regulated today, so there are some deceptive *.edu*'s on the Web.

You can easily find the Web site for your college or university of choice by entering the school's name into your favorite search engine. You'll see the *.edu* suffix in your search results.

What to Expect

If you're doing a deep search through many college and university Web sites, you'll find that some of these sites are not the easiest to navigate. These Web sites are products of Web development teams; no two teams are alike, and each has its own views on how a site should work. Be prepared to see enough differing Web site navigational features to make your eyes cross. However, most higher education Web sites are really a credit to their creators with easy-to-navigate characteristics and highly creative and eye-catching graphics and images. Let's check out one that looks very professional: Ohio University at *www.ohiou.edu*.

The Ohio University Web site is a good example of a graphically pleasing and well-composed site with lots of easy-to-find information.

Notice that everything you need to know about Ohio University can be accessed from its home page. Let's take a brief tour through one important area of the site that's of interest to us.

1. Go to *www.ohiou.edu* and click the Prospective Students heading.

2. Click the General Information link to see a brief profile of the university.

3. Click any of the links near the top of the page, including a Facts and Figures link and a Parents Guide link, for more detailed information about Ohio University.

▼ **Try It Yourself**

▲

By cruising around the Facts and Figures and Parents Guide sections, you can access enough data to become an authority on Ohio University in no time at all. That's the beauty of the Web.

Of course, there's plenty more to the Ohio University Web site in addition to what you just experienced. In the Prospective Students section, for instance, there are links to just about everything you'd need to know about attending Ohio University, including how to get admitted, finding financial aid, where to live, information about college life, and much more. There's even a button that will take you to a long list of links to Ohio University students' personal Web sites (more on this in Chapter 3, "Communicating with Undergraduates and College-Bound Peers"). By surfing through the student Web sites, you may get a good view of what campus life is really like at this university.

Did you know that every first-year residence hall room at Ohio University comes with its own computer, printer, and network connection? This is a rapidly growing trend at all college and university residence halls. To the new college student, this means that you'll be able to take advantage of online-based information and services that will help you do research, find jobs, plan your future career, have fun, and even take some of your classes from the privacy of your room if that suits you. But we're getting ahead of ourselves. After all, you haven't even decided which school you want to attend. So, let's dig up some more information by finding more college and university Web sites to examine.

Enhance Your Web Experience

To learn everything you need to know about surfing the Web, check out *Sams Teach Yourself the Internet*. Even experienced Web surfers will find lots of helpful hints and advice in this book to enhance their Web-searching and information-digging techniques.

Web Portals to Higher Education

Now that you've taken a basic look at one well-made university Web site, you can find some Web portals that will link you to many college and university Web sites and thus make your search for the right school less cumbersome.

What's a Web Portal?

A Web portal is a Web site that provides access or a doorway to other Web sites. Portals also usually offer a large selection of other resources and services such as online shopping, free email, newsletter and e-zine subscription services, online discussion boards, and compendiums of information about various topics of interest.

Incidentally, to find the definition of just about any Internet-related term, go to *www.pcwebopedia.com*, known as "the only online dictionary and search engine you need for computer and Internet technology."

Faster Connection for Better Viewing

The best way to view and hear audio and video content on the Web is through a high-speed Internet connection. Cable modem and Digital Subscriber Lines (DSL) are currently the fastest connections you can get for your home, if they are available in your area. Your school or workplace might have a T1 or T3 phone line, both of which are also good high-speed connections.

Most portals to higher education are really all-in-one stops for locating more information than you'll ever need in relation to finding, choosing, and paying for the right college or university. Higher education Web portals are growing in numbers and changing rapidly, with each new portal better than the last as they all compete to become the leading Web portal for college students and their parents.

Touring CampusTours.com

The first portal we'll visit is *www.campustours.com*.

The CampusTours.com Web site has options unlike any other site. This site enables you to see still photos or see and hear video clips of the schools you choose, as well as link to school Web sites. Using this site is a great lesson in and of itself about what types of interactive audio and video technology is available on the Web. So bear with us as we try to explain how all these high-tech, multimedia Web features work.

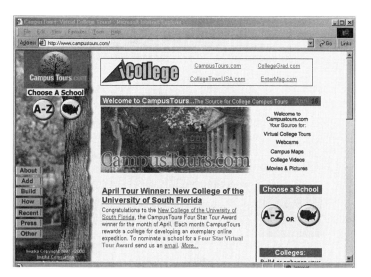

CampusTours.com is an online source for virtual college tours, interactive campus maps, college Webcams, and links to college and university Web sites.

You can start by clicking one of two circles—either A-Z or the USA map icon—that appear under the Choose a School heading. Note that this heading and the circles are conveniently located on both sides near the top of the home page Use the A-Z option by keying in the name of the school. Use the map option if you want to see lists of schools by states. After you've arrived at a school's listing, you'll have anywhere from one to six options to choose from, depending on the school. These options include Virtual Tour, Webcam, Interactive Map, Videos or Shockwave Movies, Campus Pictures or QTVR, and College Web site. Here's a brief explanation of each option:

- Click the Virtual Tour link by a school's listing, and you should be taken to that portion of its Web site that features a series of still photos with text descriptions of the campus grounds and buildings. These tours are not audio or video intensive.

- Click the Webcam link to see live images, continuously updated still images, or recently taken images of anything and everything on the college campus (usually the most picturesque views). A Webcam is a digital camera hooked up to a computer that hosts a Web page. Webcams enable viewers to see live images over the Internet. But beware: Many of these Webcams might not be operational or might show very choppy video images. Still, just having this option is a good thing for a university's Web site because, in due time, increased bandwidth will help eliminate such annoyances.

• Click the Interactive Map link to be taken to that portion of a school's Web site that shows a map image of the entire campus with links to images of exact campus locations and buildings.

• Click the Videos or Shockwave Movies link to see additional links to that portion of a school's Web site offering full-blown audio and video presentations about the campus. Each college Web site uses different file formats to accomplish these presentations. To ensure that any or all of these formats will work on your computer, you'll have to install various utilities available from other Web sites. (See "The World of Multimedia on the World Wide Web," later in this chapter.)

• Click the Campus Pictures or QTVR link to view either PICS images or QuickTime Virtual Reality images. PICS are photos that usually have internal links to other photos. A QTVR is a panoramic picture format you can view only if you have the QuickTime software installed on your computer.

• Click the College Web site link for the easiest and most expedient way to find more information about a particular college or university. This link takes you directly to the Web site of the chosen institution.

The World of Multimedia on the World Wide Web

When it comes to video and audio content on the Web, the abundance of terms in use can be confusing. Four of the primary video/audio programs (also called browser plug-ins) you should be aware of are Windows Media Player, QuickTime, RealPlayer, and Macromedia Shockwave/Flash. These programs/plug-ins—and the file formats they can handle—are the most common multimedia applications in use today. If you want to experience all the sights and sounds that many institutions provide online, you'll need some or all of these applications installed on your computer.

You'll need a video card and sound card with speakers to see and hear the audio/video formats you'll encounter at these Web sites. You'll also have to download and install the necessary programs to run multimedia files. Finally, if you can afford it, get the fastest Internet connection available in your area so that you can play video/audio content with the least amount of interruption.

If you already have the following video/audio programs installed on your computer, you can skip this section and go on to "Embarking on a Quest."

If you don't yet have these programs, here's where to go to download free versions of these four commonly used and popular video/audio applications:

- **Windows Media Player.** Most versions of Windows 98 include the latest version of this program. If you don't have Windows 98, go to *www.microsoft.com/windows/ mediaplayer/en/default.asp* and follow the instructions for downloading and installing the latest version of Windows Media Player.

- **QuickTime.** Go to *www.apple.com/quicktime/download* and scroll down to the box labeled Download the Free Player. Before clicking the Download Quicktime button at the bottom of the box, you'll have to supply your email address, first and last name, and what kind of operating system you have. The download will give you an installer that you'll save to your hard drive. When the download is complete, click the installer and follow the steps to install the QuickTime player on your computer.

- **RealPlayer.** Go to *www.real.com/player*, scroll down to the bottom of the page, and click the RealPlayer 7 Basic is our free player link. (Note: You might see a number higher than 7, which means that a newer version has come out since this has been written.) You'll have to fill out a more extensive form than the QuickTime form. Fill out all the required information and click the gray button labeled Download Free RealPlayer 7 Basic. Follow the installation instructions outlined in the preceding QuickTime bullet.

Keep Your Computer Updated

Your computer should be equipped with the latest operating system, as well as the most up-to-date version of Internet Explorer or Netscape Navigator, to effectively play video/audio files.

- **Macromedia Shockwave/Flash**. Go to
  www.macromedia.com/shockwave/download. If you have
  Windows 95/98/NT/2000, click the Auto Install Now animated button under Step 1. Make sure that you carefully read
  and click through all the pop-up dialog boxes you see.
  Macromedia installs the program for you. You'll know that
  your installation was successful when you see a short
  Macromedia promotional movie playing on your screen.

Embarking on a Quest

Some of the other Web portals to higher education are not so multimedia intensive as CampusTours.com and might be easier for
your Internet connection to handle. One of these portals can be
found at *www.embark.com*, which claims to be able to help you
"find, apply, and get into the right program for you."

Before using Embark.com's many services, you might want to
become a registered member. Membership is free. Just click on
the Register Now link in the right sidebar and fill out the necessary information. As a registered member, you'll have easy access
to Embark.com's tools that will enable you to apply to schools
online, get recruited by colleges and universities, participate in
discussion boards, conduct a career or scholarship search, and
more.

For the purpose of simply finding links to college and university
Web sites, go to the section titled Get into College and click the
Find and Apply to the Right School for You link.

Go to the section titled Choose the Right School and click the
Look Up School link. You'll be presented with four options:
Schools with Online Applications, Matchmaker Search (we'll
cover this feature in Chapter 2, "Choosing the Right College"),
College Search by Region, and Alphabetized List: Detailed
College Descriptions.

As a hypothetical student who is not quite sure where he or she
would like to go to college, click the College Search by Region
option, which enables you to browse through information about
schools by state and by American schools located in foreign
countries (including, for the truly adventurous, Bulgaria, Cayman

Islands, Guam, and Egypt). After you have picked your geographical region, you'll be supplied with a list of schools located there along with five options represented by icons: View Details, Apply Online, Send Inquiry, Strategy, and School's Web site.

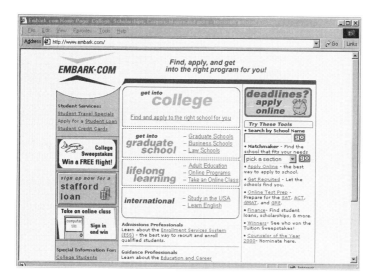

Embark.com offers plenty of services to help students find the right college online.

- Click the View Details icon to get quick access to specific information about the school broken down into six primary pages: School Description, Admissions, Curriculum, Student Body, Student Life, and Cost/Financial Aid. Each page is further divided into a number of subcategories.

- Click the Apply Online icon to access a school's online application. (Much more detailed information on the application process can be found in Chapter 4, "Applying Online.")

- Clicking the Send Inquiry icon enables you to electronically request more information from the school you've chosen.

- Click the Strategy icon to learn about the school's admission criteria along with a ranking on the importance of each admission requirement. You'll also see other admissions statistics, such as number of applications received and number of applicants accepted.

- Finally, the School's Web Site icon makes the home page of the school's Web site just a click away.

Another Web portal to higher education can be found within the expansive *www.about.com* Web site, where clicking the Education link will send you to a bountiful list of higher-education-related Web pages. Click the College Admissions link under College/University to go to a section brought to you by an About.com expert guide.

The College Admissions section in the Education area of the About.com Web site features a directory of links to colleges and universities located around the globe.

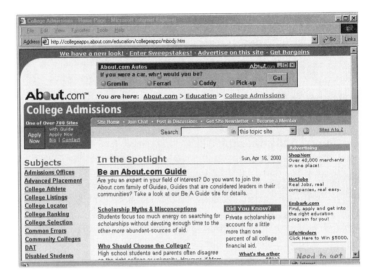

What's It All About?

The About.com Education section at *http://home.about.com/education/index.htm* covers a lot of topics of interest including adult/continuing education, primary/secondary education, art, philosophy, religion, life and earth sciences, history, physical and computer sciences, languages, literature, and social sciences.

You'll need to know the name of the school you want to link to—or at least the first letter of the school—to get a view of that institution's Web site. Just click either U.S. Colleges & Universities of the World or International Colleges & Universities. You'll get an alphabet-driven menu that will take you to the Web site of the college of your choice.

Search Engine Directories

Most of the major search engines have education sections that allow you to search for college and university Web sites. Two very good search engines happen to be *www.yahoo.com* and *www.snap.com*.

From Yahoo!'s home page you can access an extensive directory of links to colleges and universities worldwide. Click the subheading College and University under the Education heading.

You'll be taken to a page with more subheadings. Click the Colleges and Universities link to go to a page listing about 100 countries worldwide, including such remote places as Kazakhstan, Mongolia, and Zambia. Click a country and, voilà!, there are links to every college and university located within its boundaries. (Zambia had one university, which is called, you guessed it, the University of Zambia.)

Snap.com's navigational route for finding links to school Web sites is somewhat similar to Yahoo!'s. Click the subheading Colleges and Universities, under the Education heading to open a page where you can choose to search by state or international venue, among other categories. The international category is divided into various regions and continents, and we could not find the University of Zambia. (That country, in case you did not know, is located in the southern region of Africa and was formerly called Northern Rhodesia.)

If none of these Web portals and search engine directories strike your fancy, here's our short list, in alphabetical order, of other Web sites for linking to college and university Web pages. These sites also contain loads of helpful information for the prospective undergraduate student.

For a Deep Search
Complete information about search engines and links to every major search engine in cyberspace can be found at *http:// searchenginewatch. com.*

- All About College—*www.allaboutcollege.com*
  This Web site provides thousands of links to colleges and universities categorized under the following geographical areas: Africa, Asia, Australia, Canada, Europe, Mexico, South America and the United States.

- The College Board—*www.collegeboard.org*
  Makers of the SAT and PSAT tests, the College Board Web site is a must-see site for the college-bound student and his or her parents. This Web site is referred to frequently throughout this book.

- The College Bound Network—*www.collegebound.net*
  Ramholtz Publishing, Inc, publishers of *College Bound Magazine* and other higher-education-related publications, created this Web site in 1997. The site claims to be "devoted entirely to college-bound teens."

- Collegenet—*www.collegenet.com*
  You can apply online to 500 colleges and universities through
  Collegenet's application service. This site also has a scholar-
  ship search service called *Mach25*.

- College Prep 101—*http://collegeprep.okstate.edu*
  Created and maintained by a group of professionals at
  Oklahoma State University, this site offers plenty of benefi-
  cial advice for students listed under three primary categories:
  Pre-College, At College, and This-n-That.

- College Xpress—*www.collegexpress.com*
  This site is brought to the college-bound student by Carnegie
  Communications, publishers of *Private Colleges &
  Universities* magazine. College Xpress has a college search
  function along with a section on admissions and a financial
  aid section.

- The Education Network—*www.edunetwork.com*
  Tagged as "your complete source for college selection and
  financing," the Education Network has plenty of information
  on searching and planning for your higher education, as well
  as advice and tips related to applying for financial aid.

- FishNet: The College Guide—*www.jayi.com*
  FishNet has an interesting function titled Dear Admissions
  Guru. You can also access a college search service and link to
  areas titled Get Money for College, Read About College, and
  Get the Common App.

- GoCollege—*www.gocollege.com*
  GoCollege's online services include a GoCollege Search, a
  GoScholarship Search, GoTest Yourself function for practic-
  ing the ACT and SAT test, a GoAcademics guidance counselor section, and more.

- National Center for Educational Statistics: IPEDS COOL
  Search—*www.nces.ed.gov/ipeds/cool/Search.asp*
  This is one of our favorite Web sites for helping students find
  and choose the right college. (See the "Sites That Help You
  Choose" section in Chapter 2, "Choosing the Right
  College.")

- Peterson's College Quest—*www.collegequest.com*
  After registering to become a College Quest member, you'll
  have access to school profiles, tools for managing admissions
  and financial aid, and Peterson's database of 800,000 scholarships and awards.

- Powerstudents.com—*www.powerstudents.com*
  The three primary areas of this site are called Today in High
  School, Today in College, and Today in Jobs. You can also go
  to the pull-down menu titled Read More from Our Partner
  Sites to link to many other college-related Web sites.

- The Princeton Review—*www.review.com*
  Another must-see stop for the college bound, the Princeton
  Review, who is best known for their standardized test-preparation services, also provides admissions, scholarship, career
  information, and much more at this Web site.

- *U.S. News* Online—*www.usnews.com/usnews/edu*
  Another great Web site, *U.S. News* Online's .edu Web division has the highly regarded annual college rankings along
  with numerous articles, services, links, and advice to help
  you find, choose, and pay for the right college.

Finally, as you have seen, most of these portals and directories
provide a lot more than links to college and university Web sites.
The upcoming chapters cover many of the services provided by
these Web sites for the college bound.

Finding Guidebooks to Higher Education on the Web

There are books, books, and more books about finding, choosing,
and applying to the right college. You'll find information and
advertisements about them at the higher education Web portals
and, of course, at all the Web-based booksellers.

We found a list of "college survival guides" in the campus bookstore Special Features section of *www.collegeview.com* (the direct
Web address to this particular section is
www.collegeview.com/bookstore/special.html). We liked this special feature because it provided long excerpts from about eight of
these guides.

Check Out Bricks-and-Mortar Bookstores

Although the online
booksellers will
point you in the
right direction for
higher education
guidebooks, check
out your local book-
store's college refer-
ence section for
college guidebooks
that you may not
find on the Web.

There are also college guides available for free on the Web, one of which is published by the ERIC Review at *www.accesseric.org*, otherwise known as the Educational Resources Information Center, which is a branch of the National Library of Education and the U.S. Department of Education. This 60-page college guidebook, *The Path to College: Making Choices That Are Right for You*, can be obtained for free in either an HTML version or a PDF version. To order it, go to *www.accesseric.org/resources/ericreview/vol5no3/index.html*.

What's PDF?

Portable Document Format (PDF) is a file format developed by Adobe Systems. According to Adobe Systems, PDF "preserves all the fonts, formatting, colors, and graphics of any source document, regardless of the application and platform used to create it. PDF files are compact and can be shared, viewed, navigated, and printed exactly as intended by anyone with a free Adobe Acrobat Reader." You can download the Acrobat reader by going to *www.adobe.com/products/acrobat/readstep.html*.

Another free college guidebook can be found in the U.S. Department of Education Web site (*www.ed.gov*) at *www.ed.gov/pubs/GettingReadyCollegeEarly*. This 16-page booklet, which can also be viewed in either HTML or PDF format, is titled *Getting Ready For College Early: A Handbook for Parents of Students in the Middle and Junior High School Years*.

If you're seeking larger, all-encompassing guidebooks covering almost any topic you can think of in relation to going to college, you can always go to *www.amazon.com*, start a **college guides** keyword search, and find more than 1,400 titles listed for easy perusal. The same holds true for the other behemoth Web-based bookseller, Barnes and Noble at *www.bn.com*.

You might be interested in the less cumbersome, easier-to-digest list of recommended college guidebooks, all linked to Amazon.com, at *www.quintcareers.com/teen_books.html#college*.

Wrapping It Up

All the Web surfing in the world cannot replace an actual physical visit to a college campus to get a feel for what it's really like to live in the non-real world of college. That's an oxymoron.

Remember that word; it might be on your SAT test. (See Chapter 6, "Your Guide to the PSAT, SAT, and ACT Tests", plus the section on college visits in Chapter 2, "Choosing the Right College.")

All kidding aside, it's good to check out as many Web sites as possible to get an idea about the basic nature of a school, but the Web cannot and should not replace a real live visit to the institution. Remember, all these college Web sites have the right to provide the content they want you to read.

Nonetheless, we have given you a well-researched and tested guide to touring college and university Web sites that can be a catalyst for reaching your final destination, which is, obviously, the absolutely right school for you.

In brief, here's what was covered in this opening chapter:

- How to get a feel for what a decent college and university Web site looks like.

- How to find various audio and video programs on the Web for viewing multimedia presentations through your Internet connection.

- How to use Web portals and directories to higher education so that you can link to numerous school Web sites.

- Where to find free college guides on the Web, as well as where to go to purchase college guidebooks on the Web.

CHAPTER 2

Choosing the Right College

Now that you know how to find college and university Web sites, you can start making some informed decisions concerning where you'll eventually end up spending your college days. This chapter shows you where to find more helpful information on the Web about choosing the college or university that is right for you.

This chapter begins with information about how schools are classified. What makes a school a college? What makes it a university? What's the difference between a private school and a public school?

We'll visit some Web sites that help narrow down your choices by providing information about a school's tuition costs and more. We'll also visit a Web site that enables you to actually submit a bid for the amount of tuition you're willing to pay (applicable to only certain private institutions).

We'll talk a little about community colleges and how they might be the right alternative for some students.

Finally, we'll see what kind of information is available on the Web about taking live tours of colleges and universities. We'll also show you where to go for information about college fairs.

Most high school guidance counselors will tell students in the second half of their junior year to start making a list of colleges they might want to attend. By the beginning of your senior year, you should have narrowed down your list to only those schools you will seriously consider. Also by your senior year, you should be highly aware of admissions, financial aid, and other deadlines you'll need to meet for all the schools you've chosen.

What You'll Learn in This Chapter:

▸ How institutions of higher education are classified.

▸ How to use Web sites that help you choose the right school.

▸ How to find information about community colleges on the Web.

▸ How to find information about live college visits, campus tour videotapes, and college fairs on the Web.

Post This in a Highly Visible Place

To obtain a complete calendar regarding when and how you should start planning for college—beginning with what you can do as early as the eighth grade—go to *www.collegeispossible.org/choosing/calendar.htm*.

Our goal is to help you fine-tune your list by surfing the Web. In the chapters that follow, you'll learn about the details of applying online and where to find help online to meet your admission requirements and pay for college. For now, we'll concentrate on choice and how to make the right one for you and you alone using our good friend, the World Wide Web.

Classifying Institutions of Higher Education

In a broad sense, there are four types of higher education institutions:

- Private colleges and universities
- Public colleges and universities
- Community colleges
- Specialized trade and vocational colleges and universities

Generally speaking, the difference between colleges and universities is that colleges primarily award bachelor's degrees, some master's degrees, and possibly some associate's degrees; universities award bachelor's, master's, and doctoral degrees. Community colleges are primarily two-year institutions that award associate's degrees. Specialized trade and vocational colleges and universities confer degrees in specific areas, such as business, agriculture, liberal arts, law, education, engineering and technology, health science, military science, and theology. However, the classification of higher education does not stop here.

More Definitions

For another view of types of colleges, go to *www.newvisions.org/colguide.html* *#types of colleges*, brought to you by New Visions For Public Schools from New York City.

There are city or urban schools, such as City Colleges of Chicago, City University of New York, and Pasadena City College. There are state schools, such as the State University of New York (SUNY) system of colleges and universities and the California State University system. State systems usually require a minimum GPA admission requirement; city schools frequently offer guaranteed admission to all high school graduates who are permanent residents of a particular area.

There are also women's colleges, historically black colleges, colleges affiliated with particular religions, residential colleges and more (see the "More Classifications" section, later in this chapter).

The Carnegie Classifications

For a further breakdown of higher education classifications, you can start at the Carnegie Classification of Institutions of Higher Education's home page at *www.carnegiefoundation.org*.

Andrew Carnegie founded The Carnegie Foundation for the Advancement of Teaching in 1905, "to do all things necessary to encourage, uphold, and dignify the profession of teaching."

Developed by The Carnegie Foundation in 1970 "to provide more meaningful and homogeneous categories than are found in other existing classifications," this system of classification was intended for academic research purposes. It has, in fact, become a well-respected and highly recognized mark of status and rank within the world of higher education. For the time being, the Carnegie Foundation has come up with nine general classifications and ten classifications within a "specialized institutions" category (plans are to change some of the classification categories in the not-so-distant future). The latest classification breakdown is from 1994. When you go to this site, you can find where a particular school fits within this classification system. Let's try it out:

▼ **Try It Yourself**

1. Go to *www.carnegiefoundation.org* and click the Our Work button.

2. Click the circular button labeled The Carnegie Classification of Institutions of Higher Education. Then navigate to the

bottom of the page and click the link labeled The 1994 Carnegie Classification is available here.

3. Click the Definition of Categories heading to find out what these classifications are all about. After you have read this information, click the link, Part II: Index of Classifications (institutions listed alphabetically), located at the bottom of the page.

4. Click the proper letter for your school of choice and then scroll down the alphabetized list until you find your school's name and classification.

Carnegie Changes Forthcoming

The Carnegie Foundation is currently in the process of changing its classifications. For a complete explanation of what changes are looming, click the Millennial Edition link inside the Our Work section of the Carnegie Web site.

Going Public

Writer Joe Masters gives his personal take on why he chose a public college over a private one in the Personal Finance section of *www.fool.com*. The direct address to Master's article is *www.fool.com/ Money/ PayingForCollege/ PayingForCollege PublicVPrivate.htm*. Fool.com, The Motley Fool®, is a Web site that provides investment and personal finance strategies.

Private Versus Public: What's the Deal?

One of the biggest differences between a private school and a public school is the cost. The average annual cost for tuition, fees, room, and board at a top-dollar private school is about $30,000. The average annual cost for tuition, fees, room, and board as an in-state student at a typical public college or university is about $7,000. The average annual cost for out-of-state students is about $16,000. Another difference between private and public colleges is that the number of faculty in relation to the number of students is usually lower at a public school. (In other words, there are more teachers per student at private schools.) Also, it might be harder to get into a private school because of more stringent admission requirements. There might be more opportunities to obtain financial aid and grants at a private school, depending on your financial need and the number of scholarships available at a particular school.

For more information on the public versus private issue, you can go to *Kiplinger's Personal Finance* magazine's Web site. The September 1998 issue reviewed and ranked public colleges with a special focus on value for your dollar. You can read this entire story, with rankings, at *www.kiplinger.com/magazine/archives/1998/September/college.htm*. The September 1999 issue covered private colleges in the same manner and can be read in its entirety at *www.kiplinger.com/magazine/archives/1999/ September/college.htm*.

More Classifications

At the Education Network, Inc.'s Web site (*www.edunetwork.com*) visitors can search for colleges in six categories: Catholic Colleges, Ivy League Colleges, Military Colleges, Public Colleges, Private Colleges, and Women's Colleges.

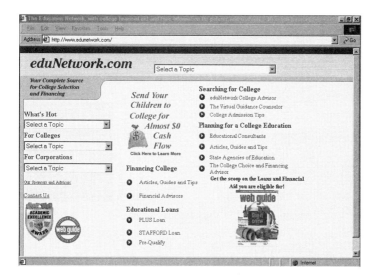

The Education Network's Web site provides a college search function as well as information on college planning and financing.

From the Education Network's home page, click the eduNetwork College Advisor link located under the Searching for College heading. Enter your email address to register so that you have access to the six college categories. Click a category, and you'll be taken to a form-driven page where you can request information by location, tuition amount ranges, whether or not you want room and board included in the tuition amount, and whether you will be an in-state or out-of-state student. Hit the Search button, and up comes a list of schools, each with total tuition expense amounts. To the right of each listing is a GO button that will give you more detailed information about that particular school, including admission requirements, percentages of male and female students, ethnic background percentages, and more.

For more Web sites that provide information and links to even more classifications of higher education institutions, check out the following:

- Historically Black Colleges and Universities—
  http://eric-web.tc.columbia.edu/hbcu/index.html
  Located primarily in the Southeastern United States, there are approximately 120 Historically Black Colleges and Universities (HBCU). Links to some of their Web sites and other HBCU resources can be accessed through this Web site.

- Seventh-Day Adventist Colleges and Universities—
  www.nadeducation.adventist.org/main.html
  This site is called Adventist Education Net and "is a service
  of the North American Division of Seventh-Day Adventist
  Church Office of Education," providing "general direction to
  over 1,000 K–12 schools and 15 colleges/universities located
  in Bermuda, Canada, and the United States of America."

- Jesuit Colleges and Universities—
  www.ajcunet.edu
  AJCUnet is the official Web site for all 28 Jesuit colleges and
  universities located in the United States. Contact information
  and links to school Web sites are provided at the List of
  Jesuit Institutions link.

- Christian Colleges and Universities—
  www.gospelcom.net/ cccu
  This is the Web site of the Council for Christian Colleges and
  Universities (CCCU). Click the About the CCCU link and
  then click the Members link to get access to the Web sites of
  70 colleges and universities who are members of the CCCU.

- Evangelical Lutheran Church of America Colleges and
  Universities—*www.elca.org/dhes/colleges/college.html*
  Links to 28 Lutheran colleges and universities are provided at
  this Web page located inside the Evangelical Lutheran
  Church in America Web site.

- Hillel: The Foundation for Jewish Campus Life—
  www.hillel.org
  Hillel is the foundation of the campus Jewish community,
  and it maintains a presence on more than 400 campuses in
  the United States, Canada, Israel, Australia, Europe, and
  South America. Click the About Hillel link and then click the
  Guide to Jewish Life on Campus/Campus Contacts link to
  find a Hillel near you.

- National Catholic College Admission Association—
  www. nccaa.org
  This is the Web site for the *Official Catholic College and
  University Guidebook*, which can be ordered online for $8.95
  (includes shipping and handling). The site also provides links

to more than 100 Catholic colleges, including profiles of each institution.

- Minority On-Line Information Service—
  www.sciencewise. com/molis
  This Web site, known as "The Workplace for Science and Engineering," is also the home of the Minority On-Line Service (MOLIS). MOLIS is "your source for information on minority institutions and minority targeted opportunities." Click the Minority Institutions link to access a form-driven search function for getting information on minority institutions and links to school Web sites.

- American Indian College Fund—
  http://collegefund.org/ main.htm
  Here you'll find links to 31 tribal colleges, "all founded by Indians to help fight high rates of poverty, educational failure, and cultural loss." Click the Where Are the Colleges link for more information about and links to these 31 schools.

- Residential Colleges—*http://strong.uncg.edu/colleges.html*
  Residential colleges are primarily small schools of a few hundred individuals "loosely modeled" on the colleges of Oxford and Cambridge. At this site, you'll find links to approximately 68 residential colleges located around the world.

Women Exceed Men

In this age of coeducation, there aren't as many strictly men's and strictly women's colleges in existence today. For instance, according to the U.S. Department of Education, in 1960 there were 300 women's colleges. Today, according to *U.S. News* Online's College Search function, there are 51 women's colleges and only 8 men's colleges, one of which is The Citadel, which is now accepting women.

U.S News Online's College Search function is located at *www.usnews.com/usnews/edu/college/cosearch.htm*. Click the Single Sex/Coed link in the opening paragraph. On the following page, you'll see a pull-down menu you can use to search for schools by one of the following three criteria: Coed, Women's College (90% or more), or Men's College (90% or more). Why the "90 percent or more"? According to *U.S. News*, "some single-sex schools admit members of the opposite sex for special programs or other unique circumstances. Contact a school directly if you have questions about its admission policies."

Sites That Help You Choose

The U.S. Department of Education's National Center for Education Statistics (NCES) is your one-stop shop to find pertinent information about every higher education institution in the country. As stated on its Web site (*www.nces.ed.gov*), "NCES is the primary federal entity for collecting and analyzing data related to education in the United States and other nations." Within the NCES Web site is an impressive college search tool (as well as an impressive acronym) called IPEDS COOL. (Don't you love our government's language?) It stands for Integrated Postsecondary Education Data System College Opportunities On-Line and can be found at *www.nces.ed.gov/ipeds/cool/Search.asp*.

In 1998, Congress authorized NCES "to help college students, future students, and their parents understand the differences between colleges and how much it costs to attend college." This was a great Congressional mandate because it created IPEDS COOL, which enables you to quickly find out the annual cost for the past three years for tuition and fees at any campus in the United States. IPEDS COOL will also tell you a school's costs for books, supplies, delete off-campus room and board, and other expenses.

IPEDS COOL links you to pertinent information from colleges and universities located throughout the United States.

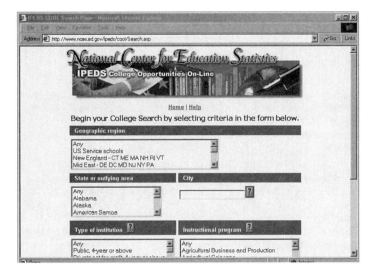

Here you can search for a college based on its location (broken down by region, state, or outlying area or city), name of institution, type of institution (2-year or 4-year, public or private), programs available, student population, and Title IV eligibility. After you navigate to your school of choice, in addition to annual cost information, you'll be given the school's phone numbers (general, financial aid office, and admissions office); a link to the school's Web site; degrees offered; Carnegie classification (aren't you glad you know all about this now?); fall enrollment figures broken down by gender, race/ethnicity, and percentage of first-time undergraduate students; and a financial aid section listing type of aid, percentage of students receiving aid, and average amount of aid students receive. Now that's some great information. Thank you, U.S. government by the people, for the people.

What's Title IV?

Title IV is part of the Higher Education Act of 1965, which establishes a school's eligibility to participate in federal student financial assistance programs that are administered by the U.S. Department of Education. Schools that are Title IV eligible have various Title IV institution codes that designate different federal financial assistance programs available at various campuses.

College Rankings by *U.S. News* Online

If you like looking at rankings, one of the most popular of all college ranking systems today is brought to you by *U.S. News* magazine. Each year, with great fanfare, this weekly magazine publishes a special issue called "America's Best Colleges." Fortunately for us, we don't have to buy it because all the results, and more, are easily accessible at *www.usnews.com/usnews/edu/college/corank.htm*. (Don't you just love how the Web can save you money?)

Some colleges and universities question the validity of this college-ranking system. To address this issue, *U.S. News* supplies a through explanation of how the ranking-system results are determined. You can read this explanation by clicking the Ranking Information link near the top of the page and then clicking the How We Rank/Methodology link.

The results of the U.S. News annual special issue that ranks colleges and universities can be found at the U.S. News Web site.

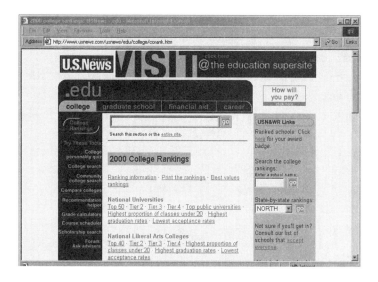

For the year 2000 rankings, *U.S. News* co-writers Amy E. Graham and Robert J. Morse stated up front, "It's absurd to think that a college's special and intangible qualities can be reduced to mere numbers, many administrators argue—even though they measure applicants by test scores and class standing. But we believe it *is* possible to objectively compare schools on one key attribute: academic excellence."

More Rankings

Go to *http:// 4colleges.4anything. com* and click the Rankings link for a Web page with information about and links to at least ten different college ranking systems.

Graham and Morse then went into the methods *U.S. News* used to come up with its highly regarded rankings, which included such factors as academic reputation, retention (proportion of freshmen who return and complete their degrees), faculty resources, student selectivity (student test scores and proportion of enrolled freshman who graduated from high school in top percentiles), financial resources (how much does the school spend per student), graduation rate performance, and alumni-giving rate.

"Modifications" of the Carnegie classifications were used to categorize ranking results. For example, the 2000 study's national universities category consisted of 222 schools that offer undergraduate, graduate, and doctoral degrees and that also place an emphasis on faculty research. The national liberal arts colleges ranked in 2000 consisted of 162 schools that offer only undergraduate degrees, with 40% of those degrees in liberal arts. Ranking results were also broken down into geographic regions.

In addition to its rankings section, the *U.S. News* Web site offers a
vast amount of information to help you choose a college or university. You can start accessing this information by going to the
home page of its .edu section at *www.usnews.com/usnews/edu/*.

*The online ver-
sion of U.S. News
magazine fea-
tures a section
titled .edu that
offers lots of
helpful informa-
tion for choosing
a college or uni-
versity.*

Like many of the popular higher education Web portals, this Web
site offers so many services that it's hard to choose which one to
access first. Fortunately, *U.S. News* has a handy feature to help
your navigational efforts. Down at the bottom of the *U.S. News*
.edu home page is a link labeled Text Index: The Low-Tech Way
to Navigate .edu. This feature will definitely help you wade
through this large site because it provides nicely organized and
titled links to everything in the *U.S. News* .edu Web site.

You might also try subscribing to one or all the *U.S. News* .edu
newsletters that can be regularly sent direct to your email box.
There are three choices:

- The *U.S. News* Online Newsletter, *"a brief weekly tip sheet
  on top stories, rankings, and interactive tools available at
  U.S. News* online."

- The High School Newsletter, a bimonthly "designed for
  college-bound high school students and their parents."

- The College Newsletter, a bimonthly "geared toward college
  students preparing for graduate school or the work force."

Ranking the Rankings

It's no secret that ranking colleges and universities is not an exact science. Nonetheless, today's society seems to have an insatiable appetite for listings of the top 10 or 100 songs, movies, businesses, colleges, and more. But rankings really have little relationship to the needs of individuals. In short, no ranking can define what's best for you. Still, for many of us, rankings are indeed fun to look at.

At the University of Illinois at Urbana-Champaign, the subject of college and university rankings was researched. Results were published on the Web at *http://www.library.uiuc.edu/edx/rankings.htm*. This site gives you plenty of information and links to many college and university ranking systems. You'll also see a section called "Caution and Controversy," wherein you'll find an extensive bibliography and links to numerous articles about the college and university rankings controversy.

MatchMaker, MatchMaker, Make Me a Match

Our friends over at Embark.com have come up with a resourceful way to find the right college. It's appropriately called MatchMaker, and it can be accessed from *www.embark.com* by choosing a category in the scroll-down menu beneath the heading MatchMaker: Find the School That Fits Your Needs, located in the right sidebar. Then click the Go button.

Embark.com's MatchMaker form-driven service provides a series of questions to help students narrow down their search for the right college or university.

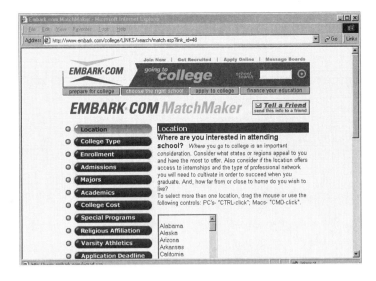

As you can see, there are 11 categories of questions, beginning with Location. Within each category are brief reminders about what you might want to consider. For example, in the School Setting section of the Location category, Embark.com tells you that urban campuses are closer to public cultural and business activities, whereas if you go to a rural campus you'll "typically rely on the social and cultural offerings of the school." (In other words, party hardy or travel over the weekends.)

Within the 11 major categories are approximately 16 subcategories. In the Special Programs category, for instance, you can let MatchMaker know that you only want to consider schools that offer cooperative education or pre-professional degree programs, which are considered advantageous for some future job prospects.

To select more than one choice in any category, drag your mouse or hold down the Ctrl key as you click options.

After you've completed the entire questionnaire, your results will quickly be revealed. You'll be shown a listing of schools that fit the criteria you have chosen. The list will be exactly the same as what was explained in the previous chapter in the discussion about Embark.com's Choose the Right School section. Each listing will have functions that help you acquire more detailed information about each school.

Going Once, Going Twice... Your Tuition Bid Is Accepted

In this new economy on the World Wide Web where auction and price bidding sites such as ebay.com and Priceline.com have gained national prominence, eCollegebid has entered the hubbub of higher education.

This Web site allows you to actually submit a bid of a dollar amount you're willing to fork over for your college tuition. Located at *www.ecollegebid.org*, this site is brought to you by Consultants for Educational Resources and Research, Inc., located in Falls Church, Virginia. Tedd Kelly, originator of eCollegebid, has 32 years' experience as a college enrollment management consultant.

Check Out the Review

Another Web site with a great college search section is offered by the *Princeton Review* at *www.review.com*. From the home page, click the College button and then click the College Search button. From there, you can do a Basic or Advanced search.

The eCollegebid. org Web site allows visitors to place bids on college tuition costs from unnamed, regionally accredited colleges.

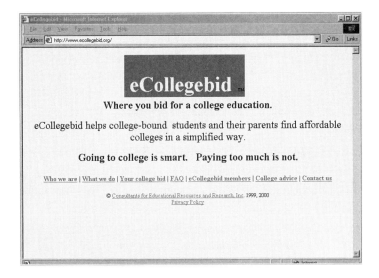

The catch—and it's a considerable one—is that you won't know which college you're bidding on, and, for that matter, which college might accept your bid. Participants can submit bids to only eCollegebid member schools that "are mostly private colleges that are not household names and do not often make the rankings found in the popular media," according to the eCollegebid Web site.

According to Kelly, there were 16 eCollegebid member schools in the spring of 2000, and he anticipated that number to increase to between 25 to 35 colleges. All schools, he added, were regionally accredited institutions (see Chapter 13, "Welcome to the Age of the Virtual Campus," for information about accreditation).

If you want more details, the eCollegebid.org Web site provides accurate and easy-to-navigate information about its service, including a succinct but relevant College Advice page, part of which is reprinted here.

The Latest in College Advice from eCollegebid.org
- Knowing what you want from a college is the first step in determining the value of the college.
- Going to college and getting a college education are not the same thing.
- College is the best place to learn to live and to earn a living.

- If you choose to go to college where your friends are going, make sure you chose your friends carefully.

- Picking a college to attend is not the biggest decision you will make about college; it's choosing the college you will graduate from.

- There are three kinds of college students: those who live at home so Mom can do their laundry daily; those who go off far enough to come home once or twice a month so Mom can do their laundry; and those who go off to college far enough away that they have to learn how to use the Laundromat. Which kind are you?

- Q. What's worse than getting into "the right college?"
  A. Getting into the wrong college.

- Getting into college shouldn't be the hardest part of going to college.

- Some college admission offices really do read those application essays (see Chapter 5, "Perfecting Your Essay Online"), and some don't. The problem is you don't know which is which.

- Meet college deadlines, or you are dead meat.

More Sites to Help You Choose

The cost of attending college is obviously an important factor to weigh when making your choice. You can find out average undergraduate costs by state from the *Chronicle of Higher Education.* Go to *http://chronicle.com/free/v46/i08/08a05201.htm*, where you can read Leo Reisberg's feature article about average college costs. Additionally there's a pull-down menu within the article that allows you to view average in-state and out-of-state tuition and fees at colleges and universities across the country by state. These figures are part of the Annual Survey of Colleges of the College Board. The College Board is an arm of Educational Testing Service (ETS), who are the creators of the SAT assessment tests. To read all about trends in college tuition and fees, go to the page within the College Board Web site at *www.collegeboard.com/press/cost99/html/991005.html.*

The College Board Web site also has a great segment all about choosing and preparing for college in its Starting Points for Students and Parents section. Go to *www.collegeboard.com/toc/html/tocstudents000.html* and check out the wealth of information provided to help you make the right choice.

Indirect Costs

When compiling a budget, don't forget to factor in the indirect costs of going to school. These can be anything from books and transportation costs to personal spending money for snacks, laundry, movies, DVDs, and whatever else may strike your fancy.

From here, you can link to the SAT Learning Center and take some SAT practice tests (more on this in Chapter 6, "Your Guide to the PSAT, SAT, and ACT Tests"), enter a chance to win a $100,00 scholarship offered by Siemens Westinghouse, and peruse the Preparing for College section.

The Preparing for College section has links to advice for the college bound, including how to think ahead and avoid potential problems, how to start thinking about a career path (see Chapter 10, "Choosing a Major and Discovering Your Career Goals"), and how to make the most of your summer vacation in relation to preparing for the college admissions process.

For information about career planning and how it relates to selecting the right school to meet your career goals, as well as information about selecting and paying for college, go to *www.mapping-your-future.org*. As stated on its home page, "this site is sponsored by a group of guaranty agencies who participate in the Federal Family Education Loan Program (FFELP) and are committed to providing information about higher education and career opportunities."

Click the Selecting a School link to go to a page listing the 10 steps to selecting the right college or university. Included in these 10 steps are links to pages that assist you with choosing a career, being academically prepared, taking standardized tests, gathering information about schools, and much more.

A Word About Community Colleges

If you're looking for schools with easy admission requirements and low tuition costs, look no further than our nation's community colleges. For a "snapshot" of statistics related to U.S. community colleges, visit the American Association of Community Colleges (AACC) Web site at *http://www.aacc.nche.edu/ allaboutcc/snapshot.htm*. According to the AACC, there are approximately 1,132 community colleges in the United States with an average annual tuition and fees cost of only $1,518. Forty-four percent of all U.S. undergraduates are enrolled at community colleges, and "95 percent of businesses and organizations using them would recommend community college workforce education and training programs."

If you're unsure about making a commitment to earning a 4-year college degree, attending a community college can be a great way to test the waters of higher education for a relatively low cost. (Tuition-paying parents, take heed.)

Most community colleges have credit transfer programs whereby students complete a program of study over two years and then transfer all credits earned to a four-year institution. Be aware, however, that transfer policies are not the same at all institutions. Transfer programs usually entail taking courses in the humanities, mathematics, sciences, and social sciences and thus mimic the first two years of a typical four-year program.

Additionally, community colleges are great for earning certificates and specialized occupational degrees in areas such as early childhood education, office management, laser optics, medical and computer technologies, automotive repair, fire science, telecommunications, and more. Health care and computer technology programs, for instance, are considered "hot" for earning decent starting salaries after graduation.

You can search for information about community colleges at the IPEDS COOL Web site mentioned earlier in this chapter. You can also go to another Web portal to higher education at *www.collegenet.com* to find detailed information about community colleges in the United States.

Transferring Credits Differs by Institution

If you're thinking about starting off in a community college and later transferring to a 4-year institution, make sure you check out transfer policies before taking the plunge.

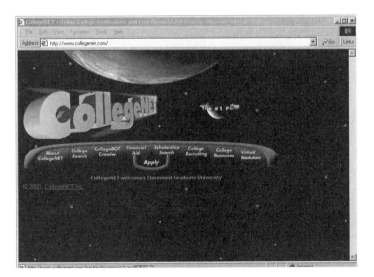

CollegeNet.com is another Web portal to higher education that provides links to and detailed information about colleges and universities in the United States, including community colleges.

Try It Yourself ▼ Let's go to CollegeNet and try it out.

1. Go to *www.collegenet.com* and click the College Search link.

2. Click the Two-Year Colleges option to direct the search to community colleges, most of which offer two-year degree programs.

3. Choose a region (all regions are chosen by default) and then fill out all or part of the form located directly below the checklist.

4. Click the Start Search button.

The result of the search is a list of community colleges based on the criteria you specified in the form, each with tuition costs, important phone numbers, enrollment figures, and a link to the institution's Web site. You can get more detailed and useful information by clicking the fields in the ACT Data Views box to the right of each listing. Click the small Apply box to the left of the listing to access the online application page of that particular

▲ school's Web site.

Enough Virtual

Even though the Web can supply you with everything you could ever possibly want to know about colleges and universities, there's one thing it can't do: The Web can't transport you to a real campus to get a first-hand look (at least not for now; beam me up, Scotty). In short, the Web cannot replace a real visit to a college campus. So, pack your bags and ask Mom and Dad to give you a ride. For some helpful advice on how to prepare for college visits, go to *http://collegeprep.okstate.edu/* and click the Campus Visits link under the Pre-College category. There's plenty you should know about before hitting the road.

For example, according to the Campus Visits section, "visits should be set up by the college's recruitment office (Admissions Office, High School Relations, or Prospective Student Services, etc.) or by the representative who visited your school. They should be able to schedule you for a tour and arrange appointments with the appropriate individuals. In some situations, you may have to call a couple of different offices before you reach someone accustomed to setting up a number of appointments for a visitor."

Also in the Campus Visits section is the Suggested Questions link, which is a list of nine important questions you should ask while taking your campus tour.

For more help with that all-important college visit, you can also go to *U.S. News* Online's page on campus visits at *www.usnews. com/usnews/edu/college/find/covisits.htm*. Writer Kelly Nelson provides a complete overview on the campus visit process, including a tutorial that begins with a phone call to each school's admission office to find out dates and times of tours available. Nelson also recommends writing down or taking photos of your impressions of each school you visit.

Nelson suggests that high schoolers check into the possibility of spending a night in a college dorm hosted by a current undergraduate. "Many schools offer this campus visit option for high schoolers during the school year (although not during the first week of classes or final exams). At nearly all schools, the bed is free. To arrange for an overnight stay, call the admissions office at least two to three weeks in advance."

Hire Someone to Tour You Around

If organizing and getting to all these campuses seems a bit too much, have someone else make the arrangements and do the driving for you. Yes, there are businesses that will take you on live campus tours. Two such services with Web sites can be found at *www.college-visits.com*, brought to you by College Visits, Inc., and *www.niep.com/pages/cp.html*, brought to you by the National Institute for Educational Planning (NIEP).

College Visits provides group tours by region in the United States; the tours originate from various cities throughout the year. All tours include student-led campus tours, meetings with admissions administrators, lodging in college housing or hotels (double occupancy), transportation, meals in student dining halls or neighborhood restaurants, recreational activities, and a workbook for keeping records and evaluating schools.

The Choice Is Yours

Even after writing down all the pros, cons, and facts in relation to your list of school choices, a good part of your decision will most likely come down to your gut feeling about which school is really right for you.

**Check Tour
Availability**

Check out the NIEP
and College Visits
Web sites for pricing
and availability of
tours for the col-
leges or universities
you are considering
attending.

NIEP group tours provide college selection seminars and workshops, transportation, accommodations, meals, admission person-
nel presentations, student-led campus tours, and sightseeing in
areas around the campuses.

As another non-Web option, you can watch videotapes of college
campuses. These tapes can be obtained through Collegiate Choice
Walking Tours Videos at *www.collegiatechoice.com*, where "the
only way to get a truer feel for a campus is to go there yourself."
Collegiate Choice sells unedited recordings of student-guided
campus tours for $15, plus $6 for shipping. The site has a long
list of tapes of colleges and universities around the world to
choose from.

Attend a College Fair

One final way to meet face-to-face with college and university
admissions counselors and other school representatives is to
attend college fairs. These are the higher education versions of
corporation trade shows and are held in convention centers around
the country throughout the year. These fairs are sponsored by the
National Association for College Admission Counseling
(NACAC) and are endorsed by the National Association of
Secondary School Principals (NASSP).

According to the NACAC Web site, college fairs allow students
and parents to "meet one-on-one, in the same day, with one of the
largest gatherings of college representatives!" Additionally,
NACAC's National College Fair program "has been one of the
most visible professional college recruitment programs since its
inception in 1972. Today, the association sponsors 36 fairs nationwide, attracting over 300,000 students each year."

NACAC also hosts a Performing and Visual Arts College Fair
Program, which was held in 27 cities in 1999.

Check with your high school guidance counselor for the next college fair coming near you or, better yet, go to the NACAC Web
page at *www.nacac.com/exhibit/fair.cfm* for a regularly updated
list of college fair dates, times, and locations—as well as print-
able lists of all the schools exhibiting at each fair.

Wrapping It Up

Well, that concludes this chapter on choosing the right college.
You should have found enough information here to make you grit
your teeth, go forward, and become the master of your college
decision-making universe in no time at all. As a memory
refresher, here's a synopsis of what this chapter covered:

- You found a wealth of information about how colleges and
  universities are classified (including the Carnegie
  Classification of Institutions of Higher Education), the differences between public and private schools, and a bevy of other
  classifications along with affiliated Web sites.

- You learned about Web sites that provide information to help
  you make a decision. You were introduced to the U.S.
  Department of Education's IPEDS COOL site, which is
  loaded with important information for helping you find the
  right school. You learned about higher education ranking systems, including "America's Best Colleges," by *U.S. News*
  Online and others. You also met Embark.com's question-
  naire-based MatchMaker service.

- You were introduced to eCollegebid.com, a Web site that
  enables its visitors to bid on college tuition costs.

- You learned that the Chronicle of Higher Education site has
  information about the average cost of tuition and fees by
  state.

- You were introduced to the College Board Web site and the
  Mapping-Your-Future.org Web site, both excellent sites for
  information about choosing and preparing for the right college.

- This chapter reviewed the benefits of attending a community
  college and showed you where on the Web you can find
  directories of these two-year institutions.

- You learned where you can go for information about visiting
  the schools you're thinking about attending. You discovered
  that there are college and university group tour services, and

you also know about the NACAC Web site that lists information about college fairs you might want to consider attending
to get first-hand information from higher education representatives.

CHAPTER 3

Communicating with Undergraduates and College-Bound Peers

This chapter covers Web sites you can visit to find alternative sources of information about the college or university you're thinking about attending.

You'll be shown how to find students' personal Web sites and how you can possibly start an electronic dialogue with an undergraduate student. The chapter moves on to talk about going to the Student Life, Student Services, or Student Affairs sections of college and university Web sites, where you can possibly communicate with the student officers of various clubs and organizations on campus.

Finally, you'll be pointed to higher-education–related discussion boards where you can engage in meaningful conversations with your college-bound colleagues and with current undergraduates at colleges and universities throughout the country. There are special discussion boards for parents, too.

Student Web Sites

There's yet another great source of information to help you choose the right college—college students themselves. Wouldn't it be nice if you could communicate with some undergraduates and get their input about college life on the actual campus you're thinking about attending? Well, you can.

One relatively easy and sensible way of communicating with undergrads is to send polite emails to them. But where do you find their email addresses? You can start at a school's Web site. Let's check one out at the University of Southern California.

What You'll Learn in This Chapter:

▶ Information about student Web sites and where you can find them.

▶ How to use student life/services Web pages to communicate with undergraduates.

▶ How to use higher-education-related discussion boards.

The University of Southern California Web site has a Student Life and Services section where you can link to USC student Web pages.

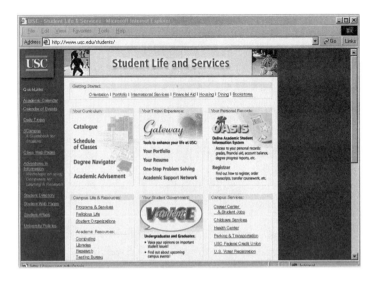

Try It Yourself ▼

1. Go to the home page of the University of Southern California at *www.usc.edu* and click the Student Life and Services link.

2. Click the Student Web Pages link located near the bottom of the left sidebar.

3. Scroll down to an alphabet-driven menu and click any letter to see a list of student Web sites whose names begin with the letter you clicked.

▲

4. Click any student name to link to his or her Web site.

Unfortunately, the only preclassification of a student's personal Web site is the student's name, which means you'll have to look through a lot of these sites before you find someone with whom you might be able to communicate. You'll also get a lot of "File Not Found" messages. When you do, in fact, connect to a student's home page, the likelihood of that person being the right one to start a dialogue with could be slim. (Depending on the student, there can be lots of content published on a personal site that may seem awfully strange to you.) Many of these sites are exercises in designing Web pages or works in progress, and many have student resumes posted for career planning purposes. Other sites are very eye-opening exposés, with information and photos about a student's major, hobbies, favorite Web sites, friends, dorm life, and a link to send them an email. These are the students you might want to contact.

For example, you might find someone who is majoring in the same field you're considering. You can send that person a friendly email introducing yourself as a prospective student who is thinking about enrolling in the same curriculum.

Our advice is that you be succinct, polite, and send only one or two email messages. If you get a response, it might open the door to more substantial communication.

Not all college and university Web sites have links to student Web pages. You'll have to search around for the ones that do. For a list of links to pages on various school Web sites where personal student Web sites are listed, go to *www.utexas.edu/world/personal*. This site is brought to you by the University of Texas at Austin, where they have provided such links to more than 250 schools.

Web Sites with Student Life, Student Services, or Student Affairs Sections

Just about every college and university Web site has sections devoted to student life, student services, or student affairs. These sections are usually labeled as such and are great places for possibly meeting up with undergraduates. In particular, student clubs and organizations are usually listed within these sections, along with email links to the clubs' officers. To give you an example of this kind of resource, check out Lehigh University's Web site at *http://www2.lehigh.edu*. Go to the Student Life heading at the top of the home page, and a scroll-down menu becomes visible. Move down the menu and click the Clubs and Organizations option.

You can now easily access information about every student club and organization at Lehigh. Each club or organization's snail mail address, along with the name and email link to its student president, is listed. You can choose the club or organization that interests you and contact these student officers as possible sources of information.

Keep Trying

Some people get offended when they are sent unsolicited email, or they get so much email each day that they only reply to what's absolutely pertinent to them. Don't get discouraged if you don't get a response from an email communication attempt with a student you've never met. Just go on to your next prospect.

The Lehigh University Web site has a Student Life section with links to information about every student club and organization on campus.

Get the Real Scoop

Reading college newspapers is a great source for alternative information about a campus that you can't get anywhere else. To find a directory of links to college newspaper Web sites, go to *www. newsdirectory.com/ college/press* where you can browse links to college and university newspaper Web sites by state, region, or city.

Rated X

Watch out for some chat rooms with the word *college* in their title, especially if the room is not monitored. You'd be surprised at the content you can find in such online talks; they are frequently littered with vulgarities and nonsensical babbling.

Lehigh's Student Life section also has a category called Student Life News. Here there are links to numerous feature articles written about students at Lehigh.

Engaging in Meaningful Discussion About Higher Education

There are a number of college-oriented chat rooms on the Web, but it's difficult, if not impossible, to find any that offer serious and meaningful discussions about college life. *Chat* is the appropriate word for such rooms, for it means idle small talk. Online chat rooms that do not have communication etiquette rules or are not monitored to ensure appropriate online behavior are where you'll find mostly meaningless conversations. There are, however, some discussion boards that are quite good for engaging in intelligent talk about a wide variety of topics related to higher education.

> **What's a Discussion Board?**
>
> A discussion board is a place online where visitors can openly exchange messages and ideas. Also referred to as bulletin boards, discussion forums or groups, or message boards, discussion boards usually consist of threaded messages. In online discourse, threaded messages are a series of posted messages in reply to a specific topic or topics.

One such discussion board can be found at the Princeton Review Web site at *www.review.com*. The Princeton Review is primarily a test preparation service (see Chapter 6, "Your Guide to the PSAT, SAT and ACT Tests"). The Web site, however, features much more than information about higher education assessment tests.

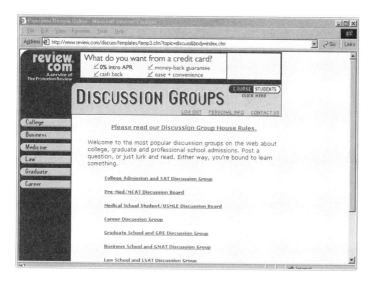

The Princeton Review's Web site has a Discussion Groups section where visitors can post questions and answers about college.

On the Princeton Review home page, click the Discussion Groups link in the left sidebar, and you'll see a page listing all the topics under discussion. At the top of the page is a link to the Review's House Rules. It might be a good idea to read them. (It's a good thing that obnoxious conversations are not tolerated.) Click the College Admission and SAT Discussion Group link. When you enter this group, you'll be presented with a long list of threaded discussions by topic, along with the date of the latest postings and the number of total postings.

A lot of the topics you'll see are related to college-bound students asking questions about schools into which they've been accepted. Some of these students are seeking advice on what school they should finally choose. Others have already made their decision and want to start discussions related to the campus academic environment. There are a number of discussions going on about the SAT and ACT tests. Still other discussion participants are seeking recommendations on what to major in at various schools and how to narrow down their options.

Check It Out

U.S. News Online's .edu Web site has a discussion forum section located at *www.delphi.com/ usnews_college/start* featuring "four forums hosted by experts who can offer advice on how to advance your education, how to pay for it, and what to do after you graduate." Peer advice is also regularly provided.

It's a simple process to join a discussion. Just click a topic, read some of the postings, and then click the Post New Message in This Thread link. You'll get a form asking for your name (nickname or real name), email address, subject (optional), and message. Type your message and click the small check box below the message area to be notified by email about all messages posted in the thread.

Discussion Group for Parents

For all you parents with questions looming about the admissions and assessment-test-taking process, the Princeton Review provides a parents-only discussion group.

If you want to start an entirely new topic, click the New Thread link and follow the instructions in the form that opens.

Got More Questions? We Got More Answers

At the Embark.com Web site, you can also take part in discussion boards. Go to *www.embark.com* and click the Get into College link. Click Message Boards in the upper-right corner, and you'll be taken to the undergraduate school forums section where, according to Embark.com, "you can bond with others going through the application process or get advice from those who have done it before."

Embark.com hosts a message board for college-bound and current undergraduates, along with a discussion forum for their parents.

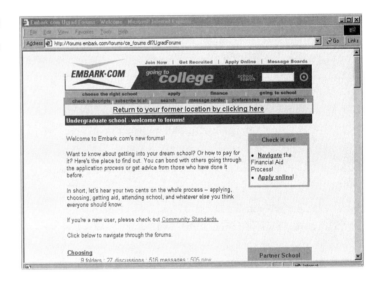

Check out the Community Standards area for information about the etiquette expected by these forums. For example, inappropriate language is not tolerated; the forums expect you to stay on the subject being discussed or to start a new subject if you can't.

You'll have to be a registered member of Embark.com to participate in these forums. Scroll down to the Guided Tour of Web Crossing category near the bottom of the page for everything you need to know about how to register and use these forums. There are five more categories of forums, including Choosing, Applying, Financial Aid, Going, and Parents. Overall, there are hundreds of threaded discussions going on here. The threaded discussions we saw covered numerous areas of interest, including gay and lesbian friendly schools, career interests, the admission process, scholarships, fraternity and sorority life, relationships, and much, much more.

Be a Good Netizen

See ten core rules for being a good *netizen* (the name for someone who uses proper behavior while communicating in cyberspace), written by Virginia Shea in a book called *Netiquette,* at *www.albion.com/ netiquette/ corerules.html.*

Another Web site where there's some decent conversation going on about higher education is located at *www.mapping-your-future.org/services/chatnight.htm.* The Chat Night page occasionally hosts scheduled live discussions and then archives these discussions for viewing at a later date.

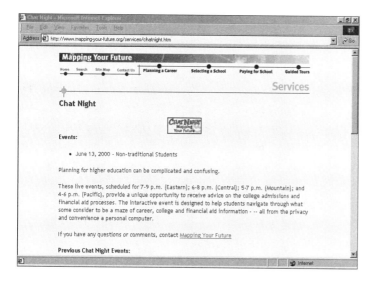

At www.mapping-your-future.org's *chat night section,* visitors can participate in moderated live chat discussions about college planning.

As stated on this Web site, "these live events, scheduled for 7-9 p.m. (Eastern); 6-8 p.m. (Central); 5-7 p.m. (Mountain); and 4-6 p.m. (Pacific), provide a unique opportunity to receive advice on the college admissions and financial aid processes. The interactive event is designed to help students navigate through what some consider to be a maze of career, college and financial aid information—all from the privacy and convenience a personal computer."

Some of the more recent chat night topics covered financial aid, career planning, and college admissions. In addition, the mapping-your-future.org Web site has a lot more advice-oriented content in four other informative sections, titled Planning a Career, Selecting a School, Paying for School, and Guided Tours.

Wrapping It Up

Although this chapter was not a lengthy one, it did provide some alternative methods to dig up more information to help you make the right college choice. In a nutshell, here's what was covered:

- Finding personal Web sites of students attending colleges and universities you might be interested in attending and learning how you might be able to communicate with some of these students by email.

- Digging into student life and student services sections of college and university Web sites to make connections with officers of student clubs and organizations.

- Visiting useful discussion boards where you can partake in threaded conversations.

This chapter concludes Part I, "Using the Internet to Find the Best College for You." Part I has enough Web sources to keep you busy for a while. These sources were chosen from among numerous higher-education–related Web sites, and it is our opinion that you have been given the best of the best. But you've only just begun. Now that you have narrowed down your choices of schools you might want to attend (or you are pretty close to accomplishing this), you have to apply, take tests, and find financial aid. Don't worry—the Web will help you go forward.

PART II

Getting Accepted

CHAPTER 4

Applying Online

Now that you know which schools interest you the most, the obvious next step is to apply for admission to them. You can begin the application process by going to college and university Web sites where you can check out their admissions sections. You can fill out the proper forms either directly online or by printing out applications and completing them by hand or with a typewriter.

In addition to showing you how two typical Web-based admissions departments work, this chapter covers some of the leading non-institutional Web sites that offer useful information about the admissions and application processes. The non-institutional Web sites provide services that enable you to fill out multiple applications while you're online and submit them to institutions electronically. One such Web site, at *www.collegeboard.com*, will also give you a free program to download so you can electronically fill out applications from your home computer offline. Additionally, these sites allow you to access and print out applications, so you can fill them out and snail mail them to the suitable institutions.

This chapter doesn't go deeply into the intricacies of actually filling out applications because most of the Web sites featured here have all the information you'll ever need to do this. Instead, you are pointed to various help sections within the featured Web sites, and you are advised to read all the instructions that everyone freely supplies, so that you can do the right thing.

What You'll Learn in This Chapter:

▶ How college and university Web sites offer admissions and application information and services.

▶ How to use non-school Web sites that provide information about admissions requirements and online application services.

Make Copies

Always print out and make copies of everything you filled out online or submitted by any other means. There's always the possibility of something getting lost along the way, so you'll want a backup.

Finally, this chapter includes an "Other Recommendations" section, which is a short list of additional relevant information on the Web about the entire admissions/application agenda.

Overall, our aim is to point you to decent Web sites that deal with admissions and applications, explain what these sites offer and how to navigate them, and in the final analysis, let you do the rest.

Good luck and keep those typing fingertips sharp!

Go to the Source

Your first stop on the road of admissions and applications can be your selected school's Web site. Most college and university Web sites have special admissions sections with application forms. Some are clearly labeled and easy to navigate, but others are not so user-friendly. Let's look at a well-thought-out admissions section at the Arizona State University (ASU) Web site, *www.asu.edu/admissions/applyingtoasu.*

Like most college and university Web sites, the Arizona State University Web site has an admissions section that guides students through the application process from start to finish.

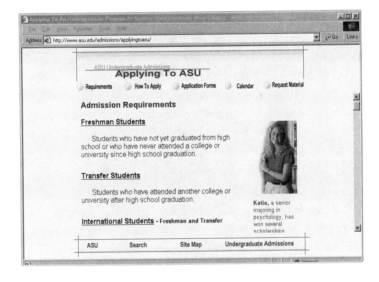

The admissions section of the ASU Web site provides succinct, easy-to-understand information about entrance requirements, how and when to apply, and how to get an application form. You can fill out your application form online, or you can download a printed version of the application in Microsoft Word or in PDF format. Instructions on how to download are also provided.

To get another perspective of an admissions section within a school's Web site, let's take a look at the University of Chicago's site at *www.uchicago.edu/uchi/admissions/menu.html.*

The University of Chicago admissions page links visitors to a wealth of information for students; there's also a special section devoted strictly to parents.

When you click the Undergraduate Admissions link under the Applying heading, you are taken to a page that has links to admissions standards, tuition and financial aid information, a connection to a special students section, and much more. When linking to the applications section, you'll be offered four options for filling out the application form:

• Request that an application be mailed to you

• Download an application in PDF format

- Apply online through a service provided by
  www.embark.com

- Apply online through a service provided by the Princeton
  Review at *www.review.com/surveys*

Notice that the last two options refer you to completely different
Web sites. Embark.com and the Princeton Review offer alternative methods for applying to the college or university of your
choice. Let's take a look at these Web sites, and two others, in the
following sections.

Go to Web Sites with Online Admissions and Application Services

Save Time

Using non-
institutional Web
sites with application
services can save you
time because they
provide a service
whereby you can
enter generic appli-
cation information
once for use on mul-
tiple applications.

You can fill out application forms through Embark.com and the
Princeton Review only if the college or university you're thinking
about attending has partnered with them. Both Emark.com and
the Princeton Review are excellent Web sites, providing, as we
have seen in Chapters one through three, a wealth of information
and services for the college-bound student.

Two additional sites similar to Embark.com and the Princeton
Review are hosted by the College Board and by what is called the
Common Application. These sites offer convenient one-Web-stops
for applying to various schools throughout the country. They also
provide a great deal of helpful information to guide you along the
way. Let's start with Embark.com and the Princeton Review, then
go on to the College Board and the Common Application Web
sites.

**Contact an
Admissions
Counselor**

Every college and
university has an
admissions depart-
ment staffed with
admissions coun-
selors. You can
always contact a
counselor by phone
or by email for
advice concerning
the admissions
and application
requirements of
the school you plan
on attending.

Embark.com

We'll start at the Table of Contents page of Embark.com's Apply
to College section located at *www.embark.com/apply*.

Options! Options! Options! Embark seems to have all the bases
covered when it comes to acquiring information about the admissions and application process. If you're new to the application
game, and you'd like to get some highly useful advice, start with
Embark's Application Tips section. There's plenty in this section
alone to keep you on the right track. If your desire for information is insatiable, go just below the Application Tips section

where you'll see an Essay Information section (see Chapter 5, "Perfecting Your Essay Online," for more on this), an Admissions section, and an Interview section. Read and retain all this information, and you might be able to consider yourself an expert on the topic of applying to colleges and universities.

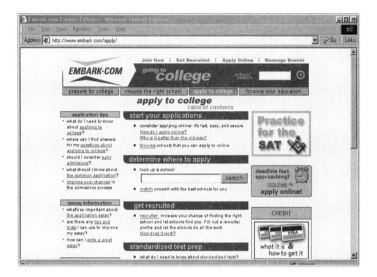

Embark.com's Apply to College section offers visitors a good amount of advice and also provides links to an online application process.

Have You Checked Out Admissions Requirements?

Before beginning with what can be a cumbersome application process, make sure that you feel comfortable with a school's admissions/entrance requirements. You can do this by checking out the admissions section at the Web site of your school of choice. You can also use Embark.com's Find School function at *www.embark.com/college/LINKS/search/ findschool.stm*. When you get to your school's listing, click either View Details or Strategy to obtain detailed information about that school's admissions requirements.

Once you understand the admissions and application processes, your next obvious step is to fill out an application. Before you consider doing this through Embark.com, make sure that your school is one of the 350 that has partnered with Embark.com. Click the See List of Schools link under the Actual Applications heading. If any of the schools you're interested in applying to is on the list, you can proceed by registering for a free account. As is true for most registration prompts on the Web, you'll set up an account with a unique user identification and password that will enable you to log in and log out to the service when necessary. After you have registered, click the Apply Online link.

As an account member of Embark.com, you can create a personal online application desktop function that will enable you to apply to multiple colleges and universities located throughout the United States.

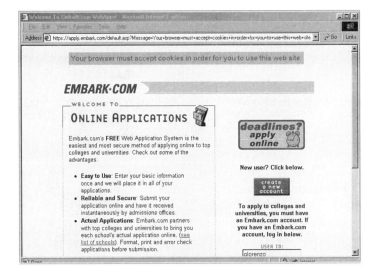

You'll be presented with a page titled WebApps and Your Application Desktop. Click the Help button to read all about how the system works.

Start the application process by clicking the Fill Out Your Profile button, where you'll find an explanation of four profile sections: Personal, Education, Family, and Other. Complete each section, which is made up of questions common to most applications. This data will appear on every application you enter wherever the information applies. As you enter your profile, you'll be able to save your data as you go along and continue at a later time or date.

After completing your profile, choose a school from the Start New Apps box and then click the Start App button. You can now start filling out the application for the school you have chosen. Embark supplies the same save-and-continue feature on this part of the application process. If you stop and come back at a later time or date, you'll see the name of the school listed in the Continue Work on Apps box. Just click the school and the Go To App button to continue where you left off.

The folks at Embark.com will also notify you by email, encouraging you to complete your application while explaining that their "automatic error-checker and data-encryption technology ensures that your application will be complete and securely transmitted."

You will find that most of these Web-based application services work in a very similar fashion to the Embark.com process: You must register a user identification and password with the service and fill out a personal profile before you can access school applications. All the services will send you an email confirmation of your user ID and password, and you'll be able to log in to the service whenever it's convenient for you to complete the application.

Proofread Everything

Web-based application services allow you to save your work and return later to proofread and correct any mistakes you may have made before you electronically submit it to your institutions of choice. Make sure that you read your completed application several times over before clicking the Submit button.

The Princeton Review

As mentioned in Chapter 3, "Communicating with Undergraduates and College-Bound Peers," the Princeton Review is noted as a leading test-preparation service for the college-bound. However, its Web site offers a lot more than test-prep stuff. In Chapter 6, "Your Guide to the PSAT, SAT, and ACT Tests," the Review's services for taking the ACT and SAT tests are covered. For now, the focus is on the Review's Apply to College service. You can start by going to *www.review.com*, scrolling down to the bottom of the page, and clicking the blue Apply! button.

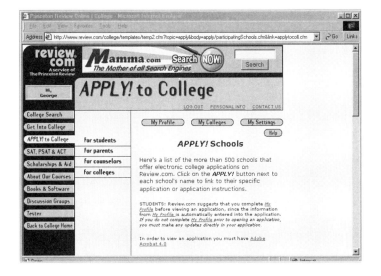

The Princeton Review has partnered with more than 500 schools (as of Spring 2000) that offer online applications through the Review.com Web site.

**Don't Discount
Your Chances**

In Review.com's
What Colleges Want
feature article, it's
stated that "even
the most selective
schools have to dip
into the general run
of humanity in order
to fill their freshman
classes. You
shouldn't discount
your chances simply
because you feel you
don't measure up to
the admissions offi-
cer's ideal."

If you want to read about the admissions process, click the Get into College button in the left sidebar. That will take you to a page titled The Admission Process. You'll see a number of feature articles on such topics as Admissions Secrets, What Colleges Want, and Surviving College Admissions, which can make you an even smarter admissions expert. After reading to your heart's content, go back to the Admissions Process page and click the College Search link in the last paragraph. You'll be taken to a page titled More College Search Options. Click the Alphabetical Listing link to see whether the schools that interest you are listed in Review.com's database.

If your school is listed, click its name and you'll be taken to a page that provides pertinent information about the school, such as tuition costs, admissions criteria, campus life information, and more. To fill out an online application to the school, click the blue Apply button and you'll be taken to a Personal Info page where you'll have to register in order to access Review.com's application processing services. Follow the prompts to register; when you're finished, you'll get access to the school's application information. To use all the features of this service, you must have version 4.0 of Adobe Acrobat Reader installed on your computer. If you don't have it, click the supplied link to download version 4.0.

After you have registered, the Princeton Review sends you an email notification welcoming you to the group and providing a link to important information about the service.

Before you start filling out applications, make sure that you click the links labeled Help and Important Instructions. This associated information explains how the entire process works. Needless to say, one of the best ways to use the Review.com service is to follow Review's help and instructions.

When you start filling out applications, you'll be able to review and update your progress by clicking the My Colleges button, where your application records are kept. You can also have your applications emailed to your parents or your guidance counselor for proofreading and back-checking by clicking the My Settings button and following the prompts. Both your counselor and parents must be registered with Review.com before they can have permission to view your application.

The College Board

The next big contender in the online application world can be found at the College Board's Web site, *www.collegeboard.com/ collapps/html/index000.html*. As mentioned in Chapter 2, "Choosing the Right College," the College Board is an arm of the Educational Testing Service (ETS), the creators of the SAT tests. In addition to the many test preparation services offered at this site, the College Board has an application section. Similar to Embark.com and Review.com, the College Board provides plenty of valuable advice and information concerning the entire application process.

The College Board provides two options for completing an actual application. You can use the Next Stop College service to apply to more than 350 colleges and universities (as of Spring 2000), or you can use the College Applications Online service, which offers free downloadable software, called CollegeLink, for applying to more than 1,000 colleges and universities (as of Spring 2000).

Check It Out

Click the Admissions and Enrollment Staff link on the College Board Web site's home page to see what kind of online services are offered to college and university admissions counselors and recruitment professionals.

The College Board's Web site provides two college and university application services, Next Stop College and CollegeLink.com.

Click the Next Stop College link, then the 375 Colleges and Universities link. If your preferred school(s) are in the displayed list, click your browser's Back button and create an account from the Next Stop College page by clicking the Create Account button. After filling out your account identifier information, you'll be

Print Out Instructions

It's a good idea to print out a hard copy of the College Board's step-by-step guide and place it next to your computer for reference instead of having to toggle back and forth from the guide to the online application.

sent to a welcome page where you are informed that a personalized desktop has been created for you. You can go to it by clicking the Continue button at the bottom of the page. From the personalized desktop, be sure to click the Step by Step Guide located in the purple box at the upper right of your screen. You'll be provided with information on how to complete applications "efficiently and effectively."

As with Embark.com and Review.com, the College Board permits you to exit, save your session, and return in the future by logging on again with the username and password created when you registered.

If you would prefer to use the other application service offered through the College Board, go back to the *www.collegeboard.com/collapps/html/apps.html* page and click College Applications Online. This will give you access to CollegeLink, which is unlike all the previous applications services presented, in that it uses software that you have to install on your computer.

CollegeLink.com and the College Board have teamed up to provide visitors with free software for applying to colleges and universities.

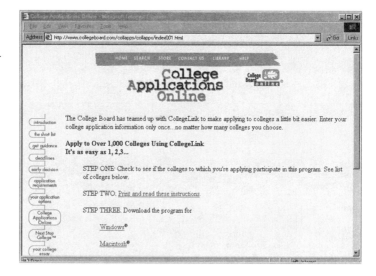

Try It Yourself ▼

To use CollegeLink, follow the three steps provided on the first CollegeLink page:

1. Scroll down to the alphabet-drive menu and see whether your school is listed as a program participant.

2. Click the Print and Read These Instructions link and do just that.

3. Download the program you'll need to install on your computer to use the application service. Instructions are provided for users of Windows 95 or later and Macintosh OS 7.5.3 or later.

After you have downloaded the CollegeLink program and saved it to your computer (preferably in your Programs File folder, if you have one), install the program and try it out. Before actually using the program, you should go to the Reference section located in the top menu bar. There you'll find online help information regarding how to use this software to apply to colleges and universities.

The Common Application

Last but not least on our list of application services is the Common Application, located at *www.commonapp.org*. As stated on the site's home page, "The Common Application is the recommended form of 209 selective, independent colleges and universities for admission to their undergraduate programs."

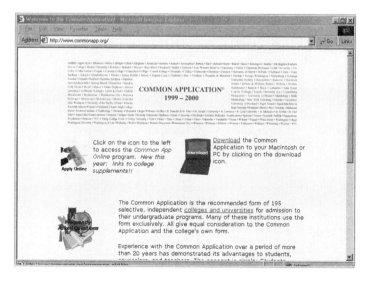

At the Common Application Web site, prospective undergraduates can choose to apply to 209 selective colleges and universities online.

The Common Application Web site is pretty straightforward. To
see the list of member institutions, click the Colleges and
Universities link in the opening paragraph. To start the application
process, you must choose from two options: Just below the main
heading, click the left icon to access the online program, or click
the right icon to download the Common Application program to
your computer.

When you access the online program, you'll be greeted by a page
with eight categories. The first category, College Information, is a
good place to start because it lists all 209 colleges and universities with links to the following information:

- Admissions requirements

- Web sites

- Admissions office email addresses

- Whether the institution accepts the application online or
  requires that you use snail mail

- The institution's phone number

- Whether the institution accepts Early Decision or Early
  Action applications

Early Decision and Early Action

Here are some definitions you should be familiar with when using the
Common Application Web site:

Early Decision (ED) is an admissions process in which a commitment is
made by a student to the institution where, if admitted, he or she will
enroll. Although the student can apply to other colleges, he/she may
have only one ED application pending at a time. If accepted by the college to which he/she has applied for ED, the student is required to withdraw all other applications and make a non-refundable deposit by a
date well before May 1.

Early Action (EA) is an admissions process in which a student is permitted
to apply to institutions of preference and receive a decision in advance
of the normal response date. The student is not committed to enroll at
the institution or to make a deposit prior to May 1. (This includes practices known as early notification and early evaluation.)

For more information about ED and EA, go to *www.perersons.com/
ugrad/earlydecision/html*.

After you have examined the College Information section, you'll
need to register in order to use the online application service.
After you've registered, you'll be supplied with a personal
account similar to all the other application services described in
this chapter. You'll also be able to complete your applications at
your leisure and return to complete the process by logging on
with the username and password that was created when you registered. It's a good idea to read all the help information so that you
use the online version of the form properly.

If you prefer using the programmed version of the Common
Application, you'll have to download the program to your computer from the home page and then install it. After the program is
installed, you'll be able to fill out the entire application step-by-
step and page-by-page on your computer; you can also save it and
come back to it at your convenience. You'll be able to submit the
application electronically to your schools of choice, or you can
print it out and snail mail the hard copy to the appropriate institutions. Use the Help feature located at the top of the menu bar to
familiarize yourself with the entire Common Application program.

Get the Disk

The Common
Application is also
available on com-
puter floppy disk in
either Macintosh or
Windows versions.
The disk costs $10.00
and can be ordered
by calling 1-800-253-
7746.

Other Recommendations

There are more places on the Web to help with admissions and
applications procedures. Here's a short list of who and where they
are and what they offer:

- **College Xpress**—*www.collegexpress.com*
  Carnegie Communications, Inc., is the publisher of this site,
  as well as *Private Colleges and Universities Magazine*. This
  site is a member of the Power Students Network, whose
  home page can be found at *www.powerstudents.com*. College
  Xpress has a relatively large admissions section at *www.col-
  legexpress.com/admissions/index.html*. There's enough information here to keep you very busy, including an Ask the
  CollegeXpress Dean of Admissions bulletin board service
  and some informative articles on understanding the admissions process, getting a jump on the admissions process,
  focusing on your interests, and more.

- *U.S. News—*

  www.usnews.com/usnews/edu/college/cohome. htm

  Scroll down to the Applying pull-down menu for a list of
  links to numerous features on the world of admissions and
  applications. Choose a link and click the Go button. For
  example, under Insider Strategy, you'll see a feature article
  titled "A Peek Behind Closed Doors," in which "*U.S. News*
  sits in as admissions decisions are made at three schools,"
  namely Brown University, the University of California-San
  Diego, and Wesleyan University. Under Application, you'll
  be treated to "a rundown of everything you'll need to do to
  apply to school." Under Consultants, you'll see an article
  about how some students hire assistants to steer them along
  the path toward acceptance into the right institution.

  You can also go to *www.usnews.com/usnews/edu/college/*
  apply/coappfaq.htm for *U.S. News* Online's Frequently Asked
  Questions About Applying section. There are 10 interesting
  questions that "are often on the minds of prospective applicants and their families," all answered by two high school
  counselors, Bonnie Fitzpatrick and Marge Loennig, who have
  a collective 47 years' experience in the field.

Is Paying for Guidance Necessary?

An eye-opening article in the November 1, 1999, issue of *Time Magazine*
profiled Achieva, a company which, according to its Web site at
www.achievaprep.com, advises students on "building strong high school
curriculums, preparing for the SATs, and crafting the personal essay most
schools require." In the *Time* article (titled "Guidance for Sale: Achieva
Does It All—Life Tips, Tutoring, Testing, and College Counseling. Is This a
Good Thing?"), writer Tamela M. Edwards examines the rise of an industry devoted to counseling students on how to get accepted into highly
competitive schools such as Stanford ("which accepted 2,700 applicants
out of 18,000" in 1998). To read the full article, go to *www.time.com/*
time/magazine/articles/0,3266,33136,00.html or read it at the Achieva
Web site at *www.achievaprep.com/article3.htm*.

- **Peterson.com**—*www.petersons.com*

  Self-labeled as "The Education Supersite," Peterson.com is
  another must-stop along the long trail of higher education-
  related Web sites. Go to *www.petersons.com/ugrad/*
  studentadvice.html for a great article titled "Been There

Done That Advice From Six High School Seniors to the
College Bound," where Peterson's Career and Education
Editor Charlotte Thomas reviewed the strategies used by six
high school students in choosing and applying to the right
schools.

- **FishNet**—*www.jayi.com*
Another must-stop Web site, Fishnet—The College Guide,
has plenty of information about college in general along with
a creatively done Dear Admissions Guru section. Don't let
the silhouetted swami look-alike head with blinking star fool
you. This guru has intelligent, advice-oriented answers to a
long list of viable questions in relation to admissions. You
can also read the article titled "Be Real, Get In" by clicking
the Read About College link at the bottom of the FishNet
home page. Written by Ron Moss, director of enrollment
management at Southern Methodist University, this article
covers the admissions decision-making process at the institutional level, and also provides advice on how applicants
should present themselves.

Wrapping It Up

Congratulations on making it to the end of this rather bulky com-
pendium about filling out applications. Actually, we tried to be as
succinct as possible so that we would not bore you to death. After
all, filling out form after form isn't exactly how you want to
spend your weekends. Nonetheless, it's a chore you have to attend
to if you want to get into any college or university. As a refresher,
here's what was discussed in this chapter:

- The sections of college and university Web sites devoted
exclusively to admissions and application criteria. Just about
every institution has one at its Web site, and they are viable
places to learn about entrance requirements, tuition costs, and
college life in general, and, of course, to apply online or
offline.

- The vast expanse of leading non-school Web sites offering
loads of free advice and information about admissions, applications, and everything else you'll find at any given college

and university in the entire universe. These sites also provide you with another way to apply online or offline to the schools you've picked, one of which will eventually become the destination of your higher-education life.

- Finally you were given directions to additional Web sites to visit that should help you along the way.

Now you're ready for Chapter 5, "Perfecting Your Essay Online," which is related to this one. Some schools require that you write an essay about yourself as part of the admissions criteria. Chapter 5 guides you through the Web for help on this all-important essay, which could turn out to be one of the most consequential pieces of writing in your life. Actually, the essay is a good tune-up for all the writing you'll be doing after you get into college. On that note, shall we go forward?

CHAPTER 5

Perfecting Your Essay Online

As mentioned in the previous chapter, when it comes to the overall admissions process, each school is different. The school you select might review a combination of these five basic admissions criteria, all to varying degrees:

- High school records

- SAT or ACT test scores

- Recommendation letters

- An interview

- An application essay

Among these five basic admissions criteria, the application essay "is still taken as a significant and reliable source of information about the applicant," according to Sarah Myers McGinty, author of *The College Application Essay*, published by the College Board. Excerpts from this book, and a link to buy it online, can be found at *www.collegeboard.org/frstlook/cae/html/cae_toc.html*.

In this chapter, you will take a close look at many of the resources available on the Web to help you write the best application essay possible. You'll begin by examining the basics: What is this essay, and what do schools typically want to see?

Next you can peruse some of the free advice that's out there. The Web offers enough free resources on this particular topic to properly guide you along your writing path. In fact, when you see the fee-based application editing services on the Web, you'll notice that these Web sites also provide a wealth of free advice and services to get your creative juices flowing so that you can enthusiastically grapple with your essay.

What You'll Learn in This Chapter:

- ▶ Some basic information about the application essay.

- ▶ Where to go on the Web for free advice on writing the perfect application essay.

- ▶ All about fee-based editing services on the Web that help you write the perfect application essay.

- ▶ How to take advantage of additional free advice and services provided by the fee-based editing services on the Web.

- ▶ What books on the application essay are available.

You'll also see what books about the application essay are available, so you can really fill your brain with every conceivable notion in relation to this important part of the application process.

Finally, a number of tips and various other information have been tossed in to keep you on top of the subject matter being discussed in this chapter.

The Basics of an Application Essay

The application essay is frequently viewed as an important piece of the overall application puzzle because it can give admissions officers a more personalized perspective of an applicant. Additionally, the essay is an obvious reflection of an applicant's writing ability, and sometimes it's seen as an indirect reflection of a student's brainpower. Regardless of how the essay is viewed, you are required to write a truly spectacular composition. Don't worry. Help is on the way!

Start with the basics and ask yourself, what exactly is an essay? For the answer, let's go to *www.m-w.com/dictionary.htm*, which is the home page for *Merriam-Webster's Collegiate Dictionary*. (You might need to use it when you're writing your essay.) A quick search will give you the following definition for the word "essay":

> "An analytic or interpretative literary composition usually dealing with its subject from a limited or personal point of view."

The key words here are "personal point of view." The topic you'll create or be asked to write about will vary from application to application. Typically, the topic relates to your "personal" experiences and perspectives on anything from your educational maturity and goals to your knowledge of classic literature or historical events and your philosophy on life. For example, a recent Common Application (see Chapter 4, "Applying Online") requested an essay of about 250 to 500 words in length on a topic or your choice or on one of the following themes:

- Evaluate a significant experience, achievement, or risk that you have taken and its impact on you.

- Discuss some issue of personal, local, national, or international concern and its importance to you.

- Indicate a person who has had a significant influence on you and describe that influence.

- Describe a character in fiction, an historical figure, or a creative work (as in art, music, science, and the like) that has had an influence on you and explain that influence.

The essay section of a recent North Carolina State University freshman application requested the following two essays, each approximately one-page in length (in no smaller than a 10-point font).

- **Essay 1: Leadership Experience Statement**

  Describe a recent successful or failed leadership experience in which you were challenged. Indicate how you grew from the experience. What were the results of your role in this event or activity?

- **Essay 2: Personal Statement**

  Cite a particular person or experience which has made a significant impact on your ideas, personal values, future goals, and/or educational or professional aspirations. Describe how this factor happened to be influential on the direction of your thinking.

Basically, admissions people want to know about the "real you." Be aware that adding fluff to your essay could be fatal. Most admissions counselors will tell you to simply "Be honest" about yourself and write a well-structured, creative essay that stays focused on the topic requested.

Free Advice

There's free advice on the Web about how to tackle the application essay. You want the good stuff and nothing less. You can start with a section in the College Board Web site at *www.collegeboard.org/collapps/essay/html/indx000.html.*

Officers with Advice

The Associated Colleges of the Midwest (ACM) is comprised of 14 independent liberal arts colleges located in Illinois, Iowa, Minnesota, Wisconsin, and Colorado. Its Web site, at *www.acm. edu/admiss/essay. htm,* offers insight from ACM admissions officers on writing the application essay.

The Your College Essay section in the College Board Web site is a good place to start looking for information and advice about the application essay.

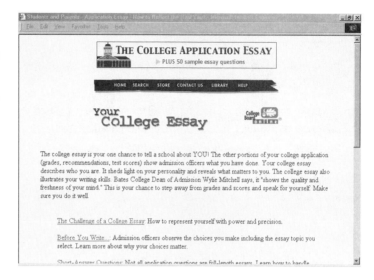

Some Advice, in Short

Follow these three simple steps when writing your application essay: Start early, write often and make revisions, and ask a teacher or parent to review your work before sending it off.

There's plenty of help available at this Web site, with links such as The Challenge of a College Essay, Before You Write, A Closer Look at the Questions, and much more. There's even an Essay Comic Relief link with several jokes about writing.

The link labeled Essay Writing Tips might be a good place to start because it provides preliminary steps you can take to ensure success. As stated here, "all writing is a process." Here are five steps to follow:

- Prewrite
- Choose a thesis
- Write a draft
- Revise
- Polish

Another Web address for free advice on the application essay is located at *www.back2college.com/essay1.htm*. The Acing the Application Essay section at Back2College.com takes you through three steps: brainstorming, selecting the essay topic, and writing the essay topic. At the end of the third step, you'll find a link to a sample essay that was written by a student accepted by Harvard. (Links to more sample essays appear later in this chapter.)

Here's a sampling of some of the advice offered at the
Back2College site:

- "You should expect to devote about 1 to 2 weeks simply to
  brainstorming ideas."

- "…admissions officers do appreciate essays that provide
  convincing evidence of how an applicant will fit into a particular academic environment. You should at least have read the
  college's Web site, and admissions catalog, and have an
  understanding of the institution's strengths."

- "Admissions officers want to learn about you and your writing ability. Write about something meaningful and describe
  your feelings, not necessarily your actions. If you do this,
  your essay will be unique."

Writer's Block

Don't get uptight if
you suddenly find
yourself unable to
scribble a word.
Writer's block is a
common ailment
that attacks every-
one. Simply walk
away, take a
breather, and return
to your writing at a
later time.

The Back2College pages also provide several links to
www.collegegate.com, a Web site that provides both fee-based and
free services related to the application essay. You'll take another
look at Collegegate.com later in this chapter. For now, let's check
out a section of the *U.S. News* Online Web site that has information about the application essay.

▼ **Try It Yourself**

1. Go to *www.usnews.com/usnews/edu* and click the College
   link in the top rectangular box.

2. Scroll down to the Applying pull-down menu, choose The
   Essay, and click Go.

3. Read the *Killer Essays* article written by Andrew Curry.

4. Review the links related to the application essay located in
   the right sidebar.

▲

In his *Killer Essays* article, Curry quotes Dean of Admissions Ted
O'Neil of the University of Chicago as saying, "sometimes the
least successful good essays are so polished they don't reveal anything about the writer." Curry also mentions a Boston College
admissions officer's favorite essays, which included "a reflection
on race by a part-time cashier in a discount clothing shop who
struggled with her conscience after a poor Hispanic woman stole
from the store."

Fee-Based Application Essay Editing Services

Grammar and Style Check-Up?
If you need help with grammar and style, visit the free electronic version of *The Elements of Style*, written by William Strunk, Jr. back in 1918. Check out this classic book online at *www. bartleby.com/141/ index.html*. Another free guide to grammar and style is at *http://andromeda. rutgers.edu/~jlynch/ Writing*, provided by English professor Jack Lynch.

In recent years, Web-based editing services and guides to help you create a top-notch application essay have grown in numbers. Professionals with experience in the college admissions process usually staff these services. In addition to offering some free, but somewhat limited, advice on the web sites, these companies will thoroughly analyze your emailed or faxed essay and provide—for a fee—feedback that should make your essay better.

Some say the stiff competition at Ivy League schools has fueled the growth of such services. Another school of thought suggests that the growth of two-parent, working families has left little time for Dad or Mom to help with their children's essay writing, a situation that has increased the reliance on such services. Still yet another theory proposes that hiring a professional to assist with the application essay can help lower the high level of anxiety that frequently accompanies this task.

What the *New York Times* Says About Application Essay Editing Services

Before you decide to use any of these application essay editing and guide services, you might want to read some articles related to this topic. A great place to go for free newspaper articles on any topic under the sun is the *New York Times* at www.nytimes.com.

To access the *New York Times* archives, click the blue Site Index box located in the left sidebar. You'll be taken to a page with a long list of category links. Click a category to begin your search, or click the black button near the top of the page with the label Site Search. If you use the Site Search function, you'll be linked to a page that offers two options: Search Today's News or Extended Search. For example, by entering **application essay** in the Extended Search box, you'll be provided with the titles of articles with matching words, each with a link to the full text of the article.

There are some very interesting articles on this topic, including "Controversy Over College Application Sites," written by Pamela Mendels in the June 23, 1999, issue. Mendels writes that "...unfairness has long been part of essay writing. The student who has a well-educated parent with time and a grasp of writing, or the student who is enrolled in a better suburban school with essay preparation courses, or the student whose parents pay for a writing coach all benefit from an unlevel playing field."

Another article, "The ———— That Changed My Life," was written by Glenn C. Altschuler in the November 7, 1999, issue. Altschuler served on

Cornell University admissions committees for 10 years. He offers plenty of sound advice, including this: "Write about your world and experiences. Seventeen-year-olds inhabit a foreign country, and adults who work in colleges and universities are curious about what it's like to live within its borders."

You can begin your look at fee-based editing services with a visit to *www.ivyessays.com*.

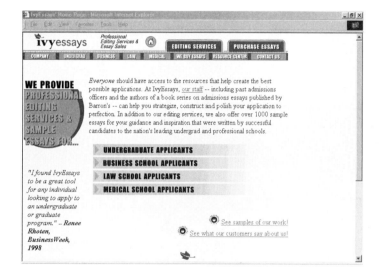

IvyEssays.com features previously written essays, editing services, and online resources that relate to that all-important application essay.

A nice feature of IvyEssays.com is that it has a complete list of the company's management and admissions teams with bios, which can be found by clicking the Our Staff link in the opening paragraph of the home page. The admissions team that assisted with the development of this Web site consisted of experienced admissions professionals from a wide range of colleges and universities.

If you now feel somewhat comfortable with the prospect of using and paying for IvyEssays.com's services, go see what they offer by clicking the Undergraduate Applicants link on the home page. The options available range from a quick second-opinion service to a complete consulting service with a former admissions counselor, who will review your entire application.

You can also take advantage of the large supply of free advice offered by IvyEssays.com. Just look to the left side of the page for a list of links to plenty of valuable information that can help you perfect your application essay without forking over one single dime.

Get a Hearty Laugh

For a nice break from the intense concentration involved with writing your essay, check out the Funny Mistakes link at IvyEssays.com. For example, one student wrote, "I enjoyed my bondage with the family and especially with their mule, Jake."

There's some sound advice here. For example, inside the Nitty Gritty link is information about paragraphs and transitions, word choice, and sentence length and structure. There's also a Beginnings and Endings link that provides numerous examples of real essay introductions and conclusions—and what admissions officers had to say about them. The site also provides suggestions for various types of essay beginning statements, such as the standard lead, the creative lead, the action lead, the personal or revealing lead, the quotation lead, and the dialog lead.

Another editing service you might want to check out is brought to you by CollegeGate at *www.collegegate.com*.

CollegeGate claims to be "the world's premier application essay editing service" with "Harvard-educated" editors.

CollegeGate gives you free access to "over 100 admissions essays accepted by the United States' top undergraduate, graduate, and professional programs." Just click the Sample Essays link in the left sidebar, and you'll be taken to a page that offers a number of options for viewing sample essays. You can search for essays by keywords or categories, view all 100 essays on file, and subscribe to a service that will send you newly arrived sample essays by email that have your keywords in them.

Another free service provided by CollegeGate can be found by clicking the Community link in the left sidebar on the home page. The Community section features a discussion forum, scheduled live chats, admission-related links, and more.

If all these freebies aren't enough, click the Editing Services link in the left sidebar on the home page. Scroll down to the bottom of the page you just linked to and click the College Applicants link. From here you can find all the information you need about CollegeGate's fee-based services.

Some Successful Samples

More sample application essays can be found at *http://user.mc.net/~moeller/essays/essays.htm*. The title of this page is College Application Essay: Five That Worked, and it's brought to you by an English teacher named Mr. Moeller. Two more interesting essays are listed at *http://www2.rogue.cc/OWL/College/exbuck.htm* and are provided by Rogue Community College in Oregon. For a humorous take on a sample essay, see "The Best College Application Essay We Ever Read" at *www.aci-plus.com/tips/tips21.htm*, provided by the ACI Writing Assistance Center.

Another major player in the application essay editing service mini-industry is myEssay.com. You'll find another large offering of sample essays and free advice here. Just click the Undergraduate link on the *www.myessay.com* home page and then click either Sample Essays or Advice at the top of the page. You can also click the Workshops link to take advantage of free online workshops that myEssay.com claims "will help you generate essay topics, understand the meaning behind essay questions, and give you tips and strategies on how to approach the admissions process." Finally, for information on myEssay's fee-based services, click either Evaluation Service or Admissions Kits.

Do the Right Thing

Don't give into the temptation to plagiarize anything from the great sample essays you'll see on the Web—or from any other written material you see on the Web. These samples have been distributed far and wide to admissions staff across the country. If you plagiarize, you'll get nailed.

What Does Plagiarize Mean?

Again using our friends at *Merriam-Webster's Collegiate Dictionary* online (*www.m-w.com/cgi-bin/dictionary*), to plagiarize is "to steal and pass off (the ideas or words of another) as one's own: use (another's production) without crediting the source."

Books on the Application Essay

Shop Around

You can always price shop for books at some of the many other booksellers on the Web. For a list of links to numerous online booksellers, go to Yahoo! and type **booksellers** at the search prompt, or go directly to *http://dir.yahoo.com/ Business_and_ Economy/Shopping_ and_Services/Books/ Booksellers.*

Based on what appears on the Web, there are not a whole lot of books in print on the topic of college application essays. We've listed five you can purchase from *www.amazon.com*. For more information and book reviews on these books, go to Amazon's home page and type any of the titles listed here at the search prompt. Included are prices listed at Amazon.com during Spring 2000.

- *How to Write a Winning College Application Essay* (3rd Edition), by Michael Mason (Prima Pub, $11.90)

- *On Writing the College Application Essay,* by Harry Bald, (Barnes & Noble, $9.60)

- *The Best College Admission Essays,* by Mark Alan Stewart, Cynthia Muchnick (Contributor)(IDG Books Worldwide, $7.96)

- *The College Application Essay (Serial),* by Sarah Myers McGinty (College Entrance Examination Board, $11.01)

- *Writing a Successful College Application Essay,* by George Ehrenhaft (Barrons Educational Series, $8.46)

Wrapping It Up

It's surprising that one relatively small piece of the college application pie can generate so much information and actually spawn its own mini-industry. Yet that's the nature of the higher education admissions and application game. In case you haven't noticed, We've been trying to make this game as easy as possible to win without spending a great deal of your hard-earned cash. That's why there was a relatively strong emphasis in this chapter on the *free* services offered on the Web concerning the application essay.

In brief, here's what this chapter reported:

- Some elementary information about the college application essay.

- How to take advantage of the abundant amount of free advice to develop and ultimately write the perfect application essay.

- The rise of the application essay-editing services that have Web sites featuring both free and fee-based services.

- Where to find sample essays on the Web.

- What books are available on the topic of the college application essay.

Writing an essay does not have to be an overly complicated process. The best way to approach any writing assignment is to clear your mind, take a deep breath, relax, and write in a style that brings out your unique personage. Also, be positive and realize that you are the single most qualified human being on the planet to write about the person you know best.

CHAPTER 6

Your Guide to the PSAT, SAT, and ACT Tests

It all starts in your junior year of high school (for some in your sophomore year) when you take the Preliminary Scholastic Aptitude Test/National Merit Scholarship Qualifying Test, also known as the PSAT/NMSQT, or most often referred to as simply the PSAT. This is the test that will prepare you for the more important Scholastic Aptitude Test, better known as the SAT.

The PSAT test is 80 minutes in length and consists of two verbal sections, two math sections, and one writing skills section. Scores are reported on a 20–80 scale with average scores near 50. It's offered once each year, typically in October.

Your PSAT scores are an indication of your academic readiness for higher education. Additionally, PSAT scores can be considered a gauge of your test-taking skills. Your PSAT score report will also tell you whether or not you qualify for a National Merit Scholarship. For more information about the National Merit Scholarship Program, go to *www.nationalmerit.org*.

After taking the PSAT, you'll have to take the SAT and/or the American College Test, called the ACT. Yes, these tests are indeed "dreaded" by most high school students. But, don't fret. You can easily get help from the higher education lifesaver of the world, also known as the forever-expanding World Wide Web.

SAT or ACT test scores are part of the admission requirements at most colleges and universities. Check with your school or schools of choice to see which scores—the SAT or ACT—are acceptable.

Many high school students take both tests during their junior and senior years, and some students repeatedly take both tests, making their final two years in high school a very serious relationship with a No. 2 pencil.

What You'll Learn in This Chapter:

▶ Where to find the official Web source for the PSAT, SAT, and ACT tests and how you can take advantage of test preparation services.

▶ Where to find additional sites offering free SAT and ACT test preparation services.

▶ Where to find two of the leading fee-based SAT and ACT test preparation services.

▶ Where you can buy SAT and ACT test preparation books and software.

What's the Meaning of This?
The SAT and ACT are not considered intelligence tests. However, a student's scores are considered an indication of his or her verbal and mathematical reasoning abilities.

The SAT (also called the SAT I) is three hours in length and consists of seven sections: three verbal, three math, and one experimental. The experimental section is either math or verbal and is used for research purposes, so it's not tallied into your score. (You won't know which section is experimental when you take the test.) You can take the SAT seven times over a period of one year.

You'll receive a score for the verbal section and a score for the math section scored on a scale of 200–800. The national average is about 500 in each section for a total of 1000. Schools that are relatively difficult to get into usually require above-average scores.

The ACT is about five minutes shorter than the three-hour SAT test. It has four sections: English, math, reading, and scientific reasoning. You can take the ACT five times over a period of one year.

Each section of the ACT is given a separate score on a scale of 1–36. You'll also be given an average composite score of all four sections. The current average composite score is approximately 20.5.

Now to confuse things a bit, there's also the SAT II, which is a series of subject-oriented tests, ranging from writing and world history to modern Hebrew and Chinese. Not all colleges require the SAT II. Each SAT II subject test is one hour long, and you cannot take more than three subject tests at one time. You can take the SAT II six times over a period of one year.

All SAT II subject tests, except for the English language proficiency subject test, are scored on a scale of 200–800.

This chapter covers where you can go on the Web for information about these exams. You'll be introduced to the official Web sites for the PSAT, SAT, and the ACT and how you can take advantage of free test preparation services offered by these sites, such as practice tests and tutorials. You'll also see some other Web sites offering free SAT and ACT test preparation materials. Then you can look at two leading private company Web sites that offer test preparation services for a fee. Finally, you can get an idea about some of the books and software related to this topic that are available for purchase online.

The SAT Controversy Goes Public

If you're interested in the history of the SAT test—and a lot of the controversy currently surrounding it—check out Nicholas Lemann's book *The Big Test: The Secret History of the American Meritocracy*. You can also go to the PBS Web page at *www.pbs.org/wgbh/pages/frontline/shows/sats/*, where you'll find an extensive PBS *Frontline* report titled "Secrets of the SAT." This report features an interview with Lemann, as well as interviews with a number of other prominent higher education professionals. The report takes a close look at the ongoing debate about the validity of standardized testing and its influence on students, parents, teachers, and the future of higher education.

Preparing for the PSAT and SAT

The first place to visit for in-depth information about the PSAT and SAT—and to register for the tests online—is the College Board at *www.collegeboard.org*, the official Web site for the SAT and PSAT.

The College Board, as stated on its Web site, "is a not-for-profit educational association that supports academic preparation and transition to higher education for students around the world through the ongoing collaboration of its member schools, colleges, universities, educational systems, and organizations."

After you've arrived at the College Board site's home page, click the Students & Parents link in the upper-left corner. This will take you to a page titled Starting Points for Students and Parents. From here, scroll down to the Taking the Tests section and click the PSAT/NMSQT link. You are now, thank goodness, at the introduction page for information about this test.

For everything you need to know about the PSAT, click the Student and Parents link on the home page and then scroll down to the section titled Taking the Tests. Click the PSAT/NMSQT link.

The PSAT section of the College Board Web site explains that you should talk to your counselor about how to sign up for the test, which is administered by high schools. Typically, this is a test you take in your junior year; however, many sophomores also take the test for practice.

Check It Out

The Educational Testing Service Network (ETS), at *www.ets.org*, develops and administers the SATs, but the College Board sponsors the SAT and decides how it will be constructed, administered, and used. ETS develops and annually administers a number of different tests worldwide on behalf of clients in education, government, and business.

The College Board Web site has a section with detailed information about the PSAT and SAT; the site also provides visitors with online test registration options.

Click on the Verbal, Math, or Writing Skills link listed under the New Interactive Practice Questions heading for sample "questions with answers and explanations that can help you prepare for test day."

For information on the SAT test, take the same navigation route as above but click the SAT I/II link. In addition to advising you to hurry up and register online for the next SAT test before it's too late, the SAT introduction page has a link to a Features section for information about test dates, deadlines, fees, and other pertinent information related to taking the test and eventually getting your scores. There's also a nifty SAT Question of the Day section, which, after you find you cannot dig into the recesses of your brain for the correct answer, might make you even more paranoid than you already are about taking this test. So, with that in mind, go get some desperately needed help by clicking the link to the College Board's SAT Learning Center.

Rules of the Test-Taking Road

Check out Embark.com's Seven Simple Rules for Taking the SAT Test at *http://testprep. embark.com/sat/ freeinfo/sat_article_ tips.asp.*

Practice, Practice, Practice

The SAT Learning Center is a great place to build your SAT test-taking skills without having to fork over any money for a book or software on the subject or to a test preparation service (more on these later). Also, if you have already taken the SAT I test, you can order a review of the test with a record of your answers and all the correct answers. There's a relatively small fee for this service, but the review might help you realize your weak points, which is especially helpful if you're a no-pain-no-gain individual, who plans on retaking the test.

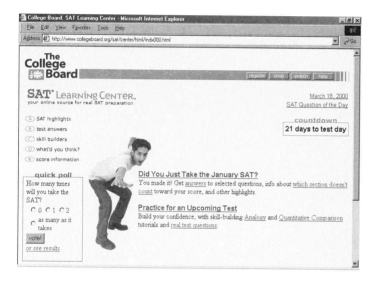

The SAT Learning Center links you to SAT practice tests and an online tutorial section.

One of the obvious ways to become familiar with the SAT test is to take the online "dress rehearsal" version before going to the real show. Let's take a look at how this can be done.

▼ **Try It Yourself**

1. Go the College Board home page at *www.collegeboard.org* and click the SAT Learning Center link.

2. Click the SAT Questions and Answers link.

3. In the menu on the left, click the kind of verbal or math questions you'd like to try.

4. Start answering questions. A link to Explanations and Tips is provided for each question.

▲

Overall, the practice questions are a great way to get a decent heads-up on what to expect on the SAT test. Remember that the SAT is a three-hour test, so you'll want to get accustomed to answering the six unique question types. The three types in the verbal section are analogies, sentence completion, and critical reading. The three types in the math section are regular, quantitative comparisons, and Grid-Ins.

You can also access some helpful—and free—tutorials from the test answers section of the SAT practice questions. Just scroll down to the Step-by-Step Skills section and click the free tutorials link for how to answer analogy or quantitative comparison SAT questions.

The test answers section also provides a SAT II Resources link for help with the SAT II subject tests. The SAT II Resources section has information on when and how to take the subject tests, as well as test-taking tips, test dates, and online registration.

Finally, if all the aforementioned options just don't satisfy your desire to be prepared beyond the call of duty, the College Board Web site sells a software test-practice package called *One-on-One with the SAT*. You can access the details about this software from the SAT introduction page. Just click the Test Prep Products link. But, before dipping into your pocketbook, you can test the waters by downloading a demo of the *One-on-One* product.

Two other test prep products are for sale by the College Board: *Essay Prep*, an online service that can help you with the SAT II writing test, and *Look Inside the SAT I*, a 30-minute videotape for developing your test-taking skills.

Preparing for the ACT

The first place you'll want to visit for information about the ACT is *www.act.org*. Click the Students icon and then click the Take Your Entrance Exam icon.

ACT was founded in 1959. As stated on its Web site, "ACT, Inc., is an independent, nonprofit organization that provides educational services to students and their parents, to high schools and colleges, to professional associations and government agencies, and to business and industry."

Just as the SAT Web site does, act.org provides you with all the necessary information about test date deadlines, test center locations, and test fees in addition to an online registration section. The site also offers free test preparation services, which is what you're really looking for because you want to somehow get a leading edge on hundreds of thousands of your peers.

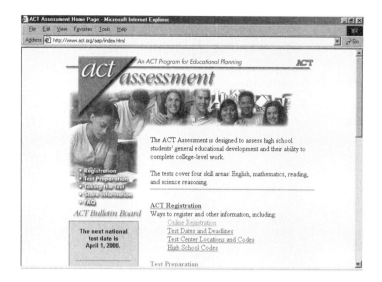

The ACT Web site covers everything you need to know about taking and registering for the ACT test.

More Practice

You can start your pretest studies by taking a complete ACT test. Just scroll down to the Test Preparation heading and click the Sample Questions link.

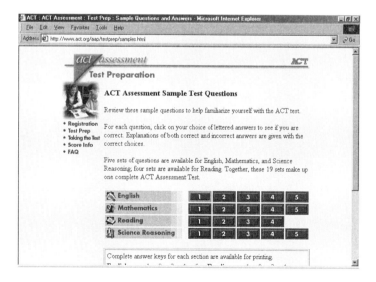

The ACT Web site has a complete online practice ACT test.

When you click the answers to the ACT sample questions, you are immediately informed whether or not you answered correctly.

If you answer correctly, you'll be given an explanation as to why the answer was correct. If you answer incorrectly, you simply get an "incorrect" response message.

Some Quick Tips

Here are some concise tips for test day: Don't answer questions too quickly or too slowly. In other words, pace yourself. Tell yourself that you will do well; answer all questions, even if you must guess; and check your answers if you happen to finish early.

From the sample questions page, you can gain access to an area called Test Prep, which covers test-taking tips. Additionally, in the Useful Test Prep Resources section, you can click the ActivePrep™ link, which takes you to information about the official software for ACT test preparation. If additional tests are what you're looking for, click the Sample ACT Test Booklets link for information on how you can buy enough practice tests to fill your backpack.

Other Test Preparation Web Sites to Consider

Choice is the key word when surfing the Web. In this vast network of human knowledge, you can always find alternative places to visit. For current purposes, you're checking out test-preparation–oriented Web sites that look like they might have some substantive matter—preferably for free—that you can download into your brain. For the sake of brevity (an entire book can be written on this subject alone), short explanations of these Web sites are provided, along with their URLs. You can easily check them out during this extremely important test phase of your life, which you might one day look back on with affection after you have finally been accepted into the college of your dreams.

Here are some alternative sites you might want to consider:

- *www.powerprep.com*
  This must-go-to site is known as the Home of SAT and ACT Prep. Run by College Power Prep in partnership with the Microsoft Corporation, PowerPrep.com offers visitors the opportunity to download four free test preparation software programs. One of the free programs features a one-hour SAT diagnostic test. Before taking the test, you input your GPA along with the college to which you're applying. After you take the test, the program compares your score with your chosen school's entrance requirements. It also compares your scores with other students throughout the country who have similar GPAs.

- *www.testprep.com*

  This site is brought to you by Scholastic Testing systems, formerly Stanford Testing Systems, Inc. In addition to accessing information on fee-based school and home-study test preparation programs, visitors can use the site's free WebWare for the SAT service. This service will diagnose your weak areas after you take the College Board–sanctioned sample SAT I test, which you can obtain from your high school guidance office. You can access this service by going to *www.testprep.com/practice.html* and clicking the WebWare for the SAT I Test link. If you just want to review your math and verbal skills, there's a link for that free service, too!

- *www.4Tests.com*

  This site is an affiliate of PowerStudents.com and Barrons Educational Series, Inc. (a publisher of test preparation manuals and school directories). Free SAT and ACT practice tests are available at this site.

Private, Fee-Based Companies Offering Test Preparation Services

It's no secret that providing test preparation services for the SAT and ACT is a multimillion-dollar industry and a natural for the World Wide Web with its almost permanent visiting herd of high school students. Nonetheless, as with almost everything on the Web, it's very difficult to pick the service that might be right for you, especially because all these test preparation services on the Web claim to be the leader "guaranteed to raise your test scores." So, keeping that in mind, we will show you two of the big players in this field, the Princeton Review and Kaplan, Inc. But, please, remember that only *you* can prevent poor test scores.

The Princeton Review

The Princeton Review provides test preparation classes in settings located throughout the United States and in many international locations. Princeton Review also sells test preparation books, software, and various types of personal tutor services. One of the quickest ways to navigate to information about Princeton Review's test preparation services is to go to its home page at *www.review.com* and click the Get Info On: Our Courses link located at the lower-left sidebar menu. From the next page, use the scroll-down menu to select the test you want information about and click the Show Me Courses button. You'll be taken to the College page, which has a test-locator function.

The Princeton Review Web site helps students locate SAT and ACT class schedules and class locations throughout the United States and Canada.

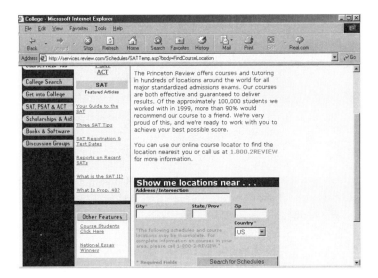

The locator function can help you find class schedules and test locations throughout the United States and Canada. Go ahead and try it by filling out the locator form with your address and ZIP Code and clicking the Search for Schedules button. First you'll get a page showing the names of Princeton Review Offices in your area along with tiny directional maps. You can click a map to show a more detailed version. You can also click an office name and be whisked to another page with the same tiny map and a click-for-more-detail function, as well as the class schedules being offered, contact information, and tuition costs.

For Princeton Review–sanctioned test preparation software, click the Books & Software link at the top of the page. The Books and Software page lets you know that to get information about test preparation software, you'll have to link to The Learning Company's online store. When you get there—surprise!—you discover you're at a page within *www.shopmattel.com*. At the bottom of this page, you'll find links to information about two

SAT/ACT test preparation software packages (regular and deluxe) authored by the Princeton Review.

Kaplan, Inc.

As does the Princeton Review, Kaplan, Inc. offers private tutoring services, classroom instruction, and test preparation software and books. In addition, Kaplan offers online courses. The obvious place to start is at *www.kaptest.com.*

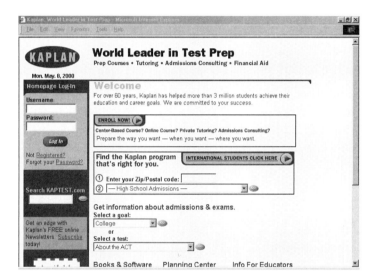

In addition to test preparation tutoring, classes, software, and books, Kaplan.com offers online test preparation learning.

Scroll down to the Get Information about Admissions & Exams section and select College from the scroll-down menu. A bit further down is another scroll-down menu, from which you select the ACT, PSAT, or SAT test and then click the Go button.

When you get to the pages for any of these tests, you'll see a scroll-down menu at the top of the page with links to programs available and information about the tests. In the left sidebar of these pages are links labeled Test Dates and Registration and Test Day Tips.

Be Prepared

For things you should know about on the day you take your standardized tests, go to the Test Day section in the College Board Web site at *www.collegeboard.com/sat/html/students/take000.html.* For example,

continues

continued

under the What to Expect link, the College Board explains that you can bring along only your admissions ticket, two #2 pencils and a good eraser, identification, an "acceptable" calculator, and an "acceptable" cassette player (if you happen to be taking the SAT II English Language Proficiency Test). Don't even think about bringing food or drink, a watch with an audible alarm, a cellular phone, or anything else other than the items on this short list and your brain. Incidentally, make sure that you get a good night's sleep the day before, eat a decent breakfast, and wear comfortable clothes so that your brain functions properly on test day.

You can check out where Kaplan's test services are available and how much they cost by using the box labeled Find the Kaplan Program That's Right for You. Enter your ZIP Code and the test you're interested in taking, and you'll be taken to a page listing tutoring-center-based classes available in your area and online courses, along with pricing for each.

Check It Out

For information about fairness and bias issues in relation to standardized tests, go to *http://fairtest.org*, the Web site of The National Center for Fair & Open Testing. This advocacy organization claims to be "working to end the abuses, misuses, and flaws of standardized testing."

What the *New York Times* Says about the SATs

We found more than 60 articles about the SAT tests going back several years in the archives of the *New York Times* Web site at *www.nytimes.com*. One particularly interesting piece, titled "Students Behaving Badly," was written by University of California, Santa Barbara, Professor Richard Flacks in the January 7, 2000 issue. The article explored the results of a study about students' academic success and its relationship to their social backgrounds and SAT test scores. Flacks and his colleague, Scott Thomas, conducted the study, which surveyed 1,000 Santa Barbara students. Of these 1,000 students, 15% had family incomes below $25,000 and 15% had family incomes above $125,000. The students from the higher-income group had SAT scores that were almost 200 points higher than their lower-income student colleagues. However, "while their dismal scores would suggest that the poor students were unprepared for the demands of college, their grade point averages were only slightly lower than those of the more privileged students: 2.80 versus 2.95," writes Flacks.

Additionally, Flacks says that within the political-sociology classes he teaches at UCSB, the students who turned in papers that were polished and showed an "obvious effort," had "demanding and difficult personal lives." On the other hand, he found that the "typical Santa Barbara student, who attends good schools and has high test scores and parents with advanced degrees" usually was not among the students who completed quality papers. According to Flacks, studies have shown that test scores are related to family income, "which determines the quality of a student's schooling and a family's ability to pay for test preparation." He also mentions that there is "growing evidence that scores are affected by biases built into test content and by the emotional effect of the test-taking experience."

Finding SAT and ACT Books and Software on the Web

You can always go to the Amazon.com Web empire to find literature, software, and more to support your quest for test preparation
material. Simply go to *www.amazon.com*. In the search box in the
upper-left sidebar, search all products by typing **SAT and ACT.**
This query will display a page that lists everything on the SAT
and ACT tests that's available for purchase either directly from or
through Amazon.com.

The Amazon.com search function allows you to find plenty of SAT and ACT test prepara-tion books and software you can purchase online.

Amazon presents four category options to choose from:
Electronics & Software, Books, zShops, and Auctions. What are
zShops you ask? When you buy from zShops, you buy from a
private seller or company, instead of buying directly from
Amazon.com, which might or might not save you some money.
zShops are similar to Web auctions except that, in a zShop, prices
are fixed. (You can't bid a price on an item.) If you're a real bargain hunter, you might find that the Auctions section of
Amazon.com will lead you to someone who is willing to sell you
the test preparation materials you want at a rock-bottom price. If
neither zShops nor Auctions is your cup of tea, you can find
plenty of new books and software for sale in the appropriate sections.

The Search for Test Prep Books and Software Continues

You should also visit Amazon's major competitor on the Web, Barnes and Noble at *www.bn.com.*

At Barnes and Noble, you'll find some software and books that were not listed on the Amazon site. Barnes and Noble also offers a Test Prep Solutions Store that you might want to check out.

You can access the B&N Test Prep Solutions Store from the B&N home page by typing **SAT and ACT** in the keyword mode of the search function at the top of the page. This search displays a page headlined Book Search Results. Just below this headline is a link labeled Increase Your Confidence, Visit Our Test Prep Solutions Store. Click this link to go shopping.

The Barnes and Noble bookstore Web site has a Test Prep Solutions store where you can find CD-ROMs and books to help you out on the SAT and ACT tests.

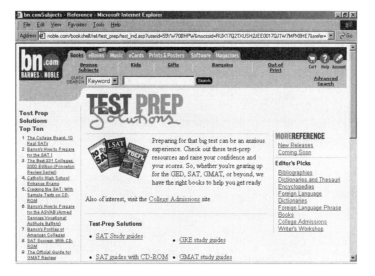

In addition (as you've undoubtedly noticed if you've been browsing the sites described in this chapter), all the test-related Web sites mentioned in this chapter have pages where you can order online or link to other sites where you can purchase SAT and ACT test preparation software or books.

Wrapping It Up

For all the high school students who are starting to really feel the pangs of paranoia regarding the SAT and ACT tests, we hope this chapter has given you some optimism that all is not lost. Here's what was covered:

- Where to go on the Web to get official information from the makers of these tests and how to use their programs and services to help prepare for the SAT and ACT.

- How to take advantage of some of the free SAT and ACT test-preparation services offered on the Web.

- Where to go on the Web to find information about SAT and ACT test-preparation classes, tutoring services, and other fee-based test-preparation programs available.

- Some places to go to on the Web for news coverage related to controversial issues surrounding standardized testing.

- Where to find printed materials and CD-ROMs for sale on the Web that can help you study for the SAT and ACT.

Remember, no test in the world can be a true measure of a person's intelligence. Some people just aren't cut out for test-taking, and others are naturals at it. Nonetheless, the bottom line is that most colleges and universities use these test scores as part of their admissions criteria, meaning that a good score can only help you. With that in mind, this chapter provided information about Web sites that can will help you do better on these tests.

But, as mentioned earlier, your ability to do well on these tests will really come from the amount of time and energy you put into reading and studying during your entire high school career. It might not be possible to cram for these tests over a short period of time. However, if you get a decent head start and use some of the test preparation services available to you on the Web, you might increase your test scores. (By how much is anybody's guess.)

One thing *is* certain: The Web allows you to study for these tests on your own time and at your own pace, which also means that you, and you alone, are the master of your fate.

CHAPTER 7

Finding and Applying for Financial Aid Online

You've arrived at the all-important chapter in this book and in your life. You've found the right school. You've made it through the cumbersome application process. You've aced your assessment tests, written an award-winning application essay, and have been accepted to attend your favorite school(s). Now you have to swim through a huge ocean of financial aid information on the Web to see what assistance might be available to help pay for your higher-education venture.

At this point, here's a good question to ask yourself: "How far can I tread water?" We're speaking figuratively, of course. The point is that navigating this vast sea of financial aid information on the Web is a sink-or-swim situation. This chapter, however, will help you stay afloat.

This chapter begins with a definition of financial aid and a visit to a typical financial aid office section inside a university Web site. You'll be introduced to the first of many terms you'll encounter, as well as the first of many forms you'll complete along the financial aid trail.

You'll be shown many great Web sites as you search for information and online services related to financial aid. We'll talk about federal and state financial aid. We'll talk about scholarships and visit Web sites devoted to the process of finding every conceivable scholarship available to the free world.

You'll pay an extensive call to the world of higher education loans, covering government and private loans. You'll also learn about financial aid tax credits and educational loan forgiveness programs.

What You'll Learn in This Chapter:

- ▶ What financial aid is and what forms you need to fill out to be considered for it.

- ▶ Where to go on the Web to learn about and calculate your (EFC) Expected Family Contribution toward the cost of your higher education.

- ▶ What kind of federal and state aid is available.

- ▶ How complete the Free Application for Financial Student Aid (FAFSA) and the CSS Financial Aid Profile.

- ▶ Everything you could possibly want to know about finding scholarships using the Web.

Throughout the entire chapter, you'll see numerous Web home
pages and numerous sections within various Web sites. The goal
is to educate you about financial aid, as well as to cut your navigation time down considerably by directing you to Web pages that
will immediately provide you with the necessary information and
online forms. These pages should help you complete the financial
aid process in record time.

An Introduction to Financial Aid

Check This Out

For a glossary of
financial aid terms,
go to the College-
Is-Possible Web
site at *www.
collegeispossible.org/
paying/glossary.htm.*

Financial aid is an umbrella term with many categories and subcategories. For instance, *loans* are one major category under the
umbrella of financial aid, even though it's easy to think of a loan
as a burden, instead of aid. There are many types of loans to consider, such as federally backed student or parent loans, private
loans, college-based loans, special loans that can be forgiven
under particular circumstances, and more.

Then there are *grants*, which can truly be considered aid because
you don't pay them back. There are two major categories of
grants, federal and state, with a host of subcategories under each.

The next broad category is *scholarships*, which you also don't
repay. Scholarships encompass numerous programs and classifications. For example, there are academic scholarships, athletic
scholarships, free scholarship contest give-aways, scholarships
from private sources, National Merit Scholarships, and more.

Another financial aid category worth mentioning can be listed
under the banner of *tuition prepayment programs* and *savings
plans.*

Finally, one more category of financial aid is called *work-study*, a
federal program that helps students find jobs to help them work
their way through college.

Finding the information you need on the Web about any or all of
these levels of financial aid can be a monumental task. There are
federal sites, state sites, lender sites, scholarship search sites,
school sites with financial aid sections, private sites and, of
course, the Web portals to higher education that all have plenty
of information on financial aid. There are links and more links,
databases and more databases, and guides and more guides.

In addition to Web-based information, there are enough books on this subject to fill an entire library.

Where to Begin

You can begin the financial aid process by visiting your high school guidance office and asking questions. Next, get plenty of information from the financial aid office of the school you plan to attend, which can be found at the school's Web site. For example, take a look at the Cornell University Web site financial aid section for undergraduate admissions at *http://cuinfo.cornell.edu/UAO/finaid.html.*

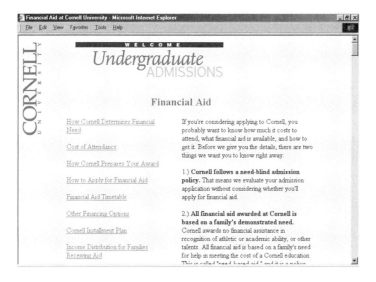

Like most college and university Web sites, Cornell University has a financial aid section that takes you through a step-by-step process to apply for financial aid.

Notice that the very first link is titled How Cornell Determines Financial Need. This is the first step along the financial aid process. Basically, Cornell determines your need in a manner similar to most other colleges and universities: They go by your EFC.

What's an EFC?

EFC is the acronym for *Expected Family Contribution.* According to the College Board, the EFC "is the amount the college will expect you and your family to pay—in other words, your share of the total college costs. The EFC is determined based on an analysis of a family's income and assets."

The EFC Stops Here
Go to the U.S. Department of Education's Student Guide section at *www.ed.gov/prog_info/SFA/StudentGuide/2000-1/need.html* for more information about the EFC. From this page, you can also download a PDF file containing the federal worksheets used to calculate the EFC.

Schools have different methods for calculating an EFC. Cornell includes both parent and student components and "weighs income, assets, family size, and the number of children enrolled full-time in college. The student's expected contribution includes a summer earning component, as well as money from personal savings and assets."

You can find more information about the EFC, as well as get an estimate of your own EFC total, by going to the three Web sites that should be your primary resources for financial aid. You'll be referred to these golden sources of online financial aid information frequently throughout this chapter:

- The College Board's financial aid section at *www.collegeboard.org/toc/html/tocfinancialaid000.html*

- FinAid at *www.finaid.org*

- The U.S. Department of Education's financial aid section at *www.ed.gov/offices/OSFAP/Students*

As do all the Web sites featured in this chapter, the College Board's financial aid section has plenty of valuable information to help you pay for college. For now, you can look at the site's online EFC calculator service at *www.collegeboard.org/finaid/fastud/html/efc.html*.

The College Board Web site has a special section where you can use a free EFC calculator service to determine how much you and your family will be expected to contribute toward your college costs.

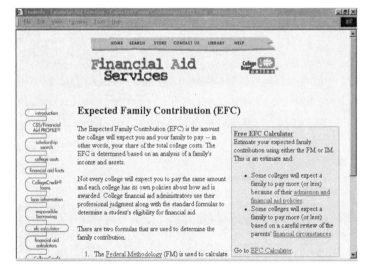

The College Board explains that there are two formulas used for calculating your EFC: the Federal Methodology (FM) or the Institutional Methodology (IM). FM is used for federal or state government financial aid programs. IM is used primarily for school or private financial aid programs (and is used in conjunction with another form, called the CSS Financial Aid Profile, covered later in this chapter). Plenty of additional information concerning the EFC can be accessed from the College Board site. You might want to go through the links to get a better understanding of what the EFC is all about. Then click the Go to EFC Calculator link.

The EFC calculator has form fields that prompt you for information about the educational status of family members, along with income, assets, and tax data that you must collect from recent tax returns. You have the option of calculating the FM EFC, the IM EFC, or both figures.

Another online EFC calculator service is in the FinAid site at *www.finaid.org/calculators/finaidestimate.phtml*. The FinAid site takes a little different approach than the College Board. Read the caveats on the opening page, then fill out the calculator form, which prompts you for information similar to that requested by the College Board's calculator service. You can also get the FM or IM calculations at the FinAid Web site. We tried both the College Board and FinAid's calculators, and there was only a miniscule discrepancy in the results.

If Necessary, You Can Appeal

If you want to appeal your EFC calculation because of a change that occurred in your financial status since you applied for aid, contact your school's financial aid office. Be ready to verbally explain your special circumstances, put your request in writing, and document everything.

Free Publications on Financial Aid from the U.S. Department of Education

While you're at the Department of Education Web site, you can take advantage of some of the HTML and PDF versions of free federal financial-aid–related publications available. From the page at *www.ed.gov/prog_info/SFA*, you'll find links to these titles:

• Funding Your Education

• Looking for Student Aid

• Student Guide—Financial Aid from the U.S. Department of Education

• Instructions for Completing the Free Application for Federal Student Aid (FAFSA)

Federal Financial Aid

The federal government awards financial aid based on need; the Free Application for Financial Student Aid (FAFSA) is the starting point for qualifying for federal aid. The EFC calculation form is found within the FAFSA.

What's the FAFSA?

FAFSA is the acronym for the U.S. Department of Education's *Free Application for Financial Student Aid*, which is the form you have to fill out to qualify for various federal financial aid programs, including the Pell Grant.

According to the U.S. Department of Education, the EFC formula is used to determine an applicant's need for assistance from the following Student Financial Assistance Programs:

- Federal Pell Grant: A financial need-based federal grant that does not have to be repaid. The maximum award for the 1999–2000 award year was $3,125.

- Subsidized Stafford Loan: According to the U.S. Department of Education, "direct and FFEL Stafford Loans are the Department's major form of self-help aid. Direct Stafford Loans are available through the William D. Ford Federal Direct Loan (Direct Loan) Program and FFEL Stafford Loans are available through the Federal Family Education Loan (FFEL) Program. The terms and conditions of a Direct Stafford or a FFEL Stafford are similar. The major differences between the two are the source of the loan funds, some aspects of the application process, and the available repayment plans. Under the Direct Loan Program, the funds for your loan are lent to you directly by the U.S. government. Under the FFEL Program, the funds for your loan are lent to you from a bank, credit union, or other lender that participates in the FFEL Program." Qualified dependent students can borrow up to $2,625 during their first academic year. Qualified independent students can borrow up to $6,625 during their first academic year.

- Federal Supplemental Educational Opportunity Grant (FSEOG): Another financial need-based grant that does not have to be repaid. According to the Department of Education, FSEOG is for undergraduate students with "exceptional" financial need—in other words, students with the lowest EFCs. The grant also gives priority to students who receive Federal Pell Grants. FESOG awards are between $100 and $4,000.

- Federal Perkins Loan: The Department of Education says "a Federal Perkins Loan is a low-interest (5%) loan for both undergraduate and graduate students with exceptional financial need. Your school is your lender. The loan is made with government funds with a share contributed by the school. You must repay this loan to your school." Currently, you can borrow up to $4,000 per year of undergraduate study.

- Federal Work-Study (FWS) Programs: These are campus-administered programs that help students find jobs, usually community-service work or jobs related to their studies. The FWS program is also based on financial need. Your total FWS award depends on when you apply, your level of need, and the funding level of your school. Pay is at least minimum wage and could be higher depending on a student's skills or the type of work involved. The total amount you earn in an FWS program can't exceed the total of your FWS award.

- PLUS Loans: These are low interest educational loans for parents who have a good credit rating. (Interest can be no more than 9%, and rates can fluctuate each year of repayment.) However, these loans are known to have more flexible standards of credit worthiness than nonfederal loans. Loans are based on your cost of attendance, less the total amount of financial aid you receive.

Get the Details and Call for More

For details and contact information on all federal financial aid programs, go to *www.ed.gov/prog_info/SFA/StudentGuide/2000-1*.

Filling Out the FAFSA

You can fill out the FAFSA online by going to a Web site especially made for you at *www.fafsa.ed.gov*. Give it a whirl. You might want to fill out the FAFSA online because it's the most expedient method for submitting the form. You'll want to do this as early as possible during the financial aid application process.

Try It Yourself ▼

1. Point your browser to *www.fafsa.ed.gov*.

2. Click Getting Started and then link to and read the informational pages covering such important topics as Requirements for Browsers, Records You'll Need, Tips and Shortcuts, Deadlines, and so on. It's suggested that you read through all the links.

3. Click the Go Back link to return to the home page and then click Entering a FAFSA Online.

4. Although you can start filling out the form right away, it's suggested that you read through all the links on this page, too. In particular, the Pre-Application Worksheet link is very helpful.

5. If you feel comfortable with the process you're about to undertake, go ahead and start by clicking the Fill Out a FAFSA link. Overall, the entire process requires your undivided attention. If you run into a jam, click the Help button at the bottom of each page. Many of the form fields also have links to more information on how to fill out a particular field. As you're going along, you'll see a color bar at the top of each page showing what percentage of the application you have completed.

6. If you want to save your form so that you can return to it at a later time before completing and submitting it, click the Save button and follow the instructions in detail. (Don't forget to change the file extension of your saved application to .HTM or .HTML.)

7. When you have completed and submitted the FAFSA, you'll see a confirmation page along with information on your estimated EFC.

You can also fill out the FAFSA form by using software called FAFSA Express. To download this software, go to *www.ed.gov/offices/OSFAP/Students/apply/fexpress.html*. Like the online version, the software allows you to complete the application and submit it via the Internet.

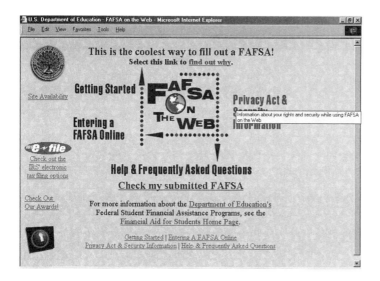

The FAFSA Web site claims to offer "the coolest way to fill out a FAFSA."

You can also download a PDF version of the FAFSA by going to *www.ed.gov/offices/OPE/express.html*. Download the file and print it; then fill out the application the traditional way and snail mail it to the Federal Student Aid Information Center.

Finally, for complete step-by-step instructions for filling out the FAFSA, you can go to *www.ed.gov/prog_info/SFA/FAFSA/instr00-1/index.html*.

The Traditional Method

To receive a paper copy of the FAFSA by snail mail, call the Federal Student Aid Information Center at 1-800-4-FED-AID (1-800-433-3243)/ TDD 1-800-730-8913.

Following Up on the FAFSA

So, what happens after you complete your FAFSA and send it off to the Department of Education's student aid center? In about one to four weeks, depending on how you completed the application, you'll receive a Student Aid Report, otherwise known as an SAR, by snail mail.

What's the SAR?

SAR is the acronym for the *Student Aid Report*, which is a precise look at the information you provided on your FAFSA. The SAR includes your calculated EFC, which is used in determining the amount of money you and your family can afford to contribute toward the cost of your higher education.

In most cases, the schools you might attend (which you listed on your FAFSA) also receive a copy of your SAR. However, be absolutely sure to contact each school's financial aid office to make sure it did, in fact, receive your SAR. Schools use SARs as the basis for compiling financial aid award letters they send to their prospective students. The award letter spells out the kind of complete financial aid package for which you qualify.

The SAR is divided into two parts. Your calculated EFC will be on the first page of your SAR. Part 1 lets you know whether you qualify for a Pell Grant and lists the information you provided on your FAFSA. Part 2 gives you the opportunity to correct any errors made on your FAFSA.

You might be selected for a process called *Verification*, which is the government's way of ensuring that this entire process is working properly. If you're chosen for Verification, you'll be required to submit copies of federal income tax returns and wage earning statements to the school you plan to attend.

Think You Can Beat the Government?

If you're contemplating the prospect of beating the government's system for calculating financial need, read about the 10 myths of financial aid provided by the University of Wisconsin-Stevens Point located on the Web at *www.uwsp. edu/stuserv/finance/ apply/myths.htm*. Each myth has a parallel, eye-opening reality check.

Federal Aid Revisited

A good place for more information about federal financial aid can be found at the U.S. Department of Education's project EASI (Easy Access for Students and Institutions) Web site, located at *http://easi.ed.gov*. Created through a joint effort of the Department of Education, students, educators, and the business community, EASI's objectives include "providing a single point of contact by which students and institutions can carry out necessary tasks associated with postsecondary education, while streamlining processes and reducing complexity, redundancy, and cost."

The CSS Profile

In addition to completing an FAFSA, many colleges and universities, as well as certain scholarship programs, require that you complete the College Board's CSS/Financial Aid PROFILE®.

What's the CSS/Financial Aid PROFILE?

CSS/Financial Aid PROFILE is a financial aid application service administered by the College Scholarship Service®, which is the financial aid division of the College Board.

CSS PROFILE is the basis for awarding nonfederal financial aid dollars. For information on the key differences between the FAFSA and CSS PROFILE, check out *www.finaid.org/fafsa/ cssprofile.phtml* at the FinAid Web site.

To fill out the CSS form online, you must go to a page within the College Board Web site at *www.collegeboard.org/finaid/fastud/ html/proform.html.*

The College Board Web site has a special section for completing its CSS/Financial Aid PROFILE online.

Click the I Wish to Complete PROFILE Online link at the bottom of the page and then click the Start a New Application button. This will give you access to all the information you need for completing CSS PROFILE. It's a good idea to check out the links at the bottom of the page before proceeding. At the Help Desk, for instance, click the Things That You Will Need link for a list of items you'll want to have handy when filling out this application. Click the Participating Institutions and Programs link to find out whether the school or scholarship program in which you're interested is among the approximately 350 colleges and universities and 350 scholarship programs that use the CSS PROFILE.

Hard Copy, Please

If you want to register for the paper version of the CSS application, call 1-800-778-6888, Monday through Friday, from 8 a.m. to 6 p.m., Eastern time. The same fees apply for the paper version.

Before you can actually start an application, you'll have to register and pay for this service with a credit card. CSS charges $6 for registration and $16 for each school or scholarship program to which you want the application delivered.

State Financial Aid

To make your financial aid quest even more unwieldy, there are numerous state financial aid programs offering an array of special programs that can include grants, scholarships, special loan packages, prepaid tuition and savings plans, and even work-study programs. Every state is different, with each providing more or less aid than the other. State aid can consist of a variety of financial need-based or non-financial needs-based aid.

Check It Out

Read "A Reason to Choose State U: Good Students Can Take a Free Ride," by Amy Saltzman, in the *U.S. News* Online Web site at *http://www.usnews. com/usnews/edu/ college/cohono.htm.* Saltzman writes about how various states are beefing up their aid programs in order to keep students in state instead of out of state.

Frequently, the results of your FAFSA form are used as part of the state aid application process in conjunction with other state-related forms. Most state aid is geared toward legal in-state residents, but some state aid programs do not have in-state residency requirements. Some state aid programs require that you attend a school within the program's respective state; others do not have that limitation. There are also programs available for specific areas of study, as well as awards based on various special interests and veteran and minority status. In short, with all these variables, it definitely pays to check out state aid.

You'll have to contact the various state aid agencies to get detailed information about their financial aid programs. Be aware that there are two types of state agencies: state grant agencies and state guaranty agencies. *State grant agencies* provide information and applications for financial aid specific to the individual state. *State guaranty agencies* are local state agencies that handle the administration of student loans under the Federal Family Education Loan (FFEL) program. To find a listing of phone numbers, addresses, contact names, and links to Web sites for both state grant agencies and state guaranty agencies, go to the project EASI Web site at *http://easi.ed.gov/studentcenter/html/apply/state.html.*

Did You Take the Prepaid Route?

Prepaid tuition and savings plans, currently offered by at least 33 states (and growing fast), allow parents to save for their children's higher education by putting money into an account that is guaranteed to increase in value in line with tuition increases at predetermined state public or private colleges and universities. Some plans allow parents to lock into current tuition rates years before their children start attending college. Many parents participate in such programs well in advance of the need for college tuition, when their children are in elementary school.

One of the primary benefits of participating in these programs is that they offer both federal and state tax exemptions.

If you've been taking part in a prepaid tuition plan, you should be aware of long-range tax implications, comparative financial investment plans, and the impact all this might have on your financial aid eligibility. For instance, depending on the state plan you have, the amount you have in a prepaid plan might be figured into the computation of your EFC.

For everything you need to know about prepaid tuition programs, go to *www.finaid.org/otheraid/prepaid.phtml*. The people at FinAid have compiled some highly informative advice about this topic, along with addresses, phone numbers, and Web site links to state prepaid tuition plan programs.

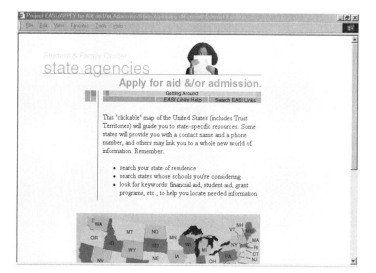

The U.S. Department of Education's project EASI Web site has a directory to state grant and guaranty agencies with a point-and-click map or text-based search features.

All About Scholarships

One of the first stops on the trail to higher education scholarships occurs when students take the PSAT/NMSQT test during the fall of their junior year in high school (see Chapter 6, "Your Guide to the PSAT, SAT, and ACT Tests"). This is a highly competitive test in which approximately 7,000 scholarships are awarded for undergraduate study. For information on how awards are offered, get the PSAT/NMSQT Student Bulletin at your high school guidance office. (It was not available on the Web at the time of this writing.)

The next step on the scholarship trail is to search through the varied and numerous private, corporate, and organizational-based scholarships, as well as scholarships available from the school you're planning to attend. There are also government-based scholarship programs you might not have discovered when you filled out the FAFSA or when you searched through the state agencies.

If all this sounds a bit overwhelming, you're right. To make matters worse, there is way too much information about higher education scholarships on the Web. However, to possibly narrow down your choices, you're about to be introduced to some more highly regarded scholarship-oriented sites. You can also check out the Web site of the school you're planning to attend.

For a great example of a school's Web pages on scholarship information, check out University of Oregon's (UO) page at *http://financialaid.uoregon.edu/SC-guide.htm*. This well-organized page comes from UO's financial aid office and is typical of many scholarship-oriented pages inside college and university Web sites.

The University of Oregon has a good example of a school Web site with a section on scholarship availability.

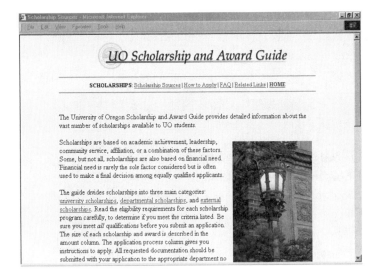

Notice how UO divides scholarships into three basic categories: university, departmental, and external. This is a good example of what's typically available throughout the world of scholarships. UO explains that university scholarships are administered by the school's financial aid or admissions office. You have to fill out a special application provided by UO to be considered for a university scholarship. (Unfortunately, filling out applications is a never-ending and mundane process that is part and parcel of the entire going-to-college scene.)

Department scholarships "are those administered by UO professional schools, colleges, academic or administrative departments, and other UO organizations such as the Alumni Association and fraternal organizations." These types of awards usually require you to fill out an additional application through the appropriate department or through UO's financial aid or admissions offices. (More apps!)

Finally, external scholarships at UO are "those sponsored and administered by individuals, agencies, or organizations not directly affiliated with the University of Oregon." These scholarships also require you to fill out special applications. (What can be said that hasn't been said already?) The external scholarships selectively listed by UO Web site are primarily local awards requiring in-state residence. To find more information on external scholarships located outside of UO's selective list and for applicants residing outside of Oregon, UO points its visitors to a popular Web site called FastWeb at *www.fastweb.com*. This site takes you to your next major stop along the scholarship trail.

Faster than a Speeding Scholarship

FastWeb has more than 6 million registered users. That fact alone tells you that it must be doing something right.

If you're not one of the 6 million already registered with FastWeb, you'll have to complete a rather extensive eight-step questionnaire to register before you can use the scholarship search service. You'll be asked plenty of questions regarding numerous facets of your life, including, but not limited to, your hobbies, special interests, employment background, ethnicity, GPA, test assessment scores, and a whole lot more. (If you don't like supplying personal information over the Internet, this is not the place for you.) After you complete the registration process, you'll realize the meaning of the label FastWeb. About as quick as you can

Keep the Record Straight

Always keep copies of every form you fill out, including online forms that you can print out as you complete them. You never know when something will get lost in the process. Maintain a copy file and date everything.

say, "I want a scholarship," up comes a page listing all the scholarships that might fit within the specifications of your profile. Moreover, each scholarship program listed links to a page with contact information, program details and, if applicable, a link to the program's Web site.

FastWeb.com's scholarship search service will build a student's customized profile and then find scholarships that fit the parameters of that profile.

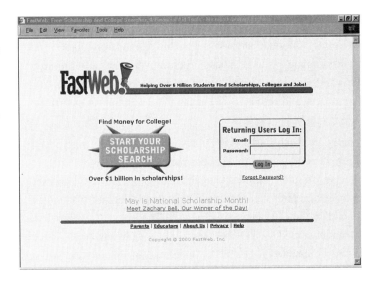

Pretty impressive! Perhaps even more impressive is that FastWeb sends you an email confirmation explaining that you now have a personal Message Center that you can access through the FastWeb site to review your list of potential scholarships. In addition, new scholarships that might match your profile are automatically added to your list as they become available. You'll also receive FastWeb's monthly email newsletter, cleverly titled *Flash*.

Do It Your Way

People who are crunched for time (or who simply don't want to deal with it) can employ a scholarship search service to find scholarships for them. However, there's enough information on the Web to enable you to find scholarships without having to pay a search service.

More Scholarship-Oriented Web Sites

As stated earlier, numerous Web sites are devoted to information about scholarships, with FastWeb being one of the premier sites. The following is a hot list of some of the other scholarship-oriented Web sites you might want to check out.

- **The College Board's Scholarship Search—** *www.collegeboard.org/fundfinder/html/ssrchtop.html* This section of the College Board's Web site is devoted exclusively to searching for scholarships. Here you'll have to fill out an online form, but it's not nearly as extensive as FastWeb's. According to the Web site, "you can locate scholarships, loans, internships, and other financial aid programs from non-college sources that match your education level, talents, and background. Complete the profile form and Scholarship Search will find potential scholarship opportunities from a database of 2,000 undergraduate scholarships, internships, and loan programs."

- *U.S. News* **Online—**
  www.usnews.com/usnews/edu/dollars/ scholar/search.htm
  U.S. News Online provides a number of quick, easy-to-use options for finding a scholarship. Additionally, the site has a personalized form-driven menu for finding scholarships that is similar to the form at the College Board site. Other features include an online worksheet that lets you compare financial aid packages from four schools, and another worksheet "to estimate the total cost of attendance for four years of school, which includes all institutional expenses, such as room and board, as well as personal expenses like entertainment, long-distance phone calls, or laundry." For more help, review the right sidebar, where there are links to highly relevant articles about scholarship-related topics such as merit awards and scholarship scam alerts.

- **Embark.com—***www.embark.com*
  From this site's home page, click the Finance link in the right sidebar. If you're registered with Embark, you can use the site's scholarship search service as well as other financial aid utilities to apply for a federal student loan and to calculate your EFC. You can also use Embark's Recruiter service "to inform scholarship organizations about yourself."

- **Sallie Mae CASHE for Education—***http://search.cashe.com*
  Sallie Mae is a leading provider of student loans. The College Aid Sources for Higher Education (CASHE) program is a 60-question, online, form-driven scholarship search service that Sallie Maie claims will take you anywhere from 15 minutes to 30 minutes to complete. After electronically submitting the completed form, "the system will compare

your data with available resources on the CASHE database
and then transmit the results to your Internet email account in
less than two hours." Sallie Mae's primary Web site,
www.salliemae.com, has plenty of information on higher education aid and financial planning.

- **Scholarships.com**—*www.scholarships.com*
  This site has loads of information about financial aid and
  another free online, personalized, form-driven scholarship
  search service. Scholarships.com also has a good deal of
  information on student loans, as well as financial aid tips and
  tools to help you plan out and manage your higher education
  finances.

- **FreeScholarships.com**—*www.freescholarships.com*
  This Web site claims to give away a $10,000 daily scholar-
  ship, a $25,000 monthly scholarship, and a $50,000 quarterly
  scholarship. If you don't believe it, check out some of the
  winners by clicking the win$ link near the bottom of the
  home page and then clicking Winners. You'll have to fill out
  a short registration form to participate in these giveaways.
  FreeScholarships.com says that your odds of winning are
  increased by frequently visiting its Web site and participating
  in various online activities that earn you what they call
  "chances."

All About Higher Education Loans

Make a Budget

Before applying for a loan, plan out a higher education budget, including those easy-to-overlook expenses such as car maintenance and travel costs, cost of books and supplies, personal entertainment expenses, parking fees, what it will cost to do your laundry, and the cost of furnishing your domicile.

You're not alone if all your hard work and determination to find
the necessary financial resources for your higher education has
resulted in the realization that you'll have to borrow money. This
is a cold, hard fact for most college students.

When you get that very important financial aid award letter from
your prospective school, you'll know whether you're eligible for
U.S. Department of Education loans, which feature lower interest
rates than other types of loans. If you're not eligible for any of
these loans, you'll have to comparison shop for alternative lend-
ing sources.

U.S. Department of Education Loans

There are basically three types of Department of Education loans: Stafford Loans, Perkins Loans, and PLUS Loans. Definitions of these loans were provided earlier in this chapter, but another good place to learn about these loans is on the *U.S. News* Online Web site at *www.usnews.com/usnews/edu/dollars/ffaid.htm*. This page is titled Flavors of Financial Aid, and you'll find a very useful and comprehensive chart here (with supportive links) that breaks down the requirements, payment plans, fees, and more for these federal loan programs.

The popular FinAid site is another good source of information about federal loans—and student loans in general. On the page at *www.finaid.org/loans*, you'll see information about consolidation loans, loan forgiveness programs, loan calculators, links to lenders, and more.

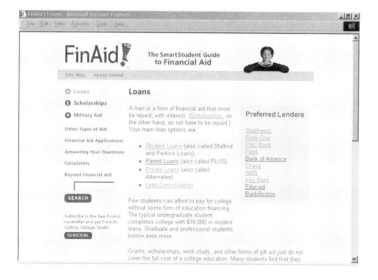

The FinAid Web site has a section dedicated to information about student loans with links to lenders.

Also, as mentioned earlier in this chapter, don't forget the state guaranty agencies that administer student loans under the Federal Family Education Loan (FFEL) program. The Web sites of state guaranty agencies have lots of useful information about education-related borrowing for both students and parents. For a list of only state guaranty agencies with contact information and links to their Web sites, go to *www.ed.gov/offices/OPE/guaranty.html*.

Private Lenders

Take your total estimated cost for education and subtract your scholarships, grants, and government loans to get your total financial need. If you still can't cover the cost of school, your next step is to find an alternative source for money. Grandparents are frequently good sources for education-related money, but obviously not everyone has that luxury. A secret philanthropic benefactor would be nice, but this is reality here. So where do you go? You can start by doing some loan comparison shopping through eStudent Loan at *www.estudentloan.com*.

eStudent Loan.com offers visitors a student loan-finder service to comparison shop for student loans offered by up to 12 loan programs from top lenders.

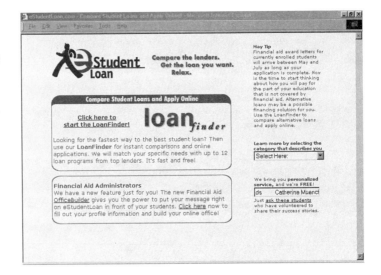

A pull-down menu on the right side of eStudent Loan's home page gives you access to information about how to apply for loans, loan eligibility requirements, types of aid, and more. The pull-down menu lists sections addressed to various audiences, such as high school students, undergraduate students, and parents. When you reach these sections, you'll see links at the bottom of the page to education loan Web sites of prominent lenders, such as Bank of America, Chase, American Express, Access Group, and Citibank. These lender Web sites also provide scads of information about student loans, including loan calculators and budgeting tools, online counseling, repayment options, and online applications.

To start a loan search, click the LoanFinder link on the home page. You'll be taken to a registration page. Check out the Frequently Asked Questions (FAQ) link at the bottom of this page. Reading the FAQs is a good way to familiarize yourself with the eStudent LoanFinder service before registering.

After you register with the LoanFinder, you'll be asked to complete a relatively easy five-page form. Let's see how the entire process works:

▼ **Try It Yourself**

1. Go to *www.estudentloan.com*, click the LoanFinder link, and register your name, password, and email address.

2. Choose the Students or Parents category. If you choose the Students category, the LoanFinder questionnaire will ask whether you'll have a loan co-signer. If you don't have a co-signer, your personal credit record will be used as the primary qualifier for a loan. Most, if not all, high school students do not have a sufficient credit history to obtain a student loan from a private lender without a co-signer.

3. Indicate whether or not you're searching for a private program or a government loan program.

4. Complete five pages of brief questions.

5. Review and compare the list of lenders that meet your loan requirements. For each lender, you'll be shown the total cost of your loan, average monthly payments, average interest payments, fees, APR, term, and rate. If any of these loans interest you, click the Send My Loan Request do-it-myself-method button or the eStudent Loan quick-method button. For the do-it-myself method, depending on the lender, you'll get an online application, a link to the application section of a lender's Web site, or an online form to fill out to get an application sent to you. For the quick method, you fill out one online form for the lender(s) you select. The lender(s) will then contact you by mail, phone, or email within seven days. You'll also get an email confirmation from eStudent Loan with the toll-free numbers of your selected lender(s).

**Working with
LoanFinder**

Click the Next but-
ton after you com-
plete each
numbered instruc-
tion in the
LoanFinder process.
If you have ques-
tions while filling
out the form, click
the yellow and red
question mark but-
tons next to the
form fields for more
details.

In addition to using the eStudent Loan service, you can always comparison shop by visiting many of the lenders' Web sites. Here's a short list of some well-known and large education loan lenders. All these sites provide a wealth of advice and services for students and parents seeking education loans.

- **Bank of America Student Banking Center—**
  www.bankofamerica.com/studentbanking
  This bank has been dishing out student loans for more than 30 years. Check out its Online Counseling link as well as a link to information about banking fundamentals called Brush Up on Banking.

- **BankOne—***http://fry.educationone.com/edonesplash.asp*
  This Web site allows you to apply online and claims to email an approval status to you in five minutes. Check out the Can I Afford College link.

- **Citibank: The Student Loan Corporation—**
  www.studentloan.com
  At its Web site, Citibank claims to be "America's #1 student loan lender working with over 2,500 schools nationwide." There are plenty of resources here, including a Budget Calculator link at the bottom of the home page to help you tally how much money you'll need for school.

- **Educaid: A First Union Company—***www.educaid.com*
  This is an expansive Web site with plenty of resources to help you along the financial aid and student loan trail. Educaid even has a sweepstakes contest where you can win one of five $5,000 scholarships.

The Rest of the Financial Aid Story

We're not through with you yet. Did you know that the U.S. Treasury Department administers tax credits related to financial aid? Did you know that the U.S. government also offers loan for-giveness programs?

Tax Credits

You should be aware of two tax credits: the Hope Scholarship Credit and the Lifetime Learning Credit. Under the Hope Scholarship, you can receive a maximum tax credit of $1,500. Under the Lifetime Learning Credit, you can receive a maximum tax credit of $1,000. For complete details on each of these tax credit programs, go to a page within the Department of Education Web site at *www.ed.gov/offices/OSFAP/Students/taxcuts/credits. html* or go to the FinAid Web site at *www.finaid.org/otheraid/tax. phtml*.

Who qualifies for these tax credits? According to the DE Web site, "single tax filers with up to $40,000 of adjusted gross income (AGI) and joint tax filers with up to $80,000 of AGI qualify for the full credit. It is gradually phased out for single filers in the $40,000–$50,000 range and for joint filers in the $80,000–$100,000 range, and it is not available for those whose income exceeds the upper limit of those ranges."

Loan Forgiveness

If you're a community-service or volunteer-oriented person, you might not have to repay your federal education loans. That's right, the government will say, "Forget it," under these specific qualifying conditions:

- If you become a teacher in what the government says is a low-income or subject-matter–shortage area, you might qualify for a loan deferment or cancellation. For more information, go to *www.ed.gov/offices/OSFAP/Students/repayment/ teachers*.

- If you decide to join and get accepted into the Peace Corps, the AmeriCorps, or the Volunteers in Service to America (VISTA), the government could cancel as much as 100 percent of your federal education loan. For more information on these programs, go to one of the most complete, all-inclusive information centers for loan forgiveness programs on the Web inside FinAid.org at *www.finaid.org/loans/forgiveness. phtml*. Here you will also find information on loan cancellation programs related to the military, law school,

medical/healthcare occupations, and other occupational programs.

Wrapping It Up

Here you are at the end of a very long and tedious financial aid
process that might have forced you to navigate through Web page
after Web page and complete enough forms to stock a paper fac-
tory. We hope it paid off with a surprise load of cash to help you
pay for your higher education. If it did not pay off, you're probably not alone, but at least you gave it the old college try. If you or
your parents don't qualify for any financial aid, including loans,
you'll simply have to bite the bullet and pay, pay, pay. If you
can't afford it, you'll have to find a way to pay through the sweat
of your own hard work and determination, which can only come
from employment. (See Chapter 11, "Finding Jobs and Internship
Programs Online.")

This chapter provided a full measure of information on the Web
concerning financial aid (without writing an entire book on the
subject), including:

- An introduction to financial aid and a brief look at Cornell
  University's Web pages on financial aid.

- The Expected Family Contribution (EFC) methodology for
  figuring out the amount of money you and your family are
  expected to pay for your higher education.

- How to access information about federal financial aid programs from the U.S. Department of Education Web site.

- Everything you need to know about the Free Application for
  Financial Student Aid (FAFSA) form, along with definitions
  of the Department of Education financial aid programs.

- What you need to know about the Student Aid Report (SAR).

- Where to go for information about CSS/Financial Aid PRO-
  FILE.

- Where to find out about state aid programs.

- The many flavors of scholarships and how to find and apply for them online.

- The world of higher education loans and where to get information that can help you make a wise choice.

- Brief explanations of tax credits and loan forgiveness programs.

PART III

Getting Help from the Web Throughout Your College Career

CHAPTER 8

Shopping for Housing Deals, Student Discounts, and More

If you are at the point where you're almost ready to pack your bags and head off to school, then this chapter will help you. That is, of course, if you're going away to school. If you're living at home while attending a local college or university, this chapter also applies to you, but you'll most likely want to skip the first section on student housing.

You'll take a good look at student housing and the many options offered by colleges and universities today for your new home-away-from-home.

You'll be shown how to be budget conscious and how to take advantage of Web sites that will save you plenty of cash. We'll also talk about buying a computer, getting a credit card, buying your textbooks online, and much more.

Finally, we'll show you how to get away from school after a grueling semester, and how you can check out what's available on the Web to help you make reservations and save money traveling during your school breaks.

Student Housing: What to Expect

According to the National Center for Student Statistics (*www.nces.ed.gov*), the average cost for on-campus room and board during the 97–98 academic year was $5,750 at private 4-year colleges and universities and $4,518 at public 4-year colleges and universities. Considering what it costs today to rent your own apartment and feed yourself, the on-campus room and board experience is definitely a bargain.

What You'll Learn in This Chapter:

▶ All about student housing options and how the Web can help you find the right housing arrangement for you.

▶ All about special Web sites devoted to student discounts and how you can take advantage of these discounts.

▶ How you can use the Web to find information and special deals for the student traveler, on both domestic and international travel.

At many schools, out-of-state resident freshmen are required to live in school-provided housing for their first year or more. At other schools, you can live wherever you like. There are also residential schools that require you to live in various school-provided domiciles during every semester of your entire undergraduate education.

Regardless of where you're going to live, most college and university Web sites have sections devoted exclusively to student housing. The headings for these sections vary from site to site, with links to housing information listed under such terms as *Student Affairs* or *Services*, *Campus Life*, *Residence Halls* or *Life*, and *Student Housing*. Sometimes you have to navigate through several pages (frequently more) before you land on the student housing information you need, so be a patient surfer. These Web pages will provide more than enough information about housing amenities and costs to help you make a wise choice. As an example, take a look at a student housing Web section of the University of Minnesota (UM), located at *http://www1.umn.edu/housing/student/index.shtml*.

Similar to most college and university Web sites, the University of Minnesota has a special section devoted exclusively to student housing.

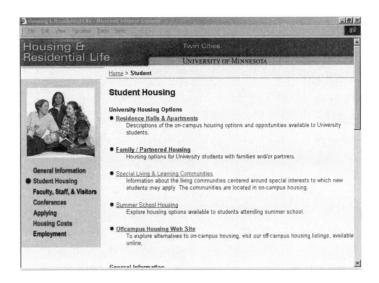

Similar to many colleges and universities, UM offers the option of living in a residence hall or a university-owned apartment complex. The cost of living in a residence hall or apartment complex can include room only or both room and board. Often you'll get to choose between a single-occupancy room for you alone or a double-occupancy room that you'll share with a roommate. UM also has triple-occupancy rooms.

Single occupancy is the most expensive option. The single occupancy room-only rate at UM residence halls for the 1999–2000 academic year (nine months, September through May) was $2,554; the double-occupancy rate was $2,299; and the triple-occupancy rate was $2,227.

At UM-owned apartments, single occupancy was listed at $485 to $495 per month, or $4,365 to $4,455 per academic year. Double-occupancy rates were $378 to $432 per month, or $3,402 to $3,888 per academic year. As you can see, there's a considerable difference in cost between residence hall life and school-owned apartment life.

Meal-plan options at UM ranged from 75 meals each semester for $435 per semester to 21 meals each week plus five guest meals each semester for $985 per semester. At UM, residence hall students are required to purchase a meal plan.

When hunger strikes and the mess hall is closed, UM's residence halls have one kitchenette and one microwave oven on each floor and one full kitchen per residence hall building. Every apartment, on the other hand, comes with its very own full kitchen with dishwasher, refrigerator, garbage disposal, electric stove, and microwave.

Apartment dwellers who aren't the best cooks can also take advantage of meal plans and take their meals at the residence hall dining commons. If you can stomach all-you-can-eat, residence-hall buffets, you can't beat the price, not to mention the time you'll save not having to prepare your own meals every day.

Depending on which school you attend, you'll definitely want to compare amenities offered by both residence halls and school-owned apartments before deciding on the living arrangement that's right and affordable for you. For example, most newer residence halls and school-owned apartments have Internet connections for personal computers; the older halls and apartments might not have Internet connections. You might want to consider that apartments usually have a lot more personal space than residence halls. Also, many double-occupancy residence hall setups have two rooms housing four students, who share one bathroom; an apartment setting might have one or two bathrooms for two people. Finally, location might be important; many of these student-housing arrangements are conveniently located near or within small shopping plazas with everything from fast-food restaurants, delis, and cafes to laundry services and small convenience stores.

Go to Work Where You Live

Colleges and universities hire plenty of students to assist with the management of student housing. Jobs such as dining assistants, night guards, and clerks are always available.

By your sophomore year, you might be eligible to become a Resident Assistant (RA). An RA is like a student housing monitor and guidance counselor, as well as an administrative aide and liaison between the student residents and the student-housing department. Being an RA is a demanding position that requires strong communication skills. The job usually takes up a great deal of time because you have to deal with many housemate concerns and issues on a 24-hour basis.

Compensation for taking on an RA position usually includes free room and board and possibly a small monthly cash stipend.

For more information on being an RA, go to *www.residentassistant.com*. This Web site is loaded with helpful advice and information about the life and times of an RA.

Relatively new developments in student housing are theme-oriented dormitories or apartment complexes where students with similar interests and studies live together in the same building or on the same floor. Another version of this is substance-free student housing arrangements, wherein residents sign pledges not to take drugs or drink alcohol. At UM, theme-oriented living arrangements were listed under Special Living and Learning Communities; those communities include a Biology House, a Global Studies House, a number of foreign-language–theme houses, and others. Depending on the school, special living arrangements cost the same as typical campus-provided student housing, and you get in simply by requesting it on your student housing contract. Frequently, theme-oriented housing fills up fast, or has very limited space, so you'll want to sign your student housing contract as early as possible, if this is what you're seeking.

The Greek Life

Another housing option worth looking at is Greek housing. Many colleges and universities have Greek Rows where fraternity and sorority chapters own houses for their members. The cost of living in a Greek house varies from campus to campus, but most are comparable to living in an apartment. Some chapter houses hire a kitchen staff to provide meal plans for their residents, which affects the cost of living there. Maintenance expenses and mortgage payments are also added into the cost of Greek housing. Additionally, Greek organizations charge yearly dues, which can range from $200 to $600, depending on which chapter you join.

Finally, at some colleges and universities, Greek housing is integrated with residence halls by setting aside various hall floors for fraternity or sorority members. In this set-up, the cost and amenities are the same for Greeks as they are for non-Greeks.

Heads Up and Sleep Tight

Before going the Greek way, you might want to consider that weekends on Greek Rows are customarily noisy, with plenty of late-night parties around to keep you awake. Many Greeks, however, are changing that custom with special non-party fraternity and sorority residences.

Off-Campus Apartment Hunting

If campus-owned housing is not your bag, you'll have to pound the pavement for the apartment of your dreams. Of course, before you wear out your shoes, you can search for an apartment or room rental on the Web. To get an idea of what rentals might be available, you can start a search through the Web site of the local newspaper published near the school you'll be attending. To find just about any newspaper Web site in the entire world, go to a great service provided by the *American Journalism Review* at *http://ajr.newslink.org*.

To find the Web site of a newspaper in your area of interest, click Newspapers in the upper-left sidebar. Here you can locate newspapers by state and various other subcategories. After you link to a newspaper's Web site, check out the classified apartment-rental section, wherein you'll find listings of rentals just as you would in any hard-copy version of a newspaper. Bookmark the newspaper Web site for future reference.

The Student Discount Game

Help From Mom

Before making the move to your college life, you'll more than likely make a list of things to take along. For some helpful advice on what to pack, ask your mother or go to CollegeMomAdvice. com at *www.college-momadvice.com/ getready/ whattopack.shtml.*

Regardless of where you decide to live, you'll have to shop for living essentials and whatever else you might need for your college residence. An excellent place to start is the Student Advantage, located at *www.studentadvantage.com.*

Student Advantage is a large Web site devoted to providing student discounts. To take advantage of the numerous student discounts offered through this Web site, you have to become a registered card-carrying member, which costs $20.

Student Advantage claims that, as a member, your card will get you exclusive savings at many spots, including CDNOW, Amtrak, Foot Locker, Staples, Textbooks.com, and more. You can purchase products and services both online and offline. You can obtain a free Student Advantage membership card by signing up for an AT&T student calling card.

Student Advantage has a rapidly growing membership, reaching more than one million. Before possibly signing up for the $20 Student Advantage membership card, let's do a test-run on the kinds of residential-oriented products you can find at a discount.

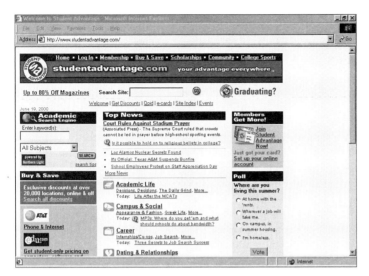

Student Advantage has a membership program in which students are provided discounts on a wide range of products and services that they can buy online or offline at more than 20,000 places in 125 cities.

1. Go to *www.studentadvantage.com*. Under the Buy and Save heading in the left sidebar, click the Search All Discounts link.

▼ **Try It Yourself**

2. You can search directly for bargains or use the directory-driven menus. For this exercise, you'll use the menus: From the Select a Category menu, select *Dorm & Apartment* to look for housing-related items (not housing units themselves) and then select a location from the Choose a Location menu.

3. Click the Continue button to go to a new page with a Select a Sub-Category menu. Select a subcategory and click the Go button.

4. You'll see a page with stores and discount details listed under the headings National Discounts and Local Discounts. To the left of each store are icons that link to more information about the discount offers and the stores themselves.

▲

Remember, to take advantage of any of the discounts, you have to register for the $20 membership card. In addition to registering online, you can print out and snail mail a registration application. Either way, it takes three to four weeks for your card to arrive.

Student Advantage is a very sophisticated Web site with numerous discounts that can easily save you the $20 membership fee

How to Buy a Computer

For an insightful look at buying a computer, visit the iVillage.com Web site (the Women's Network) where Heidi Pollock wrote a four-part series titled "How to Buy a Computer." The direct URL is *www.ivillage.com/ click/experts/ goodbuygirl/ articles/ 0,5639,38862,00.html.* If you have trouble typing this long URL, use the iVillage search function to take you to Pollock's article.

you're required to pay in advance. You can find decent savings on school supplies, clothing, furniture, entertainment, magazine subscriptions, travel services, computer hardware and software, and much more.

Buying a Computer

Speaking of computer hardware and software, let's see what kind of savings you can realize if you're in the market for that all-important computer system you'll need for your college days. After all, in today's modern world, a student without a computer is like a painter without a brush and canvas.

Before you begin the search for a computer and peripherals on the Web, check with the school you'll be attending. For example, many schools provide free computer access with an Internet connection located in campus buildings such as the library or computer labs. If you don't have the funds to purchase a computer, and you don't mind doing all your computer-based research, homework, class registration, and other electronic-oriented duties outside of the privacy of your living quarters, you can always use school-provided computers.

If you're buying a new computer, which is the highly recommended way to go, your school might suggest that the system you purchase meet certain specifications. After you know the minimum requirements, you can purchase your entire computer system in a number of ways. For example, many college and university bookstores offer considerable discounts to their students on a complete line of hardware and software, including printers, modems, scanners, and other peripherals. You can also comparison shop at national chain and local computer stores, as well as through computer mail-order companies. Last but not least, you can shop around on the Web.

The *www.edu.com* Web site offers students help with purchasing computer hardware and software, among other products and services. Edu.com's trademarked catch phrase is *students get it*. According to edu.com, "all students who attend U.S. accredited two-year or four-year colleges in the United States are eligible to enroll and make purchases at edu.com," and the site claims to confirm your student status by contacting your school registrar's office.

Edu.com is an e-commerce Web site that offers discounts exclusively to students on computer hardware and software, books and magazines, telecommunication products, and financial services.

Edu.com claims that it offers "deep" discounts on brand-name products and services. Their premium partners include such notable companies as IBM, Adobe, Citibank, Wells Fargo, Microsoft, AT&T, Fleet, Apple, and Iomega.

Edu.com asserts that its prices are lower than comparable Internet prices available at leading retail, mail order, and e-commerce resellers. Plus, whenever you purchase something through edu.com, you earn edupoints. You can redeem edupoints for free eduRewards, which include CDs, movie videos, electronic products (such as Sony Walkmans and Discmans), movie tickets, and more.

Credit Card Deals for Students

From the edu.com Web site, you can also get deals on credit card services and banking services provided by the site's premium partners. For the responsible student, these services can be a good way to establish a line of credit. For the irresponsible and highly vulnerable student, getting a credit card can do the opposite and can destroy your credit in a hurry.

A good place to review information about student credit cards is at the Student Advantage Web site (*www.studentadvantage.com*). Click the Money link on the home page and then click Credit Cards. You'll be introduced to assorted articles related to this

Go to the Source

Go directly to the manufacturer's Web site to compare prices on computer products. For example, if you go to *www.ibm.com*, you'll be able to get pricing on the IBM computer system of your choice and buy it online. Other computer manufacturers might link you to their partner resellers, where you can compare prices or buy online.

Check It Out

Another Web site that caters to students in the market for computer hardware and software is *www.gradware.com*. Like edu.com, Gradware also has a point-based system, called *PlusPoints*, for earning freebies.

topic, including "12 Secrets Credit Card Companies Don't Want You to Know," and an "Introduction to Student Credit."

Finally, if you absolutely must have a credit card, you can shop for comparable rates at *www.studentcredit.com*. In addition to offering deals on student credit cards through a number of major financial institutions, this site has an informative section titled The Importance of Credit and an Overview, which can be accessed by clicking the Learn Credit link.

Shopping for Textbooks

When you start registering for your classes, you'll be introduced to the textbook game. This is when you're forced to stand in long, meandering lines at campus bookstores to buy very expensive books that are absolutely required for your classes, and that you might or might not read, depending on your study habits.

A relatively new development in the textbook game is the burgeoning growth of virtual college bookstores where you can purchase both new and used textbooks online. We found close to 10 online bookstores devoted to college textbooks; the major online bookstores such as Amazon.com and Barnes and Noble also carry many college textbooks. The beauty of buying online is that it eliminates the long, meandering line, thus saving a great deal of your valuable time. Plus, the online world of college textbooks might even save you some money.

Before clicking your way through college textbook cyberspace, take heed of these warnings:

- If the online bookseller does, in fact, have the textbook you need, make sure that it can ship it to you in a timely fashion.

- Check out the online store's refund policy. For example, you might change your mind about the class you're about to take. What happens to the book you just bought online, and what about the shipping charges you will incur when you return it?

- Make sure that the book you find online is the same edition as the book that's required for your class.

- Be sure to shop around and compare prices. You might be surprised at the difference in prices between the various online stores and the bricks-and-mortar store on your campus, especially when considering different shipping costs.

Here's a list of some of the larger online college textbook booksellers:

- **BigWords.com**—*www.bigwords.com*
  Launched in August 1998, *bigwords.com* claims to be the "No. 1 online textbook retailer and e-commerce destination for college students." Big Words also sells music and apparel. It has a Tell-a-Friend program that earns you credit toward future purchases.

- **eCampus.com**—*www.ecampus.com*
  This site claims to be "the globe's largest college bookstore." eCampus went live with its first beta version in July 1999. The site also sells lots of other stuff, including apparel, games, and electronic instruments. If you like to enter contests, you'll surely want to visit. For example, eCampus.com recently hosted an online contest in which entrants could win anything from a fleece vest to one million dollars.

- **eFollet.com**—*www.efollet.com*
  Another Web site that sells more than just textbooks, this site is one of the pioneers in the online textbook field and was first started by the Follet Higher Education Group in August 1995. eFollet.com has partnered with 800 college campuses (and growing) to offer "immediate access to more than 16 million textbooks that can be picked up on-campus or delivered anywhere in the United States." You can also order textbooks if your school is not an eFollet partner.

- **Textbooks.com**—*www.textbooks.com*
  This site, claims to be "the world's largest textbook store." If you're a card-carrying Student Advantage member, you can get an additional 10% discount. Unlike the other online textbook sellers, Textbooks.com sells only textbooks. The site went public in August 1999.

- **VarsityBooks.com**—*www.varsitybooks.com*
  This company was founded in December 1997. In addition to selling all kinds of books, VarsityBooks partnered with Sallie

What Students Say

To read some great articles about buying books online written by college students, go to *www.studentadvantage.com*. Click the Academic Life link and then select Educational Expenses under the Issues and Interest section. Check out the links to articles in the Books category. The direct URL to this page is *www.studentadvantage.com/issue/1,1061,c4-i67,00.html*.

Mae to bring you VaristyScholars, a scholarship program awarding up to $25,000 in cash to exemplary students. The winning recipients are chosen based on "high academic achievement, strong leadership skills, and a volunteer spirit."

Now, please pay attention. This will save you a great deal of time. You can do your price shopping for many of these online textbooks by going to *www.campusbooks.com*.

Campusbooks.com searches some of the leading online textbook Web sites and then lists the prices and availability offered by each site.

Campusbooks has 15 member bookstores, including the aforementioned BigWords.com, Textbooks.com, and VarsityBooks.com. In the search field on the Campusbooks home page, simply type the title, author, ISBN number, or keywords of the textbook you want to buy. Click the Search Now button, and you'll get a Results Table that lists the price of the book, the bookstores where it's available with links to their Web sites, whether the book is available new or used, shipping costs, and approximate shipping times.

Check out some of the special promotions being offered by the member bookstores. To get coupons that can save you money, click the Get Coupons link next to the dollar sign graphic on the Campusbooks home page.

Two other sites similar to Campusbooks.com that search through online bookstores are Limespot at *www.limespot.com* and Viva Smart at *www.vivasmart.com*.

Travel the World with Your Student ID

Got a travel bug? Consider yourself lucky to be a freewheeling student about to take advantage of travel discounts created just for you.

If you're taking a trip in the continental United States and are on a typical student budget, visit Amtrak's Web site for students at *www.amtrak.com/student.html*. Amtrak offers a 15% discount to all students who have the Student Advantage card.

If you're traveling by air in the United States, a good place to find the cheapest air fares is *www.travelocity.com*. Travelocity.com is not a student-centered Web site, but it's one of the leading places on the Web for booking the lowest airfares available, as well as for finding rental car deals, reserving accommodations, and more. Click the Special Deals icon at the top of the home page for links to all sorts of travel deals.

You can also visit the Web sites of major airlines that have special student discount programs. For example, American Airlines has College SAAver Fares, which are periodic savings for students that are emailed to you after you have registered online with American. For more information, go to *www.aa.com*, click the Specials link in the top menu bar, and then select College SAAver Fares from the pull-down menu.

United Airlines has a frequent flyer program for students called CollegePlus. For more information, go to *www.collegeplus.com*.

If you're traveling outside the United States, you should visit a number of travel-oriented Web sites that are fashioned for students. You can start with Council Travel at *www.counciltravel.com*, which is billed as "America's Student Travel Leader."

At the Council Travel site, you can use the Quick Search: Round-Trip Student Airfares box to see what round-trip airfares are available for your trip abroad. Just type your departure and arrival cities and your travel dates, and you'll get a quick list of airfares

Get the ISBN

It's a very good idea to check out your college bookstore and write down all the ISBN numbers of the books you're required to buy for all your classes. The ISBN is a 10-digit number listed on the back of a book near the bar code. This will help make your search for textbooks at any of the online booksellers accurate and fast.

More Travel Deals

Go to *www.smarter-living.com/student* for links and information on plenty of student discount travel deals, for both domestic and international travel. Sign up for the free student travel newsletter to receive email messages containing information on travel bargains.

available (with a Rules link to information about travel restrictions and eligibility). The list is sorted from least expensive to most expensive fares.

Council Travel's Web site is chock-full of information and travel agency services for students traveling abroad.

Take a Ride on the Euro Rails

Go to *www. railconnection.com* for discounts and travel bonuses when you purchase the Europass or Eurailpass.

If you go down the list of links in the right sidebar, you'll get a very good idea of what you'll need to do to prepare for your trip abroad. Click the Railpasses link to see a page that links you to information about all the European train travel discount options available, such as the Eurailpass, Europass, Britrail Pass, France Pass, and Europe East Railpass. You can order any of these train passes by calling Council Travel's toll-free number or by visiting one of the Council Travel offices, which are located throughout the United States.

On the Council Travel home page, click the Int'l ID Card link to see instructions for getting your International Student ID card (ISIC). This card costs $20 and is endorsed by the United Nations and recognized worldwide. It's referred to as the "eye-zic" card, and it will get you international discounts on airfares, accommodations, travel insurance, and much more. You might be able apply for these cards at your school's international student program office. The Council Travel site has a search function that can find the issuing office nearest you. Just click the Find an ID Card Issuing Office button at the bottom of the ISIC page.

The next important page to access from the Council Travel Web site is found by clicking the Hotels/Hostels link in the sidebar. Here you'll find information about the popular youth hostels located throughout the world, as well as information on inexpensive hotels, camping, and bed-and-breakfast deals available to students.

Get the Card

Go to the Web site of International Student Exchange Cards, Inc., at *www.isecard.com* to apply for the ISIC card online and to obtain detailed information on the many discounts this card entitles you to worldwide.

Hostelling

If you're like most students who are on a very tight overseas travel budget, "hostelling" is the way to go. To find every hostel on the planet and everything you need to know about hostelling, go to *www.hostels.com*, a great budget-travel resource Web site. According to Hostels.com, hostelling is "in part, the act of traveling and staying in hostels. It's often called *backpacking* in many parts of the world, and it's perhaps best described as traveling cheaply with an adventurous spirit." Hostels usually offer dormitory-style accommodations with large shared rooms, bunk beds, and a common bathroom and maybe a self-serve kitchen area. Click the Hostelling link in the left sidebar of the Hostels.com home page and check out Hostelling 101—A Complete Guide.

Hostels.com has a lot more than just information on hostelling. Check this Web site for plenty of travel advice and links to online travel stores. There's also a bulletin board, called *Talk to People*, where you can discuss budget travel topics with other students.

The Council Travel Web site also features travel-agency services such as special travel tours and booking services, travel insurance programs, group travel rates, and car rental and bus travel deals. There are also links to information about work and study abroad programs for students.

More Student-Travel Web Sites

There are at least two more Web sites you should visit before you cross any oceans: *www.statravel.com* and *www.eurotrip.com*.

As is the Council Travel Web site, STA Travel is basically a travel agency for students that provides a host of services and resources to make your trip abroad the most economical and fulfilling. The site offers a Guidebooks section that links you to Amazon.com to purchase such titles as *Izon's Backpacker Journal*, the *Lonely Planet* travel guides, the popular *Fodor's* and *Frommer's* travel books, and more.

STA Travel also has a chat room, called Show and Tell, where you can "exchange travel information from like-minded travelers around the world." You'll also want to check out the Get the Goods link for rail passes, IDs, insurance, information on special tours, accommodation information, and services and links to study and work abroad programs.

The next stop on your student-travel Web sites tour is *www.eurotrip.com*. Eurotrip.com was made for the truly budget-oriented, backpacking traveler. For instance, you'll see a Packing and Travel Advice link that provides valuable recommendations on backpacking lists and priorities, safety issues, exchange rates, budgetary concerns, and more.

Click the Travel Destinations link for a page titled Destinations and Advice, which includes a link to Favourite Places. Among many other interesting tidbits of information in this section, you'll discover that Favourite Places is a "long and quite fascinating list of cities and places that Eurotrip's readers find special."

Other links at the Eurotrip.com site cover such things as Cheap Flight Tactics, Budget Guidebooks, and European Hostel Reviews. There's also a travel discussion board, a live chat room, and a free travel newsletter service.

At www.eurotrip.com, Founder Andrew Ogilvie from Glasgow, Scotland, has created a travel-oriented Web site tagged as "your backpackin' Europe Site."

Wrapping It Up

By now, you should feel that the price you paid for this book was well worth it. Not only did we save you a great deal of time by directing you to the right places on the Web for student discounts and more, we saved you pockets full of cold cash because you will use what these Web sites have to offer to your bank account's advantage.

Here's a brief synopsis of what was covered in this chapter:

- The kinds of living arrangements available to the new college student. You probably now realize that there are more choices than you first imagined. It's up to you to find the one that fits your lifestyle and budget.

- There are discounts galore for the savvy college student who uses the Web to his or her advantage. You were shown where to go on the Web for these discounts. You were also offered some sound advice that should help you choose wisely when plopping down your hard-earned cash.

- How to make travel plans using the Web. You were introduced to many Web sites devoted to helping you, the student traveler, reach your destination without a hitch—and hopefully with a few dollars left in your pocket when you get back.

CHAPTER 9

Conducting Research Online and Writing Papers

As a full-fledged college student, your life becomes a series of class syllabuses, each one detailing your academic responsibilities. In short, you'll be attending highly intellectual class lectures and discussions, taking copious notes, studying and reading on a regular basis, taking a variety of tests and quizzes, and last but not least, writing term papers and essays on a fairly consistent basis. The last-but-not-least part is what we're concerned about in this chapter.

If you write, you conduct research; and the Web is where it all starts. In this chapter, you'll see Web sites on how to write term papers, as well as Web sites that will help you conduct first-class research for your term papers. You'll see that there's an extraordinary number of research-related information and reference links available to students on the Web.

We'll then talk about Web sites that sell finished term papers that students frequently pawn off as their own. You'll also be introduced to a Web site that helps to curb this practice.

You'll also take a look at learning and study aids available online and how you can take advantage of Web sites that will boost your academic abilities.

How to Write a Term Paper

Before penning your very first A+ term paper, you may want to learn more about how to actually write one. You will, of course, be thoroughly instructed on this topic in your English 101 class. Plus, most schools have writing centers and tutorial services that will gladly assist you.

What You'll Learn in This Chapter:

► Where to go on the Web for information about how to write effective term papers.

► How to conduct research on the Web so that you can write highly informative term papers.

► Information about so called "paper mills" on the Web and what you need to know about plagiarism.

► Where to find some valuable learning and study aids on the Web.

Essay Tips

You can learn all about writing essays from the Paradigm Online Writing Assistant at *www.powa.org*.

If you're a Web head, you can get a complete heads-up on college term paper writing using your Internet connection on your own conditions and at your own pace. You can start by typing in the words **How to Write a Term Paper** or just **Research Papers** at your favorite search engine (our favorite is *www.google.com*). You'll find a long list of Web sites on this topic, many of which are "paper mills" that want to sell you college research papers and essays on just about every topic imaginable. All these research-paper-for-hire sites have disclaimers, stating that their papers are for research purposes only. Our advice is to stay away from these sites (more on this later).

Instead, let's take a look at the learning tools available on the Web to help you do the right thing on your own. Remember that writing and researching are primary job skills you'll need when you get to the real world after your graduation.

Our first stop will be an award-winning Web site: the Online Writing Lab Web at Purdue University, located at *http://owl. english.purdue.edu/*. Notice the acronym OWL in the URL and read the following definition.

What's an Academic OWL?

OWL is an acronym for Online Writing Lab. OWLs are college and university Web sites that provide numerous resources to help students become better writers and researchers.

The Online Writing Lab at Purdue University covers everything you need to know about writing research papers.

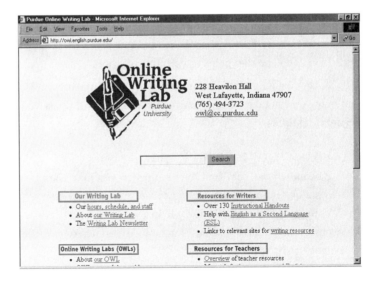

Purdue University has done an excellent job of providing a plethora of information related to writing and researching on numerous levels. Cruise around this site to get a feel for everything that's offered.

For now, we'll access basic information about how to write a term paper. You can start by clicking the Instructional Handouts link under the Resources for Writers heading. You'll get a page titled OWL Handouts Indexed by Topic. Click the Research Papers link and then click Writing a Research Paper-Hypertext Workshop. The direct URL is *http://owl.english.purdue.edu/Files/132/ introduction.html.* Writer Sarah Hamid has put together an extensive overview on the term paper process from start to finish with links to many other viable Web sites that can help you along the way.

Another great Web site that deals specifically with helping students write their research papers is at the appropriately named URL *www.researchpaper.com.* Created by Infonautics Corporation, Purdue University has partnered with this site to provide content for the Writing Center link. Macmillan Publishing USA Inc., is also a partner, with many of the topics in ResearchpPaper.com's Idea Directory adapted in part from the book *10,000 Ideas for Term Papers, Projects, Reports, & Speeches* by Kathryn Lamm. Other features of the Researchpaper.com Web site include the Researchpaper.com Chat! link and the Research Central discussion board link.

If you're searching for a topic for one of your class writing assignments, Researchpaper.com's Idea Directory can be a great help. Let's try it out.

1. Go to *www.researchpaper.com* and click the Idea Directory link.

2. Scroll down to the Search Questions field and type in a keyword relevant to the subject you're considering writing about. Then click the Search Questions button.

3. Review the list of one-sentence theme statements/topics and do further research by clicking on either the Ask eLibary button or the Net Search button underneath the topic that interests you.

OWLs Are Everywhere

For links to Online Writing Labs located at colleges and universities throughout the United States, go to *http:// departments. colgate.edu/diw/ NWCAOWLS.html.* This site is a service of the National Writing Centers Association.

Check It Out

Dushkin McGraw-Hill, an international publisher of educational textbooks, has a Web site devoted to research papers titled *How to Write Term Papers,* located at *www.dushkin. com/online/study/ dgen2.mhtml.*

▼ **Try It Yourself**

4. When you click the Ask eLibary button, you'll be taken to Infonautics's Electric Library (at *www.elibary.com*), which will give you a list of magazine articles, books, newspaper articles, maps, pictures, and TV and radio broadcast transcripts, all relevant to the topic you've chosen.

5. When you click the Net Search button, you'll be taken to another function of the Electric Library, where you'll be given a series of questions with options that will link you to more relevant information located at other Web sites and search engines.

The Researchpaper. com Web site has an Idea Directory for generating topics of interest for writing research papers, along with relevant information to support your research.

About Term Paper Styles

There are basically two citation or style methods you'll be required to use when writing a term paper: APA and MLA. You can go inside the Purdue University's OWL at *http://owl.english.purdue.edu/Files/34.html* for a complete description of how to use both methods.

APA is the acronym for the American Psychological Association. In relation to research papers, APA style conforms to specific rules for quoting and citing sources and references in a term paper, including the proper format for citing electronic sources. The emphasis in APA style is usually on the author's last name and date of publication.

If you want the official APA style guide, you can purchase *Mastering APA Style: Students Workbook and Training Guide* online at *www.apa.org/books/4210010.html*. The list price is $19.95. APA also has software, called *APA Style Helper*, designed for students in the behavioral and social sciences who need to produce manuscripts and documents written according to APA style. You can purchase this software online at *www.apa.org/apa-style*. The list price for the downloadable version of the software is $34.95. Click the Try the Free Demo link to test it out.

MLA is the acronym for the Modern Language Association. Like APA style, MLA style also conforms to very specific rules for quoting and citing sources and references in a term paper. The emphasis in MLA style, however, is more on the title of a work.

For the official MLA style guide, go to *www.mla.org*, where you can purchase the *MLA Handbook for Writers and Researchers*. Click the MLA Style link on the home page to get more information and a link to purchase this book online. The list price is $25 for the cloth-cover edition and $29 for the large-print, paper-cover edition.

Depending on which style your school requires, you may want to purchase the APA or MLA guide as a handy reference that you'll consistently use throughout your college years.

How to Conduct Research on the Web

As we all know by now, the Web is a vast network of human knowledge that you can easily tap into to conduct sophisticated and worthy electronic explorations that will help with your higher education research and writing assignments.

As a college student, you will have access to your school's online library services. For the most part, these are pretty awesome Web sites with an almost infinite number of links and more than enough information and advice about how to access the Web for research purposes.

One of the most comprehensive sites on the Web concerning how to conduct research online is the University at Albany's library site at *www.albany.edu/library/internet*, where you'll find a section titled Internet Tutorials.

Online MLA Guide

A free unofficial online guide to writing research papers using the MLA documentation method can be found at *http://webster.commnet.edu/mla.htm*. It's provided by the Humanities Department and the Arthur C. Banks Jr. Library at Capital Community College in Hartford, Connecticut

The University at Albany Web site has a section that features a host of extensive and far-reaching tutorials about how to use the Internet.

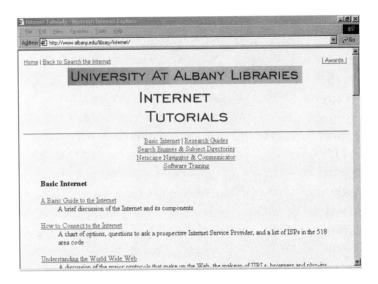

Facts at Your Fingertips

Check out *www.refdesk.com*, whose tag line is "The Single Best Source for Facts on the Web." There are plenty of interesting source links to facts on numerous topics at this site, as well as links to an extra-ordinary number of reference and research-related Web sites.

In addition to a well-written Basic Internet section and a highly informative section titled Search Engines and Subject Directories, University at Albany's Internet Tutorials has an easy-to-digest section titled Research Guides. Within this heading is a link labeled Conducting Research on the Internet. Under the subject heading labeled How to Find Information on the Internet, check out the six ways you can gather information off the Web:

- Join an email discussion group or Usenet newsgroup

- Go directly to a site if you have the address

- Browse

- Explore a subject directory

- Conduct a search using a Web search engine

- Explore the information stored in live databases on the Web, known as "the Invisible Web"

What's the Invisible Web?

The Invisible Web is a series of databases that are usually not accessible using search engines. A number of Web sites highlight these databases, including our top three: the Open Directory Project at *http://dmoz.org*, Direct Search at *http://gwis2.circ.gwu.edu/~gprice/direct.htm*, and the Big Hub at *www.thebighub.com*.

By reading through the descriptions of these six categories (succinctly described in more than 11 pages), you'll get a quick orientation on the way information can be found on the Web.

Another great place for information similar to the University at Albany Web site is the Internet Public Library (IPL) at *www.ipl.org*. This site was born way back in 1995 (eons ago in Internet time), at a graduate seminar at the School of Information and Library Studies at the University of Michigan. It is known as "the first public library of and for the Internet community," and it has grown into an ongoing project now staffed by both professionals and students and supported by grants from the University of Michigan, the W.K. Kellogg Foundation, and Bell & Howell Information and Learning.

IPL has a great section titled A+ Research & Writing for High School and College Students, which can be found at *www.ipl.org/teen/aplus*. Click the Info Search link, and you'll be taken to a section that claims to "help you learn how to become a skilled researcher, both in the library and in cyberspace." Written by Kathryn L. Schwartz, this section has the following six subcategory links for you to read and heed. (Although it was last updated in 1997, most of the information here is still highly relevant today.)

- Learning to Research in the Library
- Learning to Research on the Web
- Skills for Online Searching
- Information Found—and Not Found—on the Web
- Search Strategy: Getting a Broad Overview of a Subject
- Search Strategy: Finding Specific Information

For our purposes here, click the Learning to Research on the Web link. As you read through this section, you'll notice that there are many links that can help you with your current research project.

Virtual Library at Regents College

Another virtual library worth looking at is brought to you by Regents College at *www.library.regents.edu*. Check out the links provided by this Web site's Virtual Reading Room and Virtual Reference Room sections.

The Internet Public Library's section on researching the Web has links to numerous reference resources and search techniques.

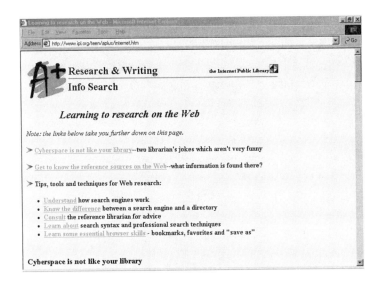

Try It Yourself ▼

As a brief example, let's see where the IPL's Learning to Research on the Web page can take us.

1. Direct your browser to *www.ipl.org/teen/aplus/internet.htm* and click the Get to Know the Reference Sources on the Web link.

2. Scroll down and click on The On-Line Books Page link. (The direct URL for this link is *http://digital.library.upenn.edu/ books.*)

3. You are now at the University of Pennsylvania Digital Library, where you can access more than 10,000 completely digitized books available for free on the Web. The Digital Library was founded in 1993 by John Mark Ockerbloom at Carnegie Mellon University; Ockerbloom is the current Digital Library planner and researcher at the University of Pennsylvania and is the editor of this impressive library.

▲

What Students Say About Conducting Research on the Web

For the opinions of students about where to go online for research, go to *www.studentadvantage.com.* Click the Community option in the top menu bar, which is the link to the Student Advantage discussion boards section. Scroll down to the box labeled *Other Discussions* and click on the Academic Life link. Here you'll see a list of online discussions by title. Scroll until you find the Online Research: Which Sites Kick Ass and Which

Just Suck? link. This is a continuous online discussion, with links, where students candidly express opinions about the Web sites that have helped them do their best research work.

A Not-Too-Cumbersome List of Research Links

For a compact list of links (with brief comments) to search engines, directories, indexes, databases, periodicals, reference materials, news sites, and more, go to *www.vanguard.edu/faculty/R_Harris/search.htm*, created by English professor Robert Harris.

Paper Mills of a Different Sort

The Internet changed the way research is conducted so that students can find what they need to write term papers almost completely online. It has also changed the way students can cheat on term papers. This is an unfortunate aspect of the Internet that we have to address here. We're talking about the sites littered all over the Web that sell literally thousands of complete term papers. Some students, who may be strapped for time because of other responsibilities or who are just plain irresponsible, will buy these finished term papers and turn them in as their own work.

These so-called "paper mills" can easily be found through search engines. In fact, paper mills have become so prevalent that *U.S. News* did a special issue on student cheating in their November 22, 1999, edition. You can check out one of the cover stories, "The Great Term-Paper Buying Caper," as well as link to related stories and information, by going to *www.usnews.com/usnews/issue/991122/cheating.b1.htm*.

Measures have been taken, however, to deter the use of paper mills. One Web site, *www.plagiarism.org*, claims to prevent term paper cheating with a program than interfaces with the major search engines and other academic Web sites and then compares a student's term paper with a huge database of previously written papers. An "Originality Report" is generated that analyzes and compares content from these numerous sources. Professors are starting to use the site (check out the Testimonials link) and so far, the results of these reports have frequently brought about dire consequences for those college students who unwisely chose to copy another's work.

Plagiarism.org offers a service to professors that can determine whether a student has submitted a plagiarized term paper.

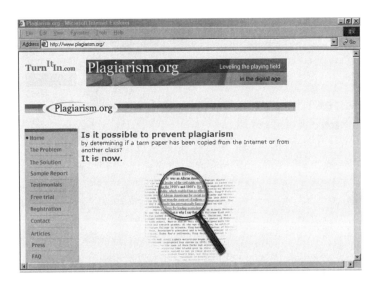

For the Writer Needing Help

The *Write Place Catalogue* at *http://leo.stcloudstate.edu/catalogue.html* is a great online source for information on the process of writing. It covers such topics as how to cite sources, rules of punctuation and grammar, and organization and cohesion.

Student Press on Plagiarism

For some eye-opening information about paper mills and plagiarism, you can go to the Student Advantage Web site at *www.studentadvantage.com*. Click the Daily Grind link under the Academic Life heading. Scroll down to the Papers & Researching and Cheating sections where you'll find links to many articles about this topic. Here are some of the headlines: "Resist the Plagiarized Paper, Profs Plead;" "Anti-Plagiarism Site Continues Rise in Popularity;" and "Downloading Papers from the Web Is Tempting, But Risky." All the articles in these sections were written by students from campus newspapers located across the country.

About Learning and Studying

Whoso neglects learning in his youth, loses the past and is dead for the future.

—Euripides 484-406 B.C.

This quotation was culled from *John Bartlett's Familiar Quotations: A Collection of Passages, Phrases, and Proverbs Traced to Their Sources in Ancient and Modern Literature*, which can be found at the Bartelby.com online bookstore at *www.bartleby.com/99*. To find worthy quotations from this work, simply type a keyword in the Search field and click Go; you'll be provided with a long list of famous quotations with your keyword inside them. For example, we typed **learning** to get the Euripides quotation. The Bartelby.com Web site also has an online encyclopedia, thesaurus, dictionary, quotes from *Simpson's Contemporary Quotations*, and a section on English usage.

Just what are we getting at here? Referring back to the statement made by Euripides, the art and act of learning is your guide to the future, so you want to be good at it. To help you become an ace learner, you can go to the Web. Yes, there are sites that teach you how to study and learn. One very good one was created by Joe Landsberger, Supervisor of the ISS/Learning Center at the University of St. Thomas in St. Paul, Minnesota. Check out Landsberger's Study Guides and Strategies located at *www.iss.stthomas.edu/studyguides*.

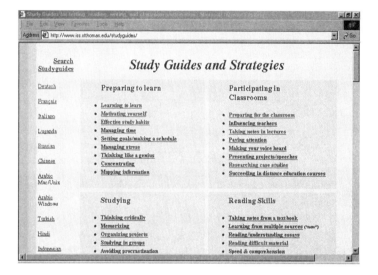

The Study Guides and Strategies Web site is a great place to find information about the art of learning and studying.

The Study Guides and Strategies Web site is chock-full of learning and studying aids, including how to participate in class, how to prepare for and take tests, links to learner self-assessment tools, and a whole lot more. At this Web site, you'll be sure to find something that applies to your individual needs for keeping pace with your academic responsibilities.

The Preparing to Learn section and the Studying section are both good places to start an evaluation of your ability to meet the challenges of higher education. From these sections, you can access information on proper study habits, how to motivate yourself, how to think critically, and more.

A Site for Life

A great interactive Web site for studying and learning all about biology is provided by the University of Arizona at *www.biology. arizona.edu*. This site was designed for high school and college students but also claims to be "useful for medical students, physicians, science writers, and all types of interested people."

Check It Out

Many college and university Web sites have sections on learning and studying that can usually be found by typing keywords such as **Learning Resource Center, Student Development Center,** or **tutoring** at the site's search function field.

The Participating in Classrooms section and the Reading Skills section are also good starting points. You'll get advice on such topics as taking lecture notes, how to read difficult material, and how to present projects and speeches in class.

Overall, this is a great site with more than enough information for helping you become an academic success.

Need Help with Math or Science?

Another site that can help you keep pace with your academic demands is the Interactive Learning Network (ILN) Web site at *www.iln.net.* If you're especially lacking in science and math skills, this site's for you.

The Interactive Learning Network provides high school and college students with interactive online math and science lessons.

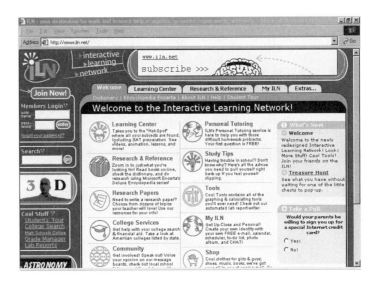

According to its Web site, the ILN includes "truly interactive" math and science lessons that "may incorporate animation, simulations, narration, and video instruction."

This Web site has so much information that it's difficult to decide where to start. In fact, a Web banner at the top of the home page promoting the site proclaimed that ILN has "so many features, your head will spin!"

You'll need the latest version of Windows Media Player and Macromedia Flash Player to experience the many video and audio capabilities of this site. To download the latest versions of these two plug-ins, click the Help option in the top menu bar. At the next page, you'll see a Download link as well as a FAQ link, a First Time User link, a Member Services link, and a Tech Support link. Use the Download link to get the latest versions of the plug-ins; check out the other links to get a good overview of what the ILN Web site is all about.

If you need immediate help with science or math, you can easily access a relatively large database of math and science lessons by clicking the Learning Center link. Before you begin, however, you'll need to register as a member of ILN to take full advantage of this Web site's features. Just click the Join Now link in the top left sidebar and fill out the short form. There's no fee to become a member.

Moonlighting and the Web

The best time to view intensive multi-media files, such as what's provided at *www.iln.net*, is during the wee early morning hours when traffic on the Internet in your area is at its lowest. You'll see that working on the Web while most people are asleep has its benefits.

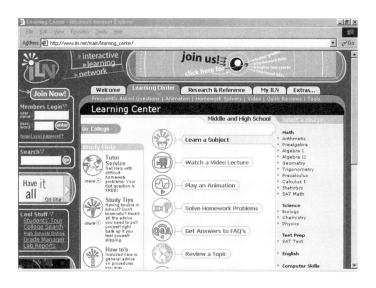

The Interactive Learning Network's Learning Center has online courses in math, science, English, computer skills, and history that you can take advantage of for free.

Everything from the Learning Center section of the ILN Web site is provided for free except for the Tutor Service link, which is priced at $99.95 annually. The Tutor Service is an email-based question-and-answer service that allows you to ask 10 questions per month. Students tend to use the service to help with difficult math or science homework problems. Check out the Sample link

Math for the Curious
Impress your professor and friends with math tricks and math trivia by going to the Curious and Useful Math Web site at *http:// personal.cfw.com/ ~clayford*.

to see what a typical question looks like. If you registered with ILN, you can test the service by sending in one question at no charge.

The Learning Center's online classes feature plenty of options and links to choose from for learning about the subjects you're studying. Check it out:

- The Learn Subject and the Watch a Video Lecture links allow you to see and hear lectures through the Microsoft Media Player.

- The Play an Animation link shows you moving representations of how math equations are solved using the Macromedia Flash Player.

- The Homework Problems link allows you to input data into a math problem or equation and then shows you how the answers are computed.

- You can use the Take a Test link to take practice tests to see how well your brain is digesting all this information.

- You can click the Review a College Topic link to view a chapter-by-chapter summary of the online courses being offered at the specific institution.

- The Get Answers to FAQ link has typical questions and answers related to all the online courses offered by the Online Learning site.

- The Glossaries and Key Terms link provides definitions related to the class you're taking online.

In addition to the Learning Center link, the ILN home page has many other features worth mentioning. Here's a brief synopsis of these features:

- *Research and Reference*—The Research and Reference link will take you to such interesting features as a tour of the solar system, links to historic documents, online access to encyclopedia Encarta, a Net resources section, and much more.

- *Research Papers*—This link provides a listing of topics, categorized by subject, and a number of links to reference sites you can use to do research on your topic.

- *College Services*—The College Services links has a college search feature and information about financial aid.

- *Community*—This section includes message boards on numerous topics, a variety of polls with their results, a high-schools-by-state search function, a Boy-Scout-Troops-by-state search function, and a Big-Brothers/Big-Sisters-Agencies-by-state search function.

- *Study Tips*—Math-related general advice concerning study habits, along with a number of helpful math tips, are provided in this section.

- *Tools*—This section gives you lots of online graphing and calculating tools for math and science subjects.

- *My ILN*—With the My ILN feature, you can create lab reports, keep track of your grades, and monitor your online test results.

- *Shop*—One word says it all. This is the e-commerce section of the site where you can link to other online shopping Web sites for books, electronics, video games, movies, music, and more.

Wrapping It Up

If you have read and reviewed all the links in this chapter, you are now one extremely intelligent and Web-savvy individual who can research and write about any topic your heart desires. Indeed, by knowing how to access all the research and reference-related resources available to you on the Web, you can write like an expert about anything.

However, if you're still a little vague about where to start in relation to writing, researching, learning, and studying during your academic life, here's a brief review of what this chapter covered:

- You were shown several Web sites that give you the basics about how to write a term paper. The two primary formats for writing term papers, MLA and APA, were also discussed.

- You were introduced to Web sites that guide you through the research phase of your term paper, including the University of Albany's online Internet Tutorials and the Internet Public Library's Learning to Research the Web link. We also mentioned a site where students discuss the research-related sites that work for them.

- Details about Web sites that sell research papers were also covered in this chapter. Web site listings of these so-called "paper mills" were not provided (for obvious reasons). Instead, you were introduced to *www.plagiarism.org*, a Web site that helps detect when students cheat on their term papers.

- The final section of this chapter reviewed two phenomenal Web sites that can help you with your learning and studying habits: The Study Guides and Strategies Web site and the Interactive Learning Network Web site.

CHAPTER 10

Choosing a Major and Discovering Your Career Goals

Decisions, decisions, decisions. Just what are you going to do with your life now that you're on a solid path to an exciting future? You need a major. You need a career path. You need help. Don't worry. You have plenty of time to make such decisions. For the time being, enjoy the luxury of simply thinking about where you want to take your education and career—and, of course, always do your homework.

If you do make a decision at this early stage in your educational planning, you can always change and refine your plans while you're still in school. So, mull things over for a while and use the Web to assist you with making wise and highly informed decisions. After all, you're an expert Web researcher now that you've read the previous chapter. Now let's fly forward into cyberspace for the next part of your journey.

This chapter covers Web sites that help you plan your higher education and your future career path. You'll start by checking out sites that are focused on the process of choosing a major. As you're touring these sites, you'll see what professional counselors and students have to say about this topic.

Then you'll go to Web sites for assistance with a course of action to find career options. You'll be introduced to a number of informative career-oriented Web sites that can lead to a career discovery that never before crossed your mind. "Eureka, I found it," you'll say, and your college days will be like an arrow traveling toward its target.

What You'll Learn in This Chapter:

► What Web sites to visit to assist you with choosing your college major.

► What Web sites to visit to assist you with discovering your career goals.

► How to use the online *Occupational Outlook Handbook* to conduct research on prospective career choices.

A Major Choice

Just about every school has an academic and career advising office that you should visit. These offices have academic advisers to assist you with setting your academic goals, selecting and declaring a major, plotting your academic path toward a viable career, and much more. For some unknown reason, many students do not use these advice services and thus lose out on the possibility of getting some great professional assistance at no out-of-pocket cost. (The cost of tuition and fees can be considered payment for such on-campus services.)

Of course, if you want information to augment or supplant on-campus academic advisement services, you can always go to the Web.

Try It Yourself ▼

Careers&Colleges.com is a good place to start looking at college majors and their relationship to career paths. Located at *www.careersandcolleges.com*, this Web site has an awesome service called the Virtual Guidance Counselor. Let's take a test drive:

1. Go to *www.careersandcolleges.com* and click the VGC link under the Take Control of Your Life heading in the left sidebar.

2. Click the Majors link and then scroll down the list of fields of study. Click one that interests you.

3. A list of related majors within your field of study will be supplied. Click a related major that interests you.

4. A list of possible career paths within your related major will be supplied. Click a career path that interests you.

5. A list of links to career information related to your career path will be supplied. Check out these links for more detailed information about your possible career.

▲

Another interesting service that provides information about choosing a major is offered through the University of North Carolina at Wilmington's (UNCW) Career Services department at *www.uncwil.edu/stuaff/career/majors.htm*.

Careers&Colleges. com has a Virtual Guidance Counselor (VGC) section with information on academic majors and career choices.

What Can I Do With a Major In...? is the title of a Web section provided by the University of North Carolina at Wilmington.

Just click a course of study that interests you, and you'll be taken to a page that lists related career titles along with a list of links to associated Web sites. There are links to various job and internship opportunities (more on this in Chapter 11, "Finding Jobs and Internship Programs Online"), associations, and other informational sites—all related to the major you have chosen.

Choosing and Using Your Major

Bell Atlantic Information Systems offers information about choosing a major at *gopher:// minerva.acc. virginia.edu/00/pubs/ career/handouts/1/6*. The Web pages at this site are text only and provide some very sound advice.

Ask an Expert Online

Go to CollegeView.com's Guidance Office at *www.collegeview. com/guidance/expert s/choosingmajor/ index.epl* to ask professional guidance counselors and college admissions professionals questions concerning choosing a college major. You can also view an archive of past questions and answers.

Misconceptions Exposed

Penn State University has an interesting Web page titled Some Common Misconceptions About Choosing a Major, located at *www.psu.edu/dus/ md/mdmisper.htm.* From the same state, at the University of Pennsylvania, is a page titled Choosing a Major: Factors to Consider, located at *www.college.upenn. edu/requirements/ factors.html.*

Embark.com also has a special section devoted to choosing a college major. The direct address is *www.embark.com/college/cm/ maj/art/majart.stm.* The home page for this section is titled Information About College Majors. Some of the links include Tips for Double Majoring, Making the Most of Your Major, and Finding the Best College for Your Major.

There's another section at Embark.com, The Inside Scoop on Top Majors, which is located at *www.embark.com/college/cm/maj/ majint/toc.stm.* Here you'll find links to Web pages of transcribed interviews with students who answered questions about their academic life; the links are categorized by majors.

Quotable Quotes from Student Advantage

Student Advantage has put together a section at its Web site called Decisions, Decisions. Go to *www.studentadvantage.com* and click the Decisions, Decisions link under the Academic Life heading. Under the Topics heading, you'll see a list of links to articles written by Student Advantage staff writers and by student journalists at colleges across the country. Here are some excerpts from these articles:

In "Major Stressing: How to Choose Your Major," writers Mary Anne Feeney and Elizabeth Onusko said, "Taking an assortment of classes can also be beneficial in several ways. Not only will it allow you to narrow down the list of subjects you're interested in, but you'll also be able to broaden your knowledge about a variety of things at the same time."

In "Major Stressing: How I Became a Photography Major," Melanie Chambers wrote, "I chose photography as my major for two simple reasons: I like it and it's fun. I can't sit behind a desk all day and stare vacantly at a computer screen."

In "Don't Hassle Me About My Impractical Major," student journalist Kelly Morris from the *Daily Utah Chronicle* wrote, "The simple fact is that I'm an English major because I like to read. I don't like to balance accounts, I don't like drawing little pictures of mouse traps I might build, and I don't like the idea of being in big business."

Finally, in "Pursue Your Passion in College," student writer Alexandria Scia, at the *Brown Daily Herald*, wrote, "I don't plan to sell you on how fabulous economics is, but I will tell you there is passion to be found in my concentration. Alan Greenspan is one of the most, if not the most, powerful men in the world. He's an economist."

Discovering Your Career Goals

What's the big deal about a career anyway? Today, people change careers like hats. What you major in might not apply to what you end up doing, and a lot of what you learn in college today will most likely be outdated by the time you reach the job market. Nonetheless, you have to do the dance. Your parents want to know what you're going to be when you grow up. (This is not a good question to ask anyone, by the way.) Your aunts and uncles want to know what you plan on doing for the rest of your life. Your grandmother is awfully curious even though she has no idea what it's like out there in today's rapidly changing world of work.

Charting a Career Path

"Your major in college is important for your first job after graduation, but studies show that most people will change careers about four or five times over the course of their lives—and no major exists that can prepare you for that," writes Randell S. Hansen, Ph.D., at the Quintessential Careers Web site (*www.quintcareers.com*). Hansen's article, titled "Choosing a College Major: How to Chart Your Ideal Path," is located at *www.quintcareers.com/choosing_major.html*.

Will You Succeed?
To peer into the crystal ball, go to *www.queendom. com/tests/success. html* for the Success Likelihood Test, comprised of 40 online questions. After completing this test, you'll get explanations of your scores in five categories: success likelihood ratio, fear of success, fear of failure, fear of social consequences of success, and drive/ambition.

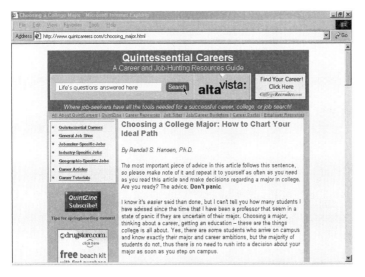

The Quintessential Careers Web site includes a section all about charting your career path.

Hansen's article is a great place to start examining your future career path options. He covers six "stops on your journey" that will help you assess what career path you might want to pursue, including an examination of your interests, your abilities, and what you value. He also provides a list of books you can check out in relation to education and career planning.

Hansen's article also gives you a number of career-oriented links, one of which is titled Quintessential Careers: Career Assessment. This link takes you to a page where you can access online assessment tests that can help you figure out the kind of career you might want to consider pursuing. Many of these assessment tests are available online for free. Such tests, from a pure vanity standpoint, are fun to take, but they can also spur on some interesting thoughts concerning your future.

Taking Online Interest Assessment Tests

Let's start the online assessment process with The Career Key at *www.ncsu.edu/careerkey*. This Web site was created by Lawrence K. Jones Ph.D., professor at the College of Education and Psychology at North Carolina State University where he specializes in the areas of school counseling and career counseling and development.

The Career Key Web site offers an expansive online assessment test that can help students realize what career options are available to them.

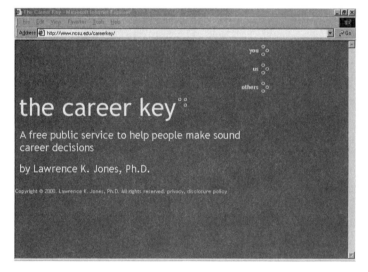

If you want to use all the features of the Career Key Web site, you'll have to sign in by filling out a short, one-page form. Just click the You link at the top of the home page and then the Sign On to Begin link. After you fill out the form, click the Continue button to access a page with 10 options listed under the Your Choices heading.

For example, start by clicking the Take the Career Key Measure link. In the next five pages, you answer a short list of multiple-choice questions on each page. The five pages have these labels:

- Which jobs interest you?

- What do you like to do?

- What are your abilities?

- How do you see yourself?

- What do you value?

After you have completed the questions, you'll be sent to a page that lists your career key test scores divided into six personality types:

- Realistic

- Investigative

- Social

- Artistic

- Enterprising

- Conventional

Scores from these six categories are the basis of what's called *Holland's Personality Life-Styles*, the creation of leading career-theory expert Dr. John Holland. The highest score you get is considered your personality type. The theory is that people who work in places that are congruent to their personality type will more than likely be successful and happy in their careers.

Another Version of Holland's Test

You can take a more in-depth, online self-assessment test based on Holland's Personality Life-Styles at the Self-Directed Search Web site, located at *http://self-directed-search.com*. After taking the test online, there's a $7.95 fee to get your results in an 8-to-12–page personalized report.

Myers-Briggs

One very popular personality-assessment test used today by many employers is called the Myers-Briggs Type Indicator (MBTI®) instrument. Scores from the MBTI identify an individual as one of 16 possible personality types; these scores can be interpreted to reveal learning, leadership, and managerial styles. For more information, go to the Web site of Consulting Psychologists Press Inc., the publishers of the MBTI, located at *www.cpp-db.com/products/mbti/index.html*. According to this Web site, MBTI "is the most widely used personality inventory in history.... Last year alone, 2 million people gained valuable insight about themselves and the people they interact with daily by taking the MBTI instrument."

The Career Key Web site also helps you gather information about jobs that fit your personality type. To start this process, click the Learn About Jobs That Fit My Holland Personality Type link under the Your Choices section. Follow the steps provided. You'll be shown listings of job titles that fit your personality type. The last step takes you to a page that lists jobs related to those you chose during this process. If you click any of the jobs listed here, you'll be taken to that job's description at the *Occupational Outlook Handbook* (OOH) Web site, located at *http://stats.bls.gov/ocohome.htm.*

The Occupational Outlook Handbook *Web site is a good place to find detailed information about possible career choices.*

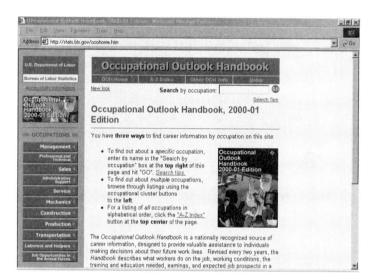

Considering the *Occupational Outlook Handbook*

According to the OOH Web site (which is published by the Bureau of Labor Statistics, U.S. Department of Labor), "the *Occupational Outlook Handbook* is a nationally recognized source of career information, designed to provide valuable assistance to individuals making decisions about their future work lives. Revised every two years, the *Handbook* describes what workers do on the job, working conditions, the training and education needed, earnings, and expected job prospects in a wide range of occupations."

To use this site to your advantage, simply follow one of the three ways to find career information listed on the home page. As you navigate through this site, you'll find lots of information about numerous occupations. Click the *Other OOH Info* link in the top menu bar; then click the How to Interpret Occupational Handbook Information Included in the Handbook link. From here, you'll get an overview of some of the site's important features. For example, for every occupation listed, there are eight categories of information:

- Nature of Work

- Working Conditions

- Employment

- Training, Other Qualifications, and Advancement

- Job Outlook

- Earnings

- Related Occupations

- Sources of Additional Information

You might want to also check out the Bureau of Labor Statistic's take on the future of work. You can access this information from the How to Interpret Occupational Handbook Information Included in the Handbook page just mentioned. Go there by clicking the Tomorrow's Jobs link in the second paragraph. There's some great information here that can help you plot your future career. For instance, in the Occupation section of this page, the Bureau of Labor Statistics predicts that from now through 2008, some of the fastest growing occupations will be computer systems analysts, computer engineers and scientists, special education teachers, and social and recreation workers.

The OOH site also has a great section on industry in general. Click the Career Guide to Industries link in the lower-left sidebar on the site's home page. Here you'll find the beginning pages of another OOH online publication, *The Career Guide to Industries*. According to the Web site, this companion publication to the *Handbook* "provides information on available careers by industry,

Free Career Options Booklet

To obtain a free booklet titled *Career Options*, go to *http://mooni.fccj.org/ ~gharr/free.htm*. This booklet claims to be "an introduction to the career exploration process" that "has been used by thousands of high school and college students as a way to begin their career planning."

including the nature of the industry, working conditions, employment, occupations in the industry, training and advancement, earnings and benefits, employment outlook, and lists of organizations that can provide additional information. This edition of the *Career Guide* discusses over 42 industries, accounting for over 7 out of every 10 wage and salary jobs in 1998."

Wrapping It Up

If you traversed the Web sites suggested in this chapter, you should have at least considered some ideas about where you want to point your brain during your years at your selected institution of higher education. However, if you still have no idea whatsoever concerning what educational path you may want to take, don't fret. Try these sites again at a later date. After all, you don't have to choose a major until your junior year—and even then you can change direction midway through the year. Regarding a career— don't believe anyone who tells you that you absolutely have to know what kind of job you want after you graduate. As mentioned earlier, many people do not end up within the professional area they studied in college.

If you need a review, here's what this chapter covered:

- Some Web sites that provide loads of information and counseling in relation to choosing your major course of college study.

- How to use online self-assessment tests to help find where your talents lie and where you might want to look for a career.

- Some other career-based Web sites, such as the *Occupational Outlook Handbook* site, that provide lots of information about the nature of today's and tomorrow's work force.

CHAPTER 11

Finding Jobs and Internship Programs Online

If you're like most college students today, you are or will be working at least part-time while attending school. Unfortunately, exploring available job opportunities through the Web can be a daunting task. There are simply too many Web sites in cyberspace, all claiming to have the right mix of services and job listings to help you find fulfilling work.

Moreover, many of these Web sites can have you spinning your wheels as you email resume after resume to prospective employers, only to find that the job listing you applied for was filled a long time ago.

In this chapter, those Web sites with outdated and superfluous information will be avoided, and your browser will be pointed in the right direction for reliable online resources to help you find jobs or internship programs.

The first stop will be at a university Career Center model Web site that happens to provide an efficient way to gather information about jobs and internship programs. You'll also be introduced to Web sites that help you find part-time employment with a strong focus on finding unique and exciting summer employment.

You'll then go to a Web site devoted to finding internship programs online. You'll also be introduced to a Web site section that features numerous articles by students who can provide valuable viewpoints and advice related to the world of internships.

Interspersed throughout this chapter are a lot of tips you should find useful in your search for employment or internship programs.

Good luck!

What You'll Learn in This Chapter:

▸ What a typical higher education Career Center Web site looks like.

▸ Three methods for finding part-time employment online.

▸ Where to go on the Web to find summer employment.

▸ Where to go on the Web to find internship programs.

Campus Career Centers

All colleges and universities have Career Centers staffed with professionals who are more than willing to help you find work while you're in school and after you graduate. In addition to occupying physical office space on campus, these centers usually provide information through the schools' Web sites. A good example is the one hosted by University of California, Berkeley.

The University of California, Berkeley, Career Center Web site helps students find jobs and internship programs.

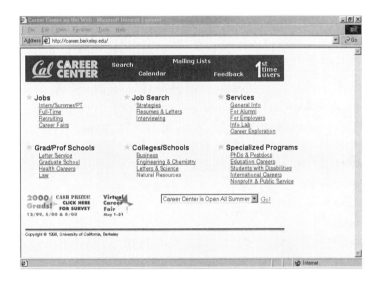

Your School's Employment Office

Most Career Center offices have large bulletin boards where numerous jobs are posted. Obviously, you can stroll over to your school's Career Center and see, first-hand, what's available.

Navigating to UC Berkeley's Career Center is easy. Just go to UC Berkeley's Web site at *www.berkeley.edu* and click the Student Life link. Then scroll down to the Jobs, Internships and Career heading and click the Career Center link. Typically, most school Web sites have similar navigation routes to their Career Centers. However, if you have difficulty finding your school's Web-based Career Center, use the site's Search function (if they have one) and type in the words **Career Center** or **jobs**. This search should tell you where the school's Web-based Career Center is located.

Inside the UC Berkley Career Center site, notice the Jobs heading in the upper-left corner, and the first link titled Intern/Summer/PT. The PT stands for part-time. As an undergraduate, this is where you want to start your search, unless, of course, you're seeking a full-time job. In that case, click the Full-Time link.

The Intern/Summer/PT section has a Frequently Asked Questions (FAQ) link that is very informative. For instance, one FAQ explains that a good time to start looking for an internship is during the second semester of your freshman year. The Career Center then provides information about available internships online through various UC Berkeley services (exclusively for UC Berkeley students).

Regarding summer internships, the FAQ section advises students to begin searching for summer work during the preceding Fall semester.

If you're looking for a part-time job and have no job experience, the FAQ section explains that employers frequently "value skills developed through academic work, volunteer experiences, extracurricular experiences, or other experiences which demonstrate skills useful in work."

How many hours should you put in? UC Berkeley recommends that full-time students work no more than 20 hours per week.

Who's Working?

According to information from the U.S. Department of Labor Bureau of Labor Statistics, a little more than half of all college students under the age of 25 hold down jobs. Students at two-year colleges are more likely to have a job than students at four-year colleges. Almost two-thirds of students at two-year colleges work, whereas slightly more than half of those at four-year colleges are employed.

Part-time college students are more likely to work than full-time students. For instance, in October 1998, 84.1% of part-time students under age 25 had jobs, whereas only 50.2% of full-time students in the same age category held down jobs.

Finding Part-Time Employment Online

Finding decent part-time job opportunities for undergraduates with little experience is not exactly the easiest thing to accomplish on the Web. Most of the job-finding sites focus primarily on full-time positions for students who are about to, or have already, graduated.

All is not lost, however. There are at least three ways to find part-time work over the Web. The first method for finding part-time work was already mentioned: Go to your school's Web site and

It's Resume Time Already

Incoming students interested in landing part-time jobs or an internship (usually available to students by the second half of their freshman year) should have a proper resume prepared, highlighting all their accomplishments in a comprehensive and intelligible format. Your school's Career Center can help you put together a decent resume.

Teach Yourself e-Job Hunting

For a clear, step-by-step tutorial for planning a career and searching for jobs using online resources, get *Sams Teach Yourself e-Job Hunting Today*, by Eric Schlesinger and Susan Musich.

find the section hosted by your school's Career Center. From
there you'll be shown what opportunities exist in your area.

Another relatively easy way to find part-time job listings
online is to go to the granddaddy of all job-finding Web sites at
www.monster.com. Let's give it a whirl:

1. Point your browser to *www.monster.com* and click the Find
   link under the Search Jobs category.

2. Choose the location in which you want to work from the
   Location Search pull-down menu.

3. Choose a job type from the Job Category Search pull-down
   menu. Using this function might help you find a job within
   an occupation that interests you the most.

4. Type **part-time** in the Keyword Search box and click the
   Search Jobs button. You'll be taken to a page listing part-time
   jobs based on the criteria you specified.

5. Click any of the jobs listed for a full description of the job
   and how to apply for it.

▲

*At Monster.com,
students can
search for part-
time job opportu-
nities by type and
location.*

Another way to find part-time employment online is to visit the
help-wanted sections of your local newspapers. As mentioned in
Chapter 8, "Shopping for Housing Deals, Student Discounts, and

More," you can go to the *American Journalism Review* Web site at *http://ajr.newslink.org* to locate all the newspapers in your state that have Web sites. When you arrive at a newspaper's Web site, it should be easy to find a clearly visible link that will take you to the help-wanted listings.

Words of Wisdom About Part-Time Work

For some words of wisdom offered by current and former college students concerning the world of part-time employment, go inside the Epinions.com Web site at *www.epinions.com/educ-FA_Jobs*, where the following two questions are posted:

- How does a campus job or work study position compare to outside employment?
- How does working your way through college affect your studies?

Forty-six viable opinions (or epinions, if you like) were logged. One student said, "on-campus jobs are more likely to be more flexible, but the jobs are more likely to be more menial. Jobs in the real world can give you some valuable, needed experience, but you have to be able to fit their schedule into yours and not vice versa."

One former student wrote, "don't ever settle for a job at a fast-food joint. It will be the worst days of your life and make you extremely depressed."

Another student veteran offered the following: "It might be a good idea to take a hard look at where income from a part-time job during the school year is going. If the answer is car insurance, and also luxury items such as DVDs, students might want to think twice. Is the time away from school really worth it?"

Finally, another former student said, "knowing that I was paying for at least part of my education each semester made me feel obligated to study more and do my best. Also, working is an education in itself no matter where you are employed."

Part-Time Learning

Perhaps the best part-time job you can find is one that's related to your anticipated career path. Approaching your job search as a means to acquire educational experiences related to your career goals might be more important than the amount of money you earn.

Finding Summer Jobs Online

For many students, the summer break away from school is not a time when they get to enjoy some vacation time. Instead, it's a time for some serious full-time work to stockpile some badly needed cash for all the expenses they'll encounter during the next Fall and Spring semesters. This does not mean, of course, that you have to rush into a job that you will not in the least bit enjoy. You can use the Web to avoid this type of scenario.

You can start your search for cool summer employment at *www.coolworks.com.*, whose tag line is "Live and Work Where Others Only Visit."

At CoolWorks.com, students can find summer employment opportunities listed by state.

Get a Head Start

Give yourself a head start and a good chance for landing a summer job by conducting your search and applying for jobs as early as late winter or early spring.

If location is an important consideration in your choice of summer employment, CoolWorks.com allows you to search for jobs by state. Click the Jobs Listed by State link inside the Search Tools box on the right side to be taken to a page with links to all 50 states. Depending on the state you click, you'll be shown summer job opportunities in national parks, beaches, amusement parks, camps, and more.

You can also search for summer employment by job category by clicking inside the Job Listings by Category box on the home page. In addition to links to national parks, amusement parks, and camps, you'll find links to resorts, guest ranches, and state parks. Other links from this section include Jobs on Water (fishing lodges, lakes, beaches, cruise ships, river jobs); Other Cool Work (gift shop jobs in Alaska, cultural exchange opportunities in Australia and New Zealand, jobs with adventure travel companies, and more); and Volunteering (a long list of summer volunteering opportunities with worthwhile organizations).

Here are some other sites related to seasonal employment:

- **About.com's Job Searching: College Grads section—**
  http://collegegradjobs.about.com/careers/collegegradjobs/msubseasonal.htm
  Guide Virginia Smith provides plenty of information about and links to seasonal jobs listed under the following

categories: Holiday Jobs, Island & Beach, Mountain, Parks, Wild West & Alaska, Summer, and Winter.

- **JobMonkey**—*www.jobmoney.com*
  JobMonkey's mission is to "help you find seasonal or year-round jobs working for employers who can offer you unique opportunities to travel the world, have fun, and earn good money doing it."

- **Student.com**—*www.student.com/subsection/summerjobs*
  The folks at Student.com have put together a special section on summer jobs with some highly informative reviews written by special Student.com correspondents regarding seasonal jobs, such as working for start-up Internet companies, being a political campaigner, and working as a camp counselor. Additionally, Student.com members post insightful comments relating to these reviews.

Finding Internship Programs Online

One of the best ways to see whether what you're learning in your classes has any relationship to the real world is to take part in an internship program. According to UC Berkeley's Career Center, an internship is "an on-site work experience that is either directly related to your major field of study or your career interest."

The right internship can be an invaluable experience, leading to an immediate job after graduation. Internships are definite resume boosters that can set you apart from the competitive crowd, especially because most students do not acquire firsthand experience in their chosen careers while still in college.

Pay rates for internship programs vary from zero pay (you're getting invaluable training and experience) to minimum wage to substantially more than minimum wage. In many cases, you can also obtain college credit for taking part in an internship program. (Check with your academic advisor.) The duration of an internship program can vary from part-time to full-time and from seasonal to year-round.

So, where do you start to find the right internship program? Your first stop should be the Career Center at your campus. Professional counselors are more than willing to help you find an internship

Are You Ready?

Monster.com has an online quiz titled What's Your Intern Potential at *http://campus. monster.com/tools/ internquiz.* Take the quiz "to see how ready you are for this important first step of your career."

program that's right for you. Additionally, most Career Centers have a library of career manuals and internship directories, as well as bulletin boards where internship opportunities are posted.

If the Career Center does not have what you're looking for, go to a site tagged as "The Internship Search Engine™" at *www.internshipprograms.com.*

InternshipPrograms .com helps students find internship programs by location and job category.

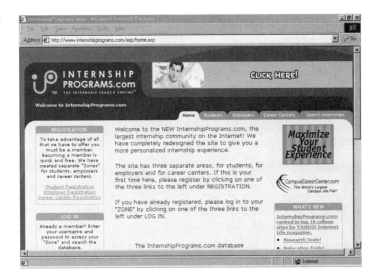

The first step in the search process is to register with InternshipPrograms.com. Click the Students tab at the top of the home page and then click the Registration link. Fill out the short form and click the Save button. You'll be taken to a page titled Student Zone that features three major links: Search Internships, Internship Experiences, and Update Student Profile.

The Search Internships link helps you find internship programs by location (U.S. city and state) and category (everything from Accounting and Finance to Travel). You can also browse for internships by clicking the International link, the U.S. City and State link, or the Company Name link, all located under the Browse Internships heading.

- The International link takes you to a Web page about a non-profit organization called the Center for Cultural Interchange (CCI). According to this Web page, "CCI organizes academic year, short-term homestay, and language study programs in the United States and in over thirty different countries around the world." For more information, click the Pre-Application link.

- The U.S. City and State link takes you to a Web page with a map of the United States and a Browse Internships by Region pull-down menu. Click a state on the map to see information about all the internship programs available in that particular state. Click a region (city and state) to see information about all the internship programs available in that particular city and state.

- The Company Name link takes you to a page with a long list of companies inside a pull-down menu titled Browse Internships by Company. Just click a company name for more information about its internship program. You'll find a detailed description of the company, a description of the position(s) being offered, and the appropriate contact information. Some listings will let you know whether a position is a paid one or not, but in most cases, the amount of pay will not be listed.

Back on the Student Zone page, you can check out internship program reviews written by actual interns by clicking the Internship Experiences link. Students are adding reviews all the time, so you might want to check back now and then to see the latest reviews.

Get a Heads-Up from Students

Another great place to obtain plenty of highly relevant information about internships directly from students is at the Internships/Co-ops section in the StudentAdvantage.com Web site. Go to *www.studentadvantage.com* and click the Internships/Co-ops link under the Careers category. (The difference between an internship and co-op work programs is that internships are usually one-time assignments whereas co-ops are repeated assignments.)

The Internships/Co-ops home page is divided into two primary sections: Features and Topics. There's also a section titled Overheard, and another titled Other Resources, both located in the right sidebar.

Review Internship Availability

Go to *www.review.com* and click the Internships link in the right sidebar for an internship search service provided by the *Princeton Review*. You can search by location, job type, and weekly compensation criteria.

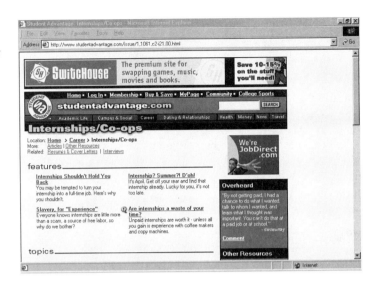

Student Advantage.com's Internships/Co-ops section posts numerous articles written primarily by students on a wide variety of topics related to internship programs.

Let's take a look at all these sections to see what students have to say about internships. Under Features, Matthew Dalton from the *Brown Daily Herald*, in a piece titled "Internships: Valuable Experience or Borderline Scam," writes, "...the mass of college folk seeking summer activities is a veritable gold mine for employers. Imagine having a huge mass of relatively educated workers who are willing to work for free." He then goes on to explain (with a healthy touch of cynicism) about the various types of internships, including internships where all you do is "spend your days doing menial tasks for your employer, for free or a measly stipend," and another that he labels "sit-on-your-butt" internships, in which you do nothing and get paid for it.

In the Topics section, there are four categories: Why an Internship, Finding One, Making the Most of It, and Examples. Each category has loads of relevant articles written by students.

In "Why You Need an Internship and How to Start the Search," in the Why an Internship category, StudentAdvantage.com writer Sophia Cordoni says, "Many students have gotten internships in their chosen field only to discover that they hate the work. Being on the inside of an industry can help you realize what you don't want to be doing just as much as it can cement your ideas about what you do want to be doing."

In "Getting An Internship: The Waiting Game, Harvard Crimson," in the Finding One category, writer Kamil Redmond provides a first-person lament concerning her seemingly interminable wait for a possible internship acceptance letter. "Each day passes without the letter and without the phone call," she says, "while I am left biting my nails contemplating a summer spent working at Banana Republic."

In the Making the Most of It section, there's a threaded discussion under the heading How Do You Cope with a Do-Nothing Internship. One former intern gave the following sound advice: "Internships are meant for you to learn; if you're not given any work, use your time to network. If your responsibilities are to answer phones and make copies, do that as efficiently as you can. Hopefully, if you hang in there, they'll see that you're reliable and they'll start giving you projects and more responsibilities."

In the Examples section, you can find a Q & A article written by Melissa Harris, from the *Daily Northwestern*, titled "One Senior's Summer Internship in Washington." (Sorry, no Monica Lewinsky jokes here.) A student who worked as a White House Letter Writer, Harris fields questions about her two-month stint with former Senator Carol Moseley-Braun.

In the Overheard section, you'll find a long list of comments inside a threaded discussion titled Are Internships a Waste of Your Time? For example, one former intern wrote, "I think the most important essence of internships is to make sure that you know what you want out of them. I wanted exposure, but if you are looking for money, that's a different avenue. Experience to me is priceless! You'll catch up to the money soon enough! Hang in there!"

Finally, for help with those sticky particulars concerning the process of applying for internships, go to the links labeled Related near the top of the Internships/Co-ops home page and click the Resumes & Cover Letters link or the Interviews link. Both links will take you to extensive sections on these topics.

Wrapping It Up

This is one chapter that, when related to life in general, never concludes. Throughout your higher education years, and thereafter, you'll more than likely be examining the job market on a pretty consistent basis. This is true especially today, when job skills change overnight, and a new global economy brings about more job opportunities than ever before.

For now, however, your concerns are more immediate. You need a job, and you need one now. You might be tired of asking your parents for spending money, or you simply don't have any other means for acquiring funds to help pay the bills (with hopefully a little left over for pizza and a cold one now and then).

This chapter was written to help you find a job or internship program that fits in with what you want out of life. The focus was not on taking any job that happens to come along. Instead, you were introduced to online services that can assist you with finding enough options to make a wise choice.

- You were given information about on-campus and Web-based Career Centers that exist for the sole reason of finding students jobs and internship programs.

- You were shown how to find part-time employment opportunities for students, including a visit to the popular Monster.com site, as well as how to access online help-wanted classified advertisements. Also included was a section on what students have to say about working their way through college.

- An entire section on finding summer jobs was provided, but the sites you visited in relation to this topic did not provide information on mundane summer jobs. Instead, you were shown where to go on the Web to find exciting summer work that can foster fond memories for many years to come.

- Last but not least, you were introduced to the online world of internship programs. Here you were able to access online search functions that attempt to find the right internship program for your particular needs and wants. You also read some highly interesting and informative internship-guidance articles written by students.

CHAPTER 12

Having Fun Online

In the previous chapters, the Web became your home for serious concerns regarding your higher education. If you did all the reading and surfing, you can consider yourself an e-College master.

All that hard work might have left you yearning for an online fun break in cyberspace. So, let's toss academics aside for now and see what kind of diversions can be found on the Web. We're talking good, clean college fun, of course.

This chapter begins with a visit to *www.uzone.com* and *www.student.com*, two relatively large Web sites that can easily help take your mind off academics for a while. Some of the topics covered include responsible drinking, dating, music, and MP3s.

You'll also be introduced to Web sites with lots of information related to electronic games on many different levels.

Then we'll cover Greek Life, with a focus on where to engage in online conversation with fellow Greeks. Online Greek-oriented shopping is also covered.

Finally, you'll take a look at sites that deal strictly with entertainment, so that you have more places to visit for escaping the academic blues.

The University of U

Yes, there are Web sites made for college students where academic-oriented content is secondary or not mentioned at all. Instead, the focus is on the social and entertainment aspects of college life. These sites want to indulge your fancy, offering everything from entertainment guides and free online music to online games, chat rooms, dating advice, and much more. One such site is at *www.uzone.com*.

What You'll Learn in This Chapter:

▸ About several Web sites that provide a host of services geared toward college students having fun online and offline.

▸ Where to find Web sites covering the vast world of electronic games.

▸ About Web sites devoted to Greek organizations and where you can go to join chat rooms and discussion boards with fellow Greeks.

▸ About a number of Web sites that cover the remarkable world of entertainment.

College culture is alive and online at Uzone.com, (*www.uzone.com*), a great site to visit for a healthy dose of college-oriented entertainment and fun. This site is divided into 12 major category links: Campus Life, Nightlife, Real World, Health and Fitness, Shopping, Sports, Fun & Games, The Hype, Love & Sex, Music & Video, Jobs & Resumes, and Academics. Each category has a lot of subcategory links, which make this Web site quite large.

Uzone.com has information and links to everything from music and video guides to health and fitness Web sites.

Zone of Influence

Uzone is part of a family of college-oriented Web sites operated by StudyFree, a Houston-based company that is a subsidiary of NetStrategy. For more information about the Uzone family of Web sites for students, go to *www.studyfree.com*.

Uzone is a truly enormous and unique Web site for college students. According to information accessed through the About Uzone link located in the left sidebar, the Uzone site "brings college culture alive online with activities, events, entertainment, and resources for the e-generation."

The Uzone site covers so many areas of interest that it might behoove you to spend some time just checking out the abundant number of links available at this Web site. When you hover the mouse over the 12 category links in the left sidebar, you'll see pop-up menu links appear. When you see something that interests you, click the link to go to sections featuring related information and even more links.

There are more than 100 subcategory links at the Uzone Web site. One seemingly arcane subcategory link in the category The Hype is titled Believe It. The Believe It Web page has links to information that could possibly make you one of the world's foremost trivia buffs. For example, did you know that there's a Web site titled the World's Sexual Records located at *www.sexualrecords.com*. (Incidentally, snakes have the longest coitus in the animal kingdom, typically remaining in union for six to twelve hours.) Some of the other unusual and unique links listed under the Believe It subcategory include Dumb Laws, Dumb Criminal Acts, Unbelievable Facts About Beer, Bad Fads, and much more—certainly all great resources for your next cocktail party conversation.

And speaking of cocktail parties, Uzone's Nightlife link has plenty of information about the art of partying, including a link titled Drinking: A Student's Guide. It's located inside the Beer, Wine, and Sprits subcategory, and it provides information about making the right choices if you happen to be over-exposed to people who might be abusing alcohol.

Of course, if you need music for your party, you can always go to Uzone's Music and Video section, where there is an enormous database of links to Web sites related to the world of sound. If you have the RealPlayer software on your computer, click the Live Radio link to hook up with a number of live Internet radio stations you can listen to while you're surfing around. Some of these live radio stations might ask you to download other audio applications, such as Macromedia's FlashRadio, that allow you to listen to a variety of music genres while online.

As mentioned earlier, Uzone is loaded with all kinds of entertainment-related matter geared specifically toward college students. So, surf around and enjoy.

Positive Student News

Click the NewsU link in the right sidebar on Uzone's home page to go to *www.newsu.com*, where there are numerous feature articles and threaded discussions about students and written by students. The content has a strong slant toward "fun stuff."

Forget About Binging

The binge-drinking culture found at many campuses puts students at risk for major health problems, drinking-related automobile accidents, rape, and other crimes. Getting drunk is really not a rite of passage into college life. The bottom line: If you drink, be sure to drink sensibly.

MP3 Is Alive and Possibly Not-So-Well on Campuses

If you're part of the growing crowd of students who go online for their music, you probably know all about MP3, the acronym for Motion Picture Experts Group Audio Layer 3, a compressed digital sound file. It's a relatively easy process to convert music on a CD to MP3 format and

continues

continued

then post the MP3 version of the music on a Web site (although it's not always legal to do this). Visitors to the Web site can then download the MP3-formatted music and listen to it on their computers for free as long as they have a freeware player installed (such as WinAmp for Windows users or MacAmp for Mac users). Computer users with the right freeware and a CD-ROM burner can take MP3 files, convert them into CD-compatible digital files, and thus make their own CDs. MP3 fans can also play MP3-formatted music on portable players. One of the more popular players on the market is called a Diamond Rio.

This whole MP3 thing has caused quite a stir in the music industry. New studies have come out saying that, in particular, college students with fast Internet connections obtained through their schools aren't buying music at their local music store anymore. Instead, they are downloading songs to their computers at no cost from a long and growing list of Web sites posting numerous MP3 files.

The most popular of the MP3-oriented Web sites is called Napster at *www.napster.com*. Napster is currently being sued by the Recording Industry of America. The lawsuit claims that that Napster's software allows computer users to acquire copyrighted music online without permission from its rightful owners. For more information on this issue, go to *www.napster.com/groundzero*.

Another piece of fallout from this controversy is that college students have been clogging up Internet lines at schools because they are frequently downloading these relatively large (although compressed) MP3 files to their computers. In fact, some schools are banning students from using Napster. (You can read an article about the bans at the Wired News Web site at *www.wired.com/news/mp3/0,1285,34382,00.html*.)

For Students Only

Another great site for some good old college fun can be found at *www.student.com*.

The Student.com home page has seven primary sections listed in the left sidebar: Campus, Culture, Sports, Travel, Jobs, Fun and Games, and Members. You might want to start off by joining this Web community so that you can take advantage of Student.com's services. Let's sign up:

Try It Yourself ▼

1. Go to *www.student.com* and click the Members link in the left sidebar.

2. Click the Join Student.Com link. (Membership is free.) Read the Web Agreement and then click the I Agree button. You'll be taken to a page with a membership form that you have to fill out.

3. Complete the form and click the Make Me a Member button.

4. You'll get a congratulatory message and be asked to log on as a member. Log on with the member name and password that you specified when filling out the form, and you will be taken back to the Student.com home page. You are now a bona fide member of Student.com.

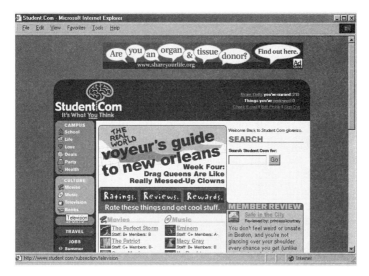

The Student.com Web site claims to be a great place to "hang out, have fun, and entertain each other."

There's enough material on this Web site to keep you entertained for quite a while. Each section has plenty of special features. When you click any of the major sections, you'll be taken to a page with a pull-down menu labeled Contents Features (except for the Travel and Jobs sections, which do not have this navigation tool). Scroll down to a feature that interests you and click the Go button to review its content. For instance, at the Love subcategory inside the Campus section, there's a segment devoted to dating issues, including such links as Pick Me Up (using the right pick-up line), Tour of Duty (meeting your significant other's parents), and More Than Friends (the dilemma of falling for a good friend).

By the way, at the bottom of every Contents Feature pull-down menu is a Discussions link. This option links to a threaded discussion area covering numerous topics. Not surprisingly, the Campus section's Love discussion group had the greatest number

The Dating Scene

See the Dating & Relationships section at the Student Advantage Website at *www. studentadvantage. com/dating* for plenty of feature articles and advice on relationships, with an emphasis on college life.

of messages posted, including more than 400 messages under a topic titled What is Love?

In the Culture section of the Student.com Web site, you'll find book, movie, music, and television reviews, as well a Seinfeld-O-Matic link, where visitors click a slot machine that generates possible Seinfeld plots.

In Student.com's Sports section, you'll find college athletics-related articles on a number of sports, including field hockey, lacrosse, volleyball, and wrestling.

In the Travel section, there are travel reviews and guides on major cities located throughout the world, as well as travel tips and links to a currency converter, a foreign dictionary, and more.

The Jobs section has lots of links to information on rather interesting jobs, such as an Alaskan fisherman, a political campaigner, and a Disney World cast member.

Finally, Student.com's Fun and Games section will keep you entertained with comics, crossword puzzles, a game called Garfunkel, and more.

Game Time

If you're a child of the 1980s, you probably have some video arcade blood in you. You might also be a Nintendo or PlayStation loyalist. If you're none of the above, you might still be a player of electronic games.

The Web can easily quench your desire for the escapism of electronic games. It can also be a catalyst for procrastination. Some students get so caught up in electronic games that it interferes with their studies.

The Web has its share of online games that make up a very large planet in cyberspace. Some of the more popular games among today's college students are Quake, Doom, Half Life, Everquest, Starcraft, and Mech Warriors. Of course, the popularity of these games changes from semester to semester. So, by the time you read this, another computer game will probably be the college craze.

Many of the most popular games are RPGs (Role Playing Games), in which users create their own characters to inhabit various three-dimensional virtual worlds that are created by the makers of these games. You purchase these games on CD-ROM and can then go to the gamemaker's Web site to play and compete against multiple players simultaneously.

A good place to go for information and links to the cyperspace planet of games is the ZDNet Gamespot at *www.zdnet.com/ gamespot.*

The ZDNet Gamespot has up-to-date information about the latest electronic games.

The Gamespot Navigation box, located in the left sidebar, is where you might want to start. Here are links to game reviews, guides, news and feature articles, and patch downloads that fix various bugs in the games you might already own. You'll also find free game demos you can download, as well as hints and strategies for some of the most popular games available today. Additionally, you can purchase games online and download some of them immediately to your computer if you are a ZDNet subscriber.

To become a subscriber and registered member of this Web community, click the box in the upper-right corner labeled Join Gamespot Elite. Membership does have its benefits, including free, private storage space for your game files on the Web; a free

Want to Be a Game Beta Tester?

ZDNet Gamespot provides links to game Web sites seeking people to test their yet-to-be released games and to report any problems they might find. Such gamers are called Beta testers. To start a search to become a Beta tester, click the Beta Center link in the Gamespot Services box.

Web-based email, voice mail, and fax service; a free online calendar; an email notification service alerting you to the latest product demos, discounts, and special offers; and access to ZDNet's gaming forums.

Just below the Gamespot Navigation box is another box titled Gamespot at E3. This is a news and game preview section with articles on the newest games that have been recently launched or are about to be launched.

Under the Gamespot at E3 box is a box titled Genres with eight categories: Action, Adventure, Driving, Role Playing, Puzzle, Simulation, Sports, and Strategy. Like the other sections of the Web site, you'll find game previews and reviews, online buying features, and various demos and patches you can download.

Finally, here are some other Web sites devoted to games (there are many more than these) that you might want to visit:

- **The Station**—*www.station.sony.com*
  Brought to you by Sony Online Entertainment, this Web site has Jeopardy and Wheel of Fortune online, as well as the official site for the popular game Everquest.

- **DMOZ Open Directory**—*www.dmoz.org/Games*
  Go here for an extensive database of links to more than 26,300 game-related Web sites. DMOZ Open Directory is a comprehensive directory of the Web that relies on volunteer editors to supply links to Web sites in their chosen areas of expertise.

- **About.com**—
  www.roleplaygames.about.com/games/roleplaygames
  Loads of information on, and links to, role-playing games, hosted by About.com guide Dru Pagliassotti.

- **FunCom Online**—*www.funcom.com*
  Plenty of free online games such as poker, spades, hearts, backgammon, blackjack, and much more are provided at this Web site

- **MSN Game Zone**—*http://zone.msn.com/default.asp*
  This site is loaded with games and is very popular among

thousands of online game players. If you're into golf, you can join the Virtual Golf Association from this Web site.

It's a Greek World

A search for fun can also take you to fraternities and sororities, also called *Greek organizations*, which are an important part of campus life for many students. These organizations offer a wide variety of social, educational, and community-service–oriented activities.

If you're thinking about joining a Greek organization or already belong to one, you can go to *www.greekchat.com* and spend some fun time chatting with your brothers and sisters.

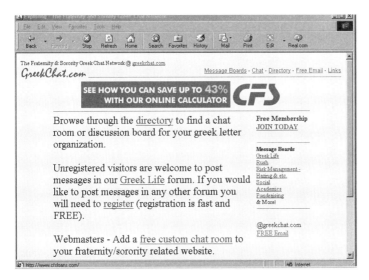

At GreekChat. com, students can participate in online discussions on numerous Greek-related topics.

GreekChat.com provides plenty of opportunities to pass time talking with your colleagues. You can enter chat rooms organized by individual Greek chapters or participate in message board discussion groups. The message boards are divided into six broad categories: Greek Life, Rush, Risk Management—Hazing & etc., Social, Academic, and Fundraising.

To join in a real-time chat with fellow Greeks, click the Directory link in the top menu section. The next page has Greek-letter-name links, from Alpha to Omega. When you click a Greek-letter-name, you'll be taken to a list of links to all the fraternities, sororities,

How to Find Greeks

To find information on just about every Greek organization in existence today, go to *www.greek-pages.com*, where you can link to information on more than 670 fraternities and sororities.

A Look at Hazing

Go to *www.stophaz-ing.org* for plenty of useful information about hazing, which are rite of passage rituals associated with pledging (also called *rush*) to gain acceptance into many Greek organizations.

and co-ed Greek organizations starting with that Greek letter. Clicking any of the organizations brings you to a page that allows you to enter a live chat room or threaded discussion board related to the organization you picked.

Another Web site devoted entirely to Greek life is located at *www.greekcentral.com*. There's a lot of interesting reading material at this Web site.

In addition to chat rooms similar to the kind found at GreekChat.com, GreekCentral offers links to contests and giveaways, an area called Greek Life, and an Online Store. The Contests and Giveaways section provides links to two Web sites you might want to check out: *www.freebiestuff.com* and *www.100percentfreestuff.com*. Both sites have information on the many free offers out there in cyberspace, such as free catalogs, free Internet services, free music online, and more (nothing earth shattering, but free nonetheless). At the Greek Life link, you'll find movie and music reviews as well as numerous news and feature articles and links related to college-oriented topics such as sports, the absurd and bizarre, and academics. The Online Store section will gladly sell you your next Greek T-shirt, hat, piece of jewelry, and more.

GreekCentral.com has news, entertainment, chat rooms, contests, and more—all about life as a Greek.

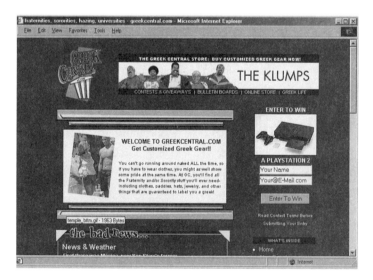

If you're in a shopping mood for Greek stuff, you can also go to *www.greek101.com*. This Web site sells T-shirts, sweatshirts, hats, jewelry, branded paddles, and much more—all with Greek lettering applied. Just click the Online Catalog link in the left sidebar to check out the numerous items for sale from this Web site.

Other links at Greek101.com include a Spring Break link, where visitors can enter contests to win a spring break vacation, and a Greek Culture link for information on Greek movies, celebrities, facts, party themes, and more.

Miscellaneous Kinds of Stuff

Yes, the title of this section is not proper English. But hey, why care? We're in the fun zone, right? There are no rules here. Therefore, let us continue to engage in mindless pursuits.

Actually, the title of this section gives us a license to talk about sites that fall under a variety of miscellaneous categories, all of which, however, are entertainment kinds of sites. (Oops, it happened again.)

Let's begin with our friend David Lettermen. If you missed his Top Ten List last night, you can always go to *www.cbs.com/lateshow/topten*, where an archive of the *Late Show with David Lettermen*'s Top Ten Lists is updated every day. You can also listen to Dave's monologue by clicking the Comedy link and then clicking Dave's Monologue. (You'll need the RealPlayer software installed on your computer.) Click the Live on Lettermen link for information on upcoming guests.

Incidentally, you can go to *www.cbs.com* to get updates on all your regularly watched programs. For instance, devotees of *The Young and the Restless (Y&R)* can go to the Show Finder pull-down menu located at the top of the CBS home page and click the show title. You'll then be able to access recaps of the shows you missed, partake in viewer polls, and get a behind-the-scenes look at the *Y&R* cast.

Other soap-related sites include Soap Opera Central at (*www.soapcentral.com*), which covers all soap operas; TV Guide Online's Soap section at *www.tvguide.com/soaps;* and ABC's official Soap section at *www.abc.go.com/soaps/soaps_home.html*.

That's the Ticket

Go to *www.ticket-master.com* for tickets and information about music, sports, arts, and family-oriented events happening across the country.

The next stop is MTV online at *www.mtv.com*. You can surf through this site's extensive index of past and current shows and interviews with artists. Again, you'll need RealPlayer software installed on your computer to see and hear the interviews and music provided. If you want to know what bands might be coming to your area, go down to the bottom of the MTV home page and choose a city from the Local pull-down menu. You'll be taken to a section covering concert dates and locations in your area, as well as listings of radio stations, clubs, and music stores.

Finally, for full-blown entertainment covering numerous areas of interest, go to Entertaindom at *www.entertaindom.com*. According to this Web site, Entertaindom "is your one-stop personalized site for everything entertainment. Movies, music, and television; previews and reviews; entertainment news; daily quizzes; TV listings; online shopping; daily horoscopes; fan pages; auctions; connecting with friends in chats and community message boards…it's all here! If it's entertainment, you'll find it in Entertaindom."

Wrapping It Up

Are you having fun yet? Many people look back on their college days for some of the fondest memories of their lives. Remember that when you're cramming for your next final exam. If you're not having the time of your life, maybe you should read over this chapter again. Better yet, read the synopsis of this chapter:

- You took a tour of two popular Web sites for college fun at *www.uzone.com* and *www.student.com*. You found a college culture alive and online at Uzone, and you found a great place to hang out at Student.com. You were also introduced to MP3s, the latest development in free online music.

- You discovered where electronic games are located on the Web, and you visited some truly awesome game-related Web sites that will keep you on top of your games of choice for the rest of your college career.

- You took a stroll down Greek Row by visiting a Web site where you can hook up with fellow Greeks in chat rooms and discussion boards. You also took an online Greek shopping trip to get that all-important Greek sweatshirt you've wanted to buy.

- You passed some time at *www.cbs.com*, where there are plenty of mindless diversions related to the world of television. You then listened to some music at the MTV Web site. To conclude your fun trip, you went to the mega site of entertainment at *www.entertaindom.com*.

That concludes Part III, "Getting Help from the Web Throughout Your College Career." Part IV, "Going to College Without Setting Foot on Campus," explores online distance learning and how it is revolutionizing the world of teaching and learning.

PART IV

Going to College Without Setting Foot on Campus

CHAPTER 13

Welcome to the Age of the Virtual Campus

There's a revolution going on today in the world of higher education, and it's called *online distance learning*.

What You'll Learn in This Chapter:
- ▶ What you need to know about online higher education distance learning.
- ▶ How higher education distance learning Web portals can help you find information about, and the availability of, online courses and degree programs.
- ▶ Where to go on the Web to learn about Advanced Placement (AP) and how to take online AP courses.

What's Online Distance Learning?

Online distance learning is where the Web and all its capabilities are used to offer classes through an Internet connection, allowing students to enroll in classes and earn credit in an anytime, anywhere environment without ever setting foot inside a bricks-and-mortar classroom.

The definition of distance learning, in a general sense, can include any or all of the following methods of delivery: television; correspondence courses that are print oriented; video tape, audio tape, or CD-ROM–based lectures; computer-based training that is not connected to a network; and online, Web-based instruction.

An online, Web-based distance learning class or program involves students linked to faculty and other higher educational resources through an Internet or intranet network and all its accompanying electronic capacity, including email, discussion boards, chat rooms, and streaming audio and video.

Over the past several years, there has been a dramatic increase in college and university courses available online to students worldwide. The World Wide Web has made it easy to deliver course material, administer tutorials and tests, and communicate with students through their computers. What was once only a few online courses being offered by a relatively small number of colleges and universities is now a rapidly burgeoning field being used by increasing numbers of cyberstudents, who prefer the flexibility of an off-campus learning environment through their anytime, anyplace Internet connections.

Section IV of this book, "Going to College Without Setting Foot on Campus," which obviously includes this chapter, takes a close look at the world of virtual education in which students are offered the opportunity to take bona fide credit and noncredit courses in an entirely new way.

This chapter starts with information about the higher education side of online learning. You'll see who typically takes online courses and look at viewpoints about which education method is better, traditional or online. You are then introduced to a model distance learning department at the Rochester Institute of Technology, and another at the University of Phoenix.

You then move on to the Web portals to higher education distance learning, which can help you learn more about the world of virtual higher education, as well as help you search for what college and university distance learning courses and programs are available in cyberspace.

Finally, online Advanced Placement (AP) is covered. You'll be introduced to some Web sites where high school students can go to learn all about AP, and where you can take online AP courses.

Going to Class Anytime, Anywhere

Typically, *adult learners*—students over the age of 24 who hold down full-time jobs and/or have family responsibilities—enroll in distance learning programs. The reasons for this are obvious. With distance education, one does not have to spend time traveling to a campus, nor does one have to sit inside a classroom at any specific time. For example, a distance learning student can view streaming audio and video class lectures and participate in threaded discussions with classmates and the instructor at a convenient time, undisturbed while in the comfort of home.

So-called *traditional students* (age 18 to 23) also take advantage of distance learning, although not nearly as much as their adult learner counterparts.

Traditional students might take a class now and then at a distance, usually to fit into their schedules a course that they otherwise could not fit in through a typical class offering. For the most part, though, traditional students need and *should* want the social setting of a typical bricks-and-mortar college environment. Obviously, the social side of higher education is a big part of the overall growth and learning experience associated with going to college. Nonetheless, under certain circumstances, an online class or classes can be beneficial.

What's a typical online class at a college or university like? Different teaching and learning methods can be applied in an online class. The basic model for a virtual classroom might entail the following:

- With the help of Web-based technology, an instructor, along with educational technology assistants and staff, create and develop the content and software for a course. The course is posted on a Web server that is usually hosted by the institution.

- Provided that they have the proper computer equipment and Internet connection, students can apply for admission, register for classes, and pay tuition for the course or courses they want to take online. After they are accepted, students are provided a username and password that allows them access to online course material. (Because the course is being offered over an Internet connection, most types of computers and operating systems will work.)

- The entire course—along with support materials such as a comprehensive orientation explaining everything you need to know to successfully complete the course—is presented through a home page that the registered student can access at any time. Lectures, assignments, quizzes, tests, tutorials, and general instructions (such as a course outline, what books you might need to purchase, technical support links, help sections, access to the school's library system, and more) can all be accessed through the course home page.

- Courses are taught using a variety of methods. In most approaches, students interact online with their instructors and fellow students through threaded discussions (asynchronous); real-time, prescheduled online chats (synchronous);

The State of Distance Learning Today

To access a report by the Council for Higher Education Accreditation (CHEA), titled *Distance Learning in Higher Education: An Ongoing Study on Distance Learning in Higher Education Prepared for CHEA by the Institute for Higher Education Policy*, go to *www.chea.org/Com mentary/distance-learning-2.html.*

email; or teleconferences. Videotaped and audiotaped lectures, CD-ROM–based learning materials, and course-specific software might also be provided. In most cases, you can also telephone your instructor or a course aide during specified office hours.

• The instructor decides what kind of written assignments, tests, or exams might be required. Most assignments and exams are submitted directly through email, fax, or snail mail. Some online courses require the student to identify a proctor, who can monitor the student as he or she takes an online exam.

What Is Asynchronous and Synchronous Learning and Teaching?

Asynchronous learning/teaching means that learning and teaching do not occur simultaneously or in conjunction with each other. A good example of asynchronous learning/teaching is a videotaped lecture that a student brings home and views at her convenience.

Synchronous learning/teaching is where the learning and teaching experiences occur in real time simultaneously, such as in an online chat room where there are text-based, real-time communications between students and teachers.

Which Method of Education Is Better?

Is distance education just as effective as traditional education? One study on this topic has been put into a book titled *The No Significant Difference Phenomenon*, by Thomas L. Russell, who is director emeritus of instructional telecommunications at North Carolina State University. Russell researched numerous studies on the viability of distance learning in comparison to traditional classes. He found that, on average, there really is no difference between the two approaches to education. In other words, technology-based instruction can deliver education just as well as traditional instruction. For more information, go to the *Chronicle of Education* article on this topic, located at *http://chronicle.com/free/2000/02/2000021001u.htm*. Excerpts from the Russell's book can be found at *http://cuda.teleeducation.nb.ca/nosignificantdifference*.

For another take on the distance learning versus traditional instruction issue, go to *www.vpaa.uillinois.edu/tid/report*. Here you'll find a full report generated through "a year-long faculty seminar convened during the 1998-99 academic year at the University of Illinois. The seminar consisted of 16 members from all three University of Illinois campuses (Chicago, Springfield, and Urbana-Champaign) and was evenly split, for the sake of scholarly integrity, between 'skeptical' and 'converted' faculty." Some of the conclusions generated from this seminar include that "online teaching and learning can be done with high quality if new approaches are employed which compensate for the limitations of technology, and if professors make the effort to create and maintain the human touch of attentiveness to their students. Online courses might be appropriate for both traditional and non-traditional students; they can be used in undergraduate education, continuing education, and in advanced degree programs. The seminar participants thought, however, that it would be inappropriate to provide an entire undergraduate degree program online. Participants concluded that the ongoing physical and even emotional interaction between teacher and students, and among students themselves, was an integral part of a university education."

Searching for Distance Learning

Many college and university Web site home pages do not have clearly marked links to their distance learning Web pages. If the home page has a search function, type the words **distance learning** or **distance education** to find the appropriate Web pages.

RIT's Distance Learning Program

Most colleges and universities have distance learning departments that are featured on the school's Web site. Let's take a look at a model distance learning department at the Rochester Institute of Technology (RIT), which has been offering distance learning courses to students for more than 20 years.

To get to RIT's distance learning section on the Web, go to *www.rit.edu* and click the links Prospective Students and then Distance Learning. The direct URL is *http://distancelearning.rit.edu.*

The same RIT faculty who teach on-campus also teach at a distance. The distance learning courses, according to RIT, "have the same objectives, rigorous workload, tuition, and academic credit as on-campus courses."

Currently, RIT offers eight graduate degrees, three graduate certificates, three undergraduate degrees, and nine undergraduate certificates, all at a distance. Students can enroll in a single course, multiple courses, or in a complete degree or certificate program.

The Rochester Institute of Technology (RIT) has a distance learning department with a large section on the RIT Web site.

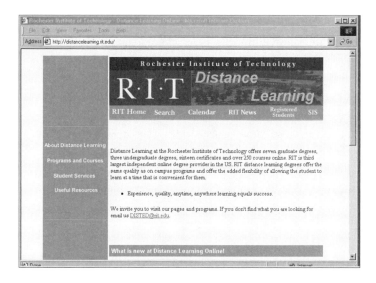

Are You a Distance Learner?

For more on how distance learning classes work and whether or not you are a good candidate for distance leaning, see Chapter 14, "Are You Cut Out for Distance Learning?"

To get an idea of how RIT provides distance learning courses to its students—which is similar to that of most colleges and universities—click the Programs and Courses link in the left sidebar. Go to the Select a Link pull-down menu and select Q&A. You'll be taken to a page that explains exactly how to register for and take a typical distance learning course at RIT.

The Accreditation of Distance Learning Programs

If you're surfing the Web for a higher education distance learning program, make sure that the institution offering the program is accredited. Most traditional bricks-and-mortar colleges and universities that also offer online courses or degree programs are, in fact, accredited. However, the more important question to ask is, Who accredits them?

What is *accreditation*? In short, accreditation is a process in which educational institutions are recognized as viable places to learn. Standards are established by various accrediting agencies that are composed of educational experts. If an institution meets the standards set down by the agency, it is acknowledged with accreditation status.

Any institution can claim to be accredited, even if its accreditation status happens to come from an accrediting agency the institution itself created. In fact, with the advent of virtual colleges and universities, a number of online con games have been played out with dire consequences. There have been incidents in which cyberstudents have paid tuition for online degree programs that had bogus accreditation. Regrettably, when exposed, these online programs disappeared into a cyberspace black hole.

With that in mind, you should know that enrolling in distance learning or traditional classes at a regionally accredited higher education institution is the most secure way to go. *Regional accreditation* means that an institution is accredited by an agency recognized by the Department of Education (DE) and the Council for Higher Education Accreditation (CHEA). For more detailed information about the process of accreditation and the standards recognized by these agencies, you can visit the DE Web site at *www.ed.gov.com* and CHEA's Web site at *www.chea.org*.

Credits earned at a distance from regionally accredited institutions can usually be transferred from one regionally accredited college or university to another. Regionally accredited institutions, which are in the majority in the United States, usually do not accept credits earned from an institution that is not regionally accredited. Additionally, many employers don't recognize diplomas earned from such non-accredited colleges or universities.

The following six regional accreditation agencies are DE and CHEA sanctioned:

- MSA (Middle States Association)

- NASC (Northwest Association of Schools and Colleges)

- NCA (North Central Association of Colleges and Schools)

- NEASC (New England Association of Schools and Colleges)

- SACS (Southern Association of Colleges and Schools)

- WASC (Western Association of Schools and Colleges)

More Information About Accreditation

Go to *http:// distancelearn.about. com/education/ distancelearn/ msubaccred.htm* for everything you could possibly want to know about higher education accreditation.

In March 1999, the North Central Association of Colleges and Schools accredited Jones International University, the first institution to be accredited by a regional accrediting body that offers its courses and services *entirely over the Internet*. The university, a subsidiary of Jones International, Ltd., headquartered in Englewood, Colorado, began offering courses in 1995.

The University of Phoenix

Another forerunner in online distance education is the University of Phoenix; the Web site's home page is at *http://online.uophx.edu.*

The University of Phoenix was formed in 1989 and currently enrolls degree-seeking adult students from all over the United States and the world.

Click the About Online link and then click the Online Students link. It's stated here that "the University of Phoenix online program currently serves approximately 9,500 students located in every corner of the world. The average age of online students is 38. Twenty percent of the students are executives or owners of their own businesses, 30 percent are middle managers in business and industry, and 44 percent are technical or licensed professionals."

Click the Programs link, and you'll see a page listing links to information on nine online undergraduate degree programs; eight online graduate degree programs; and one online doctorate program (a Doctor of Management in Organizational Leadership).

Click the Admissions link, and you'll be taken to a page about admissions requirements. Unlike typical colleges and universities, the University of Phoenix requires its prospective students to be at least 23 years of age and employed. If he or she is not employed, the prospective student "should have access to an organizational environment appropriate for the application of theoretical concepts learned in the classroom to relevant workplace issues."

To review information about how online courses are conducted at the University of Phoenix, click the About Online link and then click the FAQ's link.

Distance Learning Web Portals

Not surprisingly, there are Web portals devoted exclusively to distance learning. One very good one can be found in the About.com Web site at *http://distancelearn.about.com/education/ distancelearn/mbody.htm*.

The About.com Web site has a section with plenty of information on distance learning. The section is hosted by About.com guide Kristin Hirst.

About.com guide Kristin Hirst has really done her homework, providing a wealth of information related to distance learning on numerous levels. You can start checking things out by scrolling down to the section labeled Essentials in the middle of the home page. You'll find a number of important links to information you should know about distance learning. For instance, the Find College Degree Programs link will take you to a section where you can link to the Web sites of distance learning degree programs categorized by Associate Degrees, Bachelor Degrees, College Degree Programs by Subject, Graduate Degrees, and Virtual Campuses.

Applying an Online Course to Your Degree

Many schools do not offer full online distance learning degree programs, but they do offer a number of courses online that can be applied to a degree program of study.

For example, if you're a college student seeking to earn a bachelor's degree, you can see whether the institution you're planning to attend is listed under the Bachelor Degrees link. If it is listed, just click the school name to be taken to the Web pages of its distance learning program. If your school is not listed, that doesn't mean that distance learning courses are not being offered there. Some schools are in the early phases of developing distance learning courses and degree programs and are not yet listed on the About.com Distance Learning pages. There's also the possibility that About.com simply hasn't yet added your school to its database.

Of course, you can always go directly to the home page of any college or university Web site and search the site for information about distance learning courses or complete degree programs that might be currently offered.

Another area you might want to check out at the About.com site is the Virtual Campuses link located inside the Find College Degree Programs home page. This link takes you to the Virtual Campus Collaborations page. Here you'll find links to higher education consortiums or groups that have joined forces to offer distance learning courses in various states or regions. For example, by clicking the Illinois Virtual Campus (IVC) link, you'll be taken to its Web site where you can connect to hundreds of online and other distance learning courses and programs offered by Illinois colleges and universities.

Does this mean that you can take online courses from a number of different campuses located throughout IVC's network and then apply those courses to a degree at the institution you're attending? It depends. According to IVC, "the requirements at each individual provider institution will determine how many courses you can take from other institutions and then transfer into a program of study. You should talk with an advisor before taking a course from someone other than your home institution. A student's home institution will determine the transferability of online courses from other colleges in meeting degree requirements at the home institution."

Other statewide virtual campus collaborations you can link to are located in California, Connecticut, Florida, Idaho, Kansas, Kentucky, Maryland, Michigan, North Carolina, North Dakota, Oregon, and Washington.

There are also some regional virtual campus collaborations you can link to:

- The National Degrees Consortium—This group is comprised of nine accredited member institutions offering courses in a variety of distance education formats. Member institutions are Washington State University, Kansas State University, Mississippi State University, University of New Orleans, University of Alabama, Colorado State University, University of Maryland University College, University of South Carolina, and Oklahoma State University.

- Southwest Consortium for the Advancement of Technology in Education—Also called SCATE, this is a consortium of high schools, technical colleges, community colleges, universities, and businesses in Texas and New Mexico dedicated to advancing distance learning. Eighteen higher education institutions belong to SCATE.

- Southern Regional Electronic Campus—According to its Web site, "the Electronic Campus enables students to take electronically delivered programs and courses offered by scores of colleges and universities at times that are convenient for students." The Electronic Campus members are located in the following 16 states: Alabama, Arkansas, Delaware, Florida, Georgia, Kentucky, Louisiana, Maryland, Mississippi, North Carolina, Oklahoma, South Carolina, Tennessee, Texas, Virginia, and West Virginia.

- Western Governors University—According to its Web site, Western Governors University (WBU) "makes education more accessible by pulling together the courses and programs of dozens of existing institutions, corporations, and other entities into a master catalog. The courses offered through WGU are distance education courses designed and developed

Check Out Transferability
Be aware that not all credits earned through distance learning courses offered at institutions belonging to a consortium or a like-minded group of virtual campuses are transferable between member institutions. Policies on transferring credits into one university from another vary from institution to institution.

to allow learning to take place when you and your professor or instructor are located miles, even thousands of miles, apart."

As mentioned earlier, the About.com Distance Learning section has a great deal of valuable information for the prospective online learner. You can also search for distance learning programs by subject at this site, and there's a Bookstore link that provides information on books related to distance learning that you can purchase online.

An Education Pathway

If you want to search for complete higher education distance learning degree programs by location, you can visit another distance learning portal at *www.edpath.com.*

Edpath.com provides links to complete higher education distance learning degree and certificate programs located in the United States.

Try It Yourself ▼

Edpath.com is a constantly growing Web site that provides links to complete undergraduate and graduate degree programs, as well as complete certificate programs, all offered in a distance learning format. Check it out:

1. Go to *www.edpath.com* and click one of the four links to distance learning degree or certificate programs located at the top of the home page.

2. Click one of nine regions located on the map of the United States.

3. Click a school name listed under your state of preference. You'll be taken to the school's distance learning program Web pages.   ▲

Edpath.com also provides a free email subscription newsletter called *Educational Pathways*, which covers a number of topics related to higher education distance learning, including student and teacher profiles.

A Distance Learning Channel

Another good Web site to check out is called Ed-X.com: The Distance Learning Channel, located at *www.ed-x.com.*

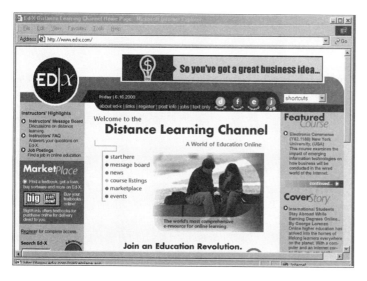

Ed-x.com provides access to thousands of distance learning courses available from colleges and universities located around the world.

According to information at the About Ed-X link, Ed-X.com "was envisioned to serve as a 'one-stop' Web community and portal site for institutions seeking to get their message out and for learners desiring to gather information regarding distance learning programs and products from around the world."

Visitors seeking higher education distance learning courses can start by scrolling down to the Pick A Subject heading, where they can access a large database of distance learning courses and degree programs, continuing education classes, test preparation classes, and more. The Leisure Learning link in this section gives you access to a host of unique distance learning courses in subjects such as entrepreneurship, gardening, personal finance, stress management, and more.

The Ed-X.com Web site also has an interesting Webzine called *The Online Learner*, where some of the feature articles profile successful distance learning students.

Distance Learning at 28 Major Universities

Another Web portal to distance learning that's worth checking out can be found at *www.r1edu.org*.

R1edu.org provides access to 28 major research universities in the United States that offer distance education programs.

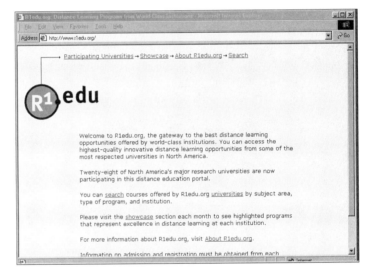

If you click the About R1edu.org link, you'll learn that "R1edu.org provides students easy access to high-quality distance learning programs from world-class institutions. It provides a one-stop portal to the most innovative distance learning programs at some of the most respected schools in North America."

R1edu.org directs students to participating institutions' distance learning course information. R1edu.org is not a degree-, certificate-, or diploma-granting institution.

Participating institutions in R1edu.org are members of the Association of American Universities and are classified as Research Universities I by the Carnegie Foundation.

What's a Research Universities I Rating?
Research Universities I institutions offer a full range of baccalaureate programs and give a high priority to research. There are currently 88 public and private universities that qualify as "R1" institutions.

Everything on the R1edu.org Web site is accessible through its home page, where there are only four category liks:

- Participating Universities—Links to 28 school Web sites

- Showcase—A monthly updated section that highlights new distance learning programs

- About R1edu.org—Descriptions of the site

- Search—A function that allows you to find a distance learning class that's right for you.

The Search function allows visitors to find distance learning programs by subject, by the manner in which courses are delivered (print, Web, CD-ROM, videotape, and so on), and by what kind of credit or degree might be awarded after completion of studies.

More Distance Learning Portals

Here are some other Web sites that will link you to distance learning courses and degree programs:

- **Petersons.com: The Lifelong Learning Channel—**
www.petersons.com/dlearn
Petersons has a Search Distance Learning Databases link that gives visitors access to information about accredited distance learning programs by name or degree category. There's also a link called Where Do You Stand, which takes you to information from Regents College, a higher education institution that grants college credit through various learning options, such as credit for work experience.

- **Yahoo!—**
http://dir.yahoo.com/Education/Distance_Learning/Colleges_and_Universities
The folks at Yahoo.com, in typical fashion, have put together an extensive list of links to distance learning courses and

Check It Out
It's difficult, if not impossible, for Web portals to keep pace with the growth of distance learning courses and programs. Always check with your institution of choice to get reliable, up-to-date information on what distance learning courses or programs are currently available.

degree programs offered by colleges and universities located throughout the world.

- **Hungry Minds: The Online Learning Marketplace—** *www.hungryminds.com*
  Hungry Minds is a gateway to online learning on many levels. For online higher education-level courses and degrees, click either the Online Courses or the Degree Programs link listed in the home page's left sidebar. (For more information about Hungry Minds, see Chapter 15, "A Smorgasbord of Online Learning.")

Advanced Placement Online

All About AP

For everything you need to know about AP, go to *www.collegeboard.org/ap/index.html*. This section in the College Board Web site tells you how to prepare for an AP course and exam and what subjects are available. It also has a great FAQ section.

If you're a high school student with college on your brain, you are well aware of Advanced Placement (AP). If you're not aware, here's a handy definition.

What Is Advanced Placement?

According to the College Board, which develops and administers the Advanced Placement program, "AP gives you the chance to try college-level work in high school, and to gain valuable skills and study habits for college. If you get a 'qualifying' grade on the AP exam, there are thousands of colleges worldwide that will give credit or advanced placement for your efforts.

"There are 32 courses in 18 subject areas, offered by approximately 14,000 high schools worldwide. In 1999, more than a million exams were taken by more than 700,000 students."

A relatively new development in the AP world is that AP courses are now available online in a distance learning format. Because AP courses are not yet being offered at every high school in the country, the online format can give some students an opportunity to enroll in an AP class that they otherwise would not have. Additionally, the online format allows especially busy and dedicated students to take AP courses at their own pace from their home computers if they can afford to pay the tuition required to take these courses (up to $400 per course).

Perhaps the premiere site for online AP classes is hosted by Apex Learning at *www.apex.netu.com*. Apex Learning was started by Paul Allen, who happens to be one of the co-founders of Microsoft.

In the About Us section, it's stated that Apex has fused "Internet technology with comprehensive curricula." Furthermore, Apex online courses feature "high-quality curricula and instructional materials in sync with College Board AP curriculum guidelines, instant online instructor support for improved communication and individualized study," and "self-paced learning made accessible anytime, anywhere."

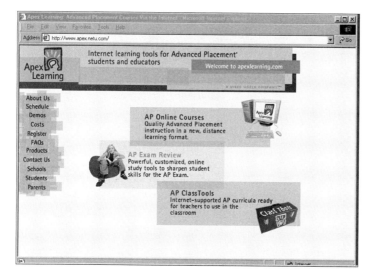

Apex Learning offers "Internet learning tools for Advanced Placement students and educators."

For more detailed information about when, where, and how Apex delivers its online AP courses, click the FAQ link. Here you'll find six links:

- Costs and Payments

- Course Operations and Schedules

- Academic Credit, Grading and Academic Policies

- Technical Requirements

- Curriculum and Materials

- Advanced Placement Programs

Before you even begin to examine the options available, you should know that the tuition cost for one course is $395, and that there are prerequisites involved. If you click the Schedule link from the home page, you'll find prerequisites for each course listed under the course title links. Read the information under the Recommended Preparation headings, which are divided into Academic, Writing, and Computer categories.

> **Feature Articles about Online College Prep**
>
> Pamela Mendels of the *New York Times* wrote an interesting and eye-opening feature article about online AP courses, titled "Advanced Placement Courses Offered Online," which can be found at *http://www.nytimes.com/library/tech/99/04/cyber/education/ 28education.html.*
>
> Another interesting article on online college prep classes for high schoolers was written by Mark Hornbeck at the *Detroit Daily News* Lansing Bureau. Titled "Students Accept Challenge of Online College Classes," Hornbeck's article is listed at *http://detnews.com/2000/ schools/0006/09/c01-70712.htm.*

Wrapping It Up

Virtual education is not for everyone. As mentioned earlier, traditional students just entering college do not see this as a viable option. You obviously can't experience the overall exuberance of college life from a computer workstation. You can, however, augment your academic life—and even your social life—by going online for some of your course work. Make sure that you know exactly what you're getting into before registering for an online distance learning course. If you're a responsible student, it can work out. If you're a bit undisciplined, it most likely won't work out. (See the following chapter, "Are You Cut Out For Distance Learning?")

If you're a responsible, time-crunched, busy adult learner, the virtual education world was made for you. Go for it!

In the meantime, here's a recap of what was covered in this chapter:

- You were introduced to the world of virtual education, also called *online distance learning.*

- You were provided with information about the viability of distance learning and how it compares to traditional learning.

- You were shown the Web pages of two model distance learning departments to give you an idea of how distance learning programs work.

- Information about accreditation and how it applies to distance learning was provided.

- You were introduced to the main Web portals for distance learning and how you can use these portal sites to guide you through the world of distance learning. You learned how to find distance learning courses and degree programs online, and you were given some advice about transferability of online courses.

- Advance Placement (AP) was covered, and you were introduced to a site that provides online AP courses.

CHAPTER 14

Are You Cut Out for Distance Learning?

This online distance learning stuff is obviously not for everyone. You're not a candidate for distance learning if you need face-to-face feedback from your instructors and on-campus interaction with fellow students in order to succeed. You're not a candidate for distance learning if you need the discipline of physically attending a time-specific, on-campus class.

For the most part, taking an online class entails working completely alone at your computer workstation. Yes, you do have some interaction through various electronic communication links, but it's obviously not the same as face-to-face interaction and feedback.

Here's the bottom line: Taking online classes takes a lot of discipline and the ability to work independently and meet deadlines at your own pace. For the adult, self-assured student, succeeding in the virtual world of education can be an important component of a lifetime of learning, which continues to play an important role in the quest for quality of life.

This chapter begins with a look at Web-based resources available to help determine if you're cut out for online distance education. You'll have the opportunity to take some online quizzes that can tell you more about the likelihood of your online education success. You'll also be introduced to some methods for evaluating distance learning programs.

You'll then see what a number of distance learning students have to say about their online education.

What You'll Learn in This Chapter:

▶ What's required to become a successful online distance learning student.

▶ What distance learning students have to say about their online education experiences.

▶ How eBooks might change the way college textbooks are purchased and read.

▶ How online distance learning is changing to benefit the disabled.

Finally, there's a section covering distance learning and its relationship to the disabled. You'll become acquainted with how the Web is changing to facilitate easier and better access for the handicapped.

Through all this, you'll learn about distance learning tuition costs; gain a valuable tip on where to go for the latest news about distance learning; and be introduced to eBooks, the wave of the future.

Resources for the Prospective Online Distance Learner

An excellent place to start investigating what it takes to be a successful online student, as well as what you should know before enrolling in any online course, is at the About.com site, in the Distance Learning section.

Here's how to get to About.com's Distance Learning section for help in determining whether you are cut out to be a distance learner:

Try It Yourself ▼

1. Point your browser to *http://distancelearn.about.com/ education/distancelearn/mbody.htm*.

2. Click the Student Resources link in the bottom half of the left sidebar.

3. Start your research by clicking the Are You a Candidate for DL? link.

You'll find some worthy advice here from Peterson's Career and Education editor Charlotte Thomas. Higher education distance learning administrators and directors, as well as students enrolled in distance learning programs, are quoted throughout this article. Here are some of the topics covered:

- What's your motivation for learning?
- How do you learn best—listening, reading, looking?
- Do you have what it takes personally?
- Are you organized enough to handle many things at once?
- Do you have the academic skills you'll need?
- Will the technical requirements unplug you?

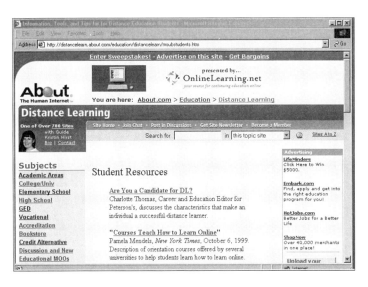

After reading Thomas's article, you might want to check out the links to online quizzes located at the end of the article. The How Ready Are You for Distance Learning? link takes you to a page where you can look at "ten indicators of readiness with successful independent study. By evaluating yourself on each indicator, you will gain a sense of your level of readiness for independent study. More importantly, you will discover specific areas of weakness and strength. Then by addressing weaknesses and building on strengths, you will be able to position yourself for success."

The other quiz link at the end of Thomas's article is titled Rank Yourself for Discipline and Motivation. This quiz was prepared by Michael P. Lambert, Executive Director at the Distance Education and Training Council in Washington, D.C. There are nine questions. Your score will tell you whether or not you are likely to succeed. As stated on this Web page, Lambert "makes no claims to scientific research in coming up with these questions but rather has drawn on his experience and deep involvement with distance education."

DL Tuition Costs Not Much Different

You can expect to pay the same tuition costs for distance learning courses as you would for a traditional class. According to the National Center for Education Statistics, in a statistical analysis report titled *Distance Education at Postsecondary Education Institutions: 1997–1998* (published in December 1999), "about three-quarters of institutions with

continues

continued

distance education always charge the same tuition for distance education and comparable on-campus courses." Approximately 90% of two-
year institutions charged the same tuition for distance learning courses
as on-campus courses, and about 72% of public four-year institutions
charged the same. The percentages are based on an estimated 1,680
institutions that offered distance education courses in 1997–98. To see
the report online in PDF format, go to *http://nces.ed.gov/pubs2000/
2000013.pdf.*

**Get the Latest
News**

To read timely arti-
cles about higher
education distance
learning, go to *The
Chronicle of Higher
Education's* Distance
Learning section at
*www.chronicle.com/
distance.*

There's a whole lot more valuable information within the Student
Resources section of the About.com Distance Learning Web site.
Back at the home page, you'll find links to a *New York Times* article about orientation courses offered by several universities, such
as Pennsylvania State University and Florida State University, that
help students wade through the world of online learning.

Also in the About.com Student Resources section is a link titled
Red Flags, which provides "warning signs to watch for when
evaluating distance learning programs." What Makes a Successful
Online Student? is another link worth checking out. This link
takes you to a section in the Illinois Online Network (ION) Web
site. ION "is a collaboration of thirty-one community colleges
and the University of Illinois working together to advance utiliza-
tion of Internet-based instruction and service throughout the state
of Illinois." The direct URL is *http://illinois.online.uillinois.edu/
model/StudentProfile.htm.*

*The Illinois Online
Network Web site
has a section
titled What Makes
a Successful
Online Student?*

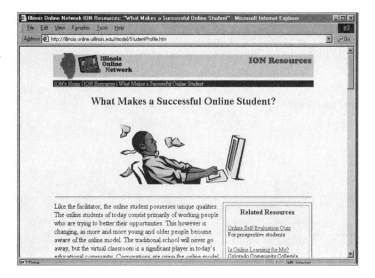

"The traditional school will never go away, but the virtual class-room is a significant player in today's educational community," according to the makers of the ION site. They then list 10 qualities the online student should possess. For example, online students need to be "open minded about sharing life, work, and educational experiences as part of the learning process." Additionally, online students must "be able to communicate through writing," and "be willing to speak up if problems arise."

Why are such qualities important to the online educational environment? Because visual and auditory biases often associated with a traditional bricks-and-mortar class are eliminated in the online environment, which means that there's usually more openness and discussions among fellow classmates. In threaded discussions, for instance, students have ample time to respond to questions and topics of interest, and thus they usually contribute more thoughtful and relevant information to the benefit of the entire class.

Some of the other qualities online students should possess include being "willing and able to commit 4 to 15 hours per week per course," and to "accept critical thinking and decision making as part of the learning process."

The ION site also has a list of Related Resources in the right sidebar. Here you'll find more self-evaluation quizzes, a Tips for Success link, and a relevant article titled "What Every Student Should Know About Online Learning," by Coordinator of Distance Education Technology at Kennesaw State University John E. Reid, Jr., Ph.D.

What Distance Learning Students Have to Say

We have interviewed at least 18 students by telephone and email, who were or are enrolled in various higher education distance learning programs. The general consensus from this small number of interviewees is that distance learning, although not for everyone, indeed has beneficial results.

This is obviously not enough student interviews for a viable statistical conclusion, but the student comments are nonetheless interesting reading.

For example, Ed Shanshala, a recent graduate of the Rochester Institute of Technology's completely online master's degree

Are You an Online Distance Learning Candidate?
Park University President Dr. Donald Breckon wrote an interesting article titled "Are You Right for an Internet Degree? What Internet Degree Completion Program Is Right For You?" Read it at *www. townsend-outlook. com/editorials/ park_u.html.*

Interview with Seven Distance Learning Students
See a *Chronicle of Higher Education* article by Jeffrey R. Young titled "Dispatches from Distance Education, Where Class Is Always in Session: Seven Students Discuss How They Learn—and Live— Through a Regimen of Online Courses," located at *www.chronicle.com/ free/v46/i26/ 26a04101.htm.*

program in Health Systems Administration, said of his online classmates: "Even though, in most cases, we have never met, we have developed relationships that will last a lifetime. Through distance learning, I have had access to a broad range of colleagues that would otherwise not be possible."

Kimberly Simon, a distance learning student studying for a master's degree in communications from Jones International University, said, "Distance education works for me, and I find this method offers more benefits to me than I experienced in the past at a traditional institution. I get almost immediate feedback and responses to any questions I have. The information from the courses is relevant to real life and my daily working situations. Group tasks in each course foster student interaction. I don't feel alone, and I enjoy the challenges."

Barb Hemschoot, who is enrolled in an online MBA program with the University of Phoenix, said, "I definitely feel that the education I am receiving has had a positive effect on my job performance. So far, the classes I have taken have been very relevant to my job and have allowed me to apply what I've learned."

Dave Dallen, who is pursuing an online bachelor's degree in Computer and Information Science from the University of Maryland University College, said he finds that "the anonymity of posting and discussing in a virtual classroom tends to bring out more discussion than in real classrooms. This anonymity reduces the natural timidity of some students and adds more to an educational discourse or setting. A similar student sitting in a real classroom might not say the same thing for fear of being wrong."

Another University of Phoenix MBA student, Adam Jagger, said, "In every class I've taken, I've learned one or two paradigms that I'll be able to take with me in the future. The instructors are very informed and knowledgeable. They all seem to have impressive backgrounds. I think that's important because they are aware of all the cutting-edge information breakthroughs that are happening today."

Another RIT student enrolled in the school's online master's degree program in Environmental Health and Safety Management, Brian Hansen, said, "I was truly unaware of just what the Internet could do before enrolling into RIT. The program forces students to tap into this resource, making us more proficient with its current usefulness as a tool. This resource helps us

---

gain access to the intellectual library of information through a click of a button."

No More Schoolbooks

Backpacks to lug your books around might become a thing of the past for the next generation of college students—or sooner. The ability to store college textbooks in digital format already exists. However, only a small number of college textbooks are currently available in digital format. And unless you have a laptop computer, you can't take those electronic textbooks with you to that little nook you found on campus for studying and reading. The solution is a thing called *eBooks*. With eBooks, you can store all your textbooks on a relatively inexpensive device that has a monitor the approximate size of one textbook. These devices are called *readers*.

A company called Softbook is one of the forerunners with this new technology. According to the Softbook Web site at *www.softbook.com*, the company manufactures a hand-held product called a SoftBook Reader®, which "is specifically designed to provide a comfortable, legible, and portable way to purchase and read electronic newspapers, magazines, books, and documents." An ergonomically designed, leather-bound device weighing only 2.9 pounds, the Softbook Reader allows the user to connect to the Internet from any phone line. The user then goes to the SoftBookstore® to purchase and download digitized books into the reader.

Currently, the reader has a rechargeable lithium-ion battery pack that provides "two to five hours of reading (depending on display settings) with a fast, one-hour recharge. The removable battery pack enables continuous reading beyond the limits of one battery." The reader has a grayscale, backlit, touch-sensitive LCD display that is 6 inches wide by 8 inches tall. The reader has a storage capacity of 5,000 pages (8MB)and "is capable of expanding to 50,000 pages with optional Flash Memory cards." It has a built-in 33.6Kbps modem that is capable of downloading approximately 100 pages per minute.

The Softbook Reader Model 200 was selling for a "one-time payment of $599.95, or for $299.95 with an agreement to purchase newspapers, magazines, or books in the amount of $19.95 per month for 24 months from the SoftBookstore."

Although the firm wasn't selling college textbooks at the time of this writing, Softbook is a good example of what the future might be like for college students seeking to lighten their backpacks.

Distance Learning and the Disabled

In addition to working adults with busy professional and personal responsibilities, other beneficiaries of distance education are those people who might have a difficult time attending classes because of physical disabilities.

See the Access Board Publication

The full text, in HTML or PDF format, of the Access Board's Notice of Proposed Rulemaking titled *Standards for Electronic and Information Technology*, published in the *Federal Register* on March 31, 2000, is located at *www.access-board.gov/RULES/ 508nprm.htm*.

Check Out Bobby

The Center for Applied Statistics, an educational not-for-profit organization, has created a Web-based tool called Bobby, that analyzes Web pages for their accessibility to people with disabilities. For more information, and a free downloadable version of Bobby, go to *www.cast.org/bobby*.

The anytime, anywhere aspect of distance learning has its obvious benefits for the disabled. As distance learning grows, more Web-based programs will be better designed for the blind, deaf, hard of hearing, and mobility impaired.

For example, in August 1998, President Clinton signed into law the Workforce Investment Act, which includes Section 508 of the Rehabilitation Act Amendments. Section 508 requires the Architectural and Transportation Barriers Compliance Board—the U.S. government agency known as the Access Board—to set standards for federal agencies to ensure that federal employees with disabilities have "comparable" access to and use of information and data as do non-disabled federal employees.

What does this have to do with virtual education? It's possible that any federal government access standards to be signed into law in the near future will eventually be required by all higher education institutions.

Section 508 also "requires that individuals with disabilities, who are members of the public seeking information or services from a federal agency, have access to and use of information and data that is comparable to that provided to the public who are not individuals with disabilities."

Moreover, Section 508 "provides that, beginning August 7, 2000, any individual with a disability may file a complaint alleging that a federal agency fails to comply with section 508 in providing accessible electronic and information technology."

The Access Board was required to publish standards by February 7, 2000. As of June 2000, the Board had not met that statutory deadline. This does not mean, however, that standards will not be implemented.

A related article, titled "New U.S. Law Required Web Sites to Become Handicapped Accessible," is posted at the Freedom Forum Online Web site at *www.freedomforum.org/ technology/1999/4/30handicapaccess.asp*. According to the article, provisions of the Access Board's standards "are expected to include a ban on any audio without simultaneous text and restrictions on animated graphics." Plus, "in addition to conventional HTML and PDF versions available online, all online information must also be available via audio text and TTY (teletypewriter also known as TDD for Telecommunication Device for the Deaf), as well as cassette tape, Braille, large print, or computer disk."

Academy Online Talks About Access Issues

A Web site covering the issues of accessibility for the disabled is located at *www.academyonline.com/access_matters/access_ 0799.htm*. In addition to providing links to the Center for Applied Statistics and the Freedom Forum Online Web sites just mentioned, the Academy Online site provides information about the issue of accessibility from the Americans with Disabilities Act of 1990 (ADA); the United States Department of Education, Office of Civil Rights (OCR); and the Workforce Investment Act of 1998.

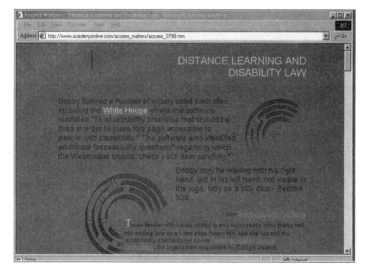

Academy Online, published by the International Association for Management Education, has a Web section titled Distance Learning and Disability Law that covers online learning accessibility issues related to the disabled.

In a section titled Planning Ahead, Senior Editor Jeff Cobb writes that "for schools and corporations developing or already offering Web-based programs, the message is clear: Careful planning will help you avoid many pitfalls in the future. Familiarize yourself now with the law and with the rules of accessible Web design."

In another section titled Related Links, you'll find a long list of links to articles, as well as Web sites that feature authoring and publishing tools related to this topic.

A Level Playing Field for the Deaf

In the meantime, some schools are developing distance learning programs with the disabled in mind. For example, through the combined efforts of RIT's National Technical Institute for the Deaf (NTID) and its distance learning program, deaf and hard-of-hearing students are learning computer programming in a totally new way. (NTID is the world's first and largest technological college for deaf students.)

For example, NTID instructor James Mallory teaches cutting-edge distance learning courses in C++ and Visual Basic with the deaf and hard-of-hearing in mind.

One of the challenges of teaching a technical discipline such as computer programming to the deaf and hard-of-hearing is that interpreters are usually not trained in translating the technical jargon of such courses. Because of this, deaf students attending traditional computer programming classes often miss out on the full benefits of an instructor's lecture. In Mallory's distance learning classes, however, such communication problems for the deaf and hard-of-hearing are eliminated.

Mallory uses close-captioned voice, sign language, graphics, cartoon animations, and executable simulation files in his videotaped instructions. For example, a typical videotaped class starts with Mallory explaining, in close-captioned voice and sign language, how a computer program works. Then the tape cuts away to an animated cartoon character drawn in his likeness, talking and emphasizing important points. Next, the computer program is displayed, animated with certain points highlighted one line at a time, showing how the program executes.

Mallory is also experimenting with the use of digital cameras that can be mounted onto the computers of deaf and hard-of-hearing students. The cameras will allow for video transmission over the Web. Mallory has also co-authored a C++ textbook at an easier-to-read level that he has brought into his distance learning classes.

"Distance learning levels the playing field for students," says Mallory. "This means that deaf and hard-of-hearing students can now participate as readily as their hearing peers can. We are now able to expand our educational audience to include geographically remote populations who may not normally be inclined to take courses at RIT, such as geographically remote deaf and hard-of-hearing adults with full-time jobs and families, or single mothers."

"As a deaf adult, distance learning courses have opened additional opportunities and avenues that have long been available to my hearing peers," wrote one deaf student, who recently took Mallory's C++ class. "Besides allowing me to focus on learning as opposed to, say, wondering how much of the essence of a teacher's message the interpreter or note-taker has captured, distance learning provides a forum where deaf adults like me can share technical and non-technical expertise unhindered by language, negative attitudes, geography, or distance. All told, distance learning gives me a fighting chance to stay current, competent, and competitive in a fast-changing technological environment."

W3C Web Content Accessibility Guidelines for Everyone

The World Wide Web Consortium (W3C), a highly regarded and internationally renowned member-supported consortium including both software vendors and a variety of consumers, has created Web Content Accessibility Guidelines. These guidelines are posted on the Web at *www.w3.org/TR/1999/WAI-WEBCONTENT-19990505.*

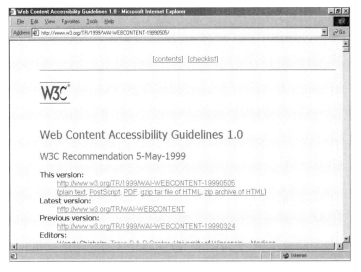

The World Wide Web Consortium's Web Content Accessibility Guidelines section covers how to make Web sites that the disabled can more easily access and understand.

The W3C primarily creates recommendations for the Web, which are effectively standards documents. According to the W3C Web site, these guidelines "explain how to make Web content accessible to people with disabilities. The guidelines are intended for Web content developers (page authors and site designers) and for developers of authoring tools. The primary goal of these guidelines is to promote accessibility. However, following them will also make Web content more available to all users, whatever user agent they are using (for example, desktop browser, voice browser, mobile phone, automobile-based personal computer, etc.) or constraints they might be operating under (for example, noisy surroundings, under- or over-illuminated rooms, in a hands-free environment, etc.). Following these guidelines will also help people find information on the Web more quickly. These guidelines do not discourage content developers from using images, video, etc., but rather explain how to make multimedia content more accessible to a wide audience."

Wrapping It Up

So, do you want to go online for your education? If you're fresh out of high school or soon to be fresh out of high school, the answer might well be "No way." If you're a working stiff with a time-bandit mentality and a penchant for technology-based learning, your virtual education is only a few mouse clicks away.

Here's what was covered in this chapter:

- What the prospective online distance learner needs to understand before enrolling in a virtual higher education program of study.

- How visual and auditory biases customarily associated with traditional classes are generally nonexistent in the online distance learning environment.

- How students voicing their personal views about online distance learning might influence your own decision.

- How student backpacks might end up being lighter through the development of eBook readers that can hold multiple textbooks in digitized format on a small, lightweight device.

- The development of a new world of Web accessibility geared for the disabled that will enable them to take advantage of online distance learning and will help facilitate an even playing field for all enrolled in an online class.

- What the World Wide Web Consortium has to say about Web content accessibility for everyone.

CHAPTER 15

A Smorgasbord of Online Learning

When it comes to Web-based education (also called *e-learning, e-education, virtual education, online distance learning*, and probably some other terms we haven't discovered yet), the Web offers a mixed bag of classes in many forms and colors. Online learning is available for elementary and secondary school (K through 12), post secondary (freshmen college students through Ph.D students), professional development, continuing education, and more. You can take a class online in vegetarian cooking, and you can take a class online in calculus. There's a vast range of tuition costs for online classes, starting at zero on up to hundreds and even thousands of dollars.

In this chapter, you'll become acquainted with some of the hottest Web sites devoted to the expansive and multifaceted world of online continuing education and everyday lifelong learning.

You should be aware that many of the non-college– or non-university–hosted online classes are frequently non-credit courses and are not provided by regionally accredited institutions. In most cases, such course work cannot be transferred to a degree program at a regionally accredited college or university. (For more information about accreditation, see Chapter 13, "Welcome to the Age of the Virtual Campus.") Nonetheless, depending on the online course you may be interested in taking, the benefits can be quite substantial. For instance, completing an online Microsoft certification program can boost your earning and job promotion potential in a computer technology-related field, even though such a program may not be offered by an accredited institution. Another example might be an online course in how to buy and sell stocks. Yes, such a course could be highly beneficial on a

What You'll Learn in This Chapter:

▶ Where to access online distance learning classes for continuing education.

▶ What kinds of options are available online for continuing your lifelong learning process.

e-Education Is Growing

An article from TheStreet.com, titled "Online Learning Excels," by Roland Jones, posted at *www.abcnews.gocom/sections/business/TheStreet/eeducation_000601.html*, quotes Eduventures.com, an education industry research firm as saying that "in the first quarter of 2000, e-education investment has already risen to 64 percent of total investment in education, or about $1 billion."

personal level, but its transferability toward a regionally accredited college degree is most likely nonexistent.

Your first stop in the world of online continuing education and lifelong learning is Hungry Minds, a forever changing and expansive Web site that provides access to numerous free and fee-based online courses. This site will give you a feel for what these large portals to online learning are all about.

Then you'll take a tour of SmartPlanet.com, another site with an extremely large database of online courses, both free and fee-based.

Then it's off to Learn.com and Learn2.com, two more dynamite Web sites where you can access plenty of online classes, from a simple online guide to making a necktie knot to sophisticated Microsoft certification classes.

Finally, you're provided with a list of nine more Web portals to online education. Although each of these sites is somewhat similar to the four previously described sites, they offer even more free courses you can take from the comfort of your home.

Hungry for Knowledge?

Our first stop is a Web site with a catchy name and lots of online classes: Hungry Minds at *www.hungryminds.com*.

Hungry Minds calls itself "the online learning marketplace."

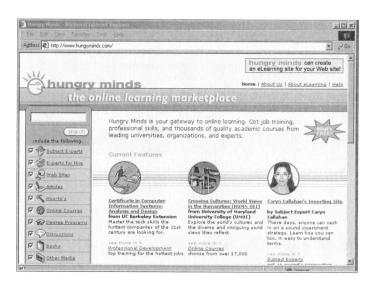

At the top of this Web site's home page, it's stated that "Hungry Minds is your gateway to online learning. Get job training, professional skills, and thousands of quality academic courses from leading universities, organizations, and experts."

So, where do you start? How about going for the free stuff?

Click the What's Free link located next to the site description, and you'll be taken to a page offering five options: Subject Experts, How-to's, Discussions, Web Sites, and Free Courses. The What's Free section alone can keep can keep you busy for quite some time. Beginning with the Free Courses link, you'll find thousands upon thousands of free online courses "on everything from first-aid to HTML."

The list of Free Courses is divided into 13 category links, including Arts & Humanities, Computers & Internet, Health, Business & Finance, Hobbies, and more. When you click any of these category links, you are taken to a page that has subcategory links listed by various subject headings. The Hobbies link, for instance, is divided into 11 subject links, such as Food and Drink, Automotive, Gambling, Pets, Photography, Animal Husbandry, and more.

For example at the time of this writing, there was one free course being offered in Animal Husbandry: Novice Beekeeping. In the Gambling subcategory, there were five free courses available, all of which were related to some form of poker and were being offered by several of Hungry Minds' partner Web sites. In the Photography category were three free courses: Camera Functions, Photography—Expert Tips, and Photography 101.

As another example of freebies, Hungry Minds offers computer programmers free online courses in HTML, Java, JavaScript, Perl, C and C++, and Web design—all available by simply clicking the Programming link in the Computer & Internet section.

Going back to the section accessed from the home page's What's Free link, visitors can also take advantage of what Hungry Minds' cadre of professional Subject Experts have to say about numerous topics of interest. Click the See All Subject Experts link, and you'll be taken to a page with 14 category links, including Personal Finance, Science & Math, Sports & Outdoors,

The Evolution of a Web Site

Hungry Minds is constantly adding new courses, links, and services to its Web site as it evolves into a massive repository of information concerning online education. By the time you read this, the Hungry Minds site may look different than what's been described here.

Price Shopping for Online Classes

You can comparison shop for fee-based online courses by going to L Guide at *www.lguide.com*. Click the L Guide Marketplace link to get online class provider and pricing information.

Government & Law, Family & Relationships, and more. Subject Experts are recruited by Hungry Minds "to teach you about their areas of expertise. These experts write original articles and recommend Web sites, books, online courses, and other resources for you to explore." For example, clicking the Professional Development link takes you to a page where you have your choice of three experts, who each have their own Web pages. The Susan Miller Career Development section, for instance, had information on the essentials of resume preparation, a link titled New Ways to Work, and much more. Miller's credentials include an M.A. in counseling psychology from UC Berkley as well as being a National Certified Career Counselor and Certified Vocational Evaluator.

For more free stuff, go back to the What's Free link home page and click the See All How-to's link. This section, according to the introduction, will allow you to "gain instant access to the world's largest variety of quick, informative courses on thousands of useful skills, from washing your dog to administering CPR. It's the ultimate online resource for real-world living."

In addition to the free stuff, you can go back to Hungry Minds' primary home page to find a whole lot more to keep you busy learning online. Click the Online Courses link in the left sidebar to go to a section titled Online and Distance Learning Courses, where "you don't have to go to a classroom to get an education." Hungry Minds adds that you can take your pick from a "directory of over 17,000 distance-learning courses—delivered via the Web, the mail, TV, video, or the phone..." The courses are listed under 18 categories and numerous subcategories. Click a course that interests you, and you'll be taken to the Web site of the provider of that course, which in most cases is a bona fide college or university.

If you're interested in earning a degree online, click the Degree Programs link in the left sidebar to go to the Degree and Certificate Programs page. There are nine major categories to choose from, including Arts & Humanities, Communications, Education, and more. When you click a category, you'll be given the option to search for associate's, bachelor's, or master's degree programs, as well as any online doctorate programs that may be available throughout the world.

You really have to test drive Hungry Minds' large site to take full advantage of its many other features, such as discussion boards and links to articles and Web sites.

A Smarter Planet

Another great Web site for online learning is SmartPlanet at *www.smartplanet.com*. SmartPlanet's tag line is "Learn Virtually Anything®"; and you navigate this site, you come to the realization that they really mean it.

The SmartPlanet Web site is "a unique personal and professional learning community where people pursue goals and lifelong interests through online courses and human interaction."

There are plenty of online courses, both free and fee-based, at SmartPlanet. To access them, you have to register by clicking the Go button under the Join Now heading. From here, you have two options to register: Free Membership or Standard Membership. With Free Membership, you're entitled to take as many free courses as you desire—and there are lots of them available at the SmartPlanet Web site. Free Membership also gives you access to all the fee-based courses you can take on an individual pay-as-you-enroll basis. Standard Membership, which costs $15.95 per month, is an option that allows you to take as many "standard" courses as you desire without paying the individual course fees.

Get Some CEUs

You can earn Continuing Education Units (CEUs) when taking some of the online classes offered by SmartPlanet. CEUs offer formal documentation, recognized by major institutions in the United States, that you've completed a class. For more information, go to *www.smartplanet. com/module.asp? module=help_ceus*.

Be Compliant

Make sure that your computer is audio and video compliant and has all the necessary browser plug-ins and software recommended by the course providers before enrolling in any online course.

There are plenty of standard courses, too. For example, as a Standard Member, you can take a 4-week online course titled *Internet Business Strategy* and not have to pay the $19.95 tuition fee that a Free Member would be required to pay.

After you have registered with SmartPlanet, you can start taking both free and fee-based courses. Like the Hungry Minds site, the SmartPlanet Web site is loaded with links to numerous online courses. A good place to start learning about being courses offered can be found by clicking the Need Help? link and then clicking Courses. Scroll down to the FAQ section, where you'll see course-related links to questions.

There are basically two types of online courses you can take: instructor-led courses or self-study courses. Here's how each is described on the SmartPlanet Web site:

> SmartPlanet offers two types of instructor-led courses: classes and workshops. Both are led by a subject-matter expert and conducted in a message board 'classroom.' Students read the messages, do the assignments or lessons, and post questions to the instructor in the message board.
>
> SmartPlanet's self-study courses have been created by professionals as well as by members just like you. We also have seminars, which combine audio and text presentations, with the majority of content supplied via audio. Text is displayed as the audio is played. Each seminar is approximately 10 to 15 minutes in length. SmartPlanet features two different types of seminars: an Executive Series, providing management-oriented overviews; and a Technical Series, providing skill-building information.

SmartPlanet's classes are listed under eight broad categories:

- Arts & Society

- Body & Mind

- Career & Business

- Computing & Internet

- Finance & Investing

- Hobbies & Recreation

- Home & Family

- Science & Technology

The Easy Learner

For more online learning, go to *www.learn.com*, which bills itself as "the ultimate destination for learning for individuals as well as corporations." At this Web site, all the courses are free.

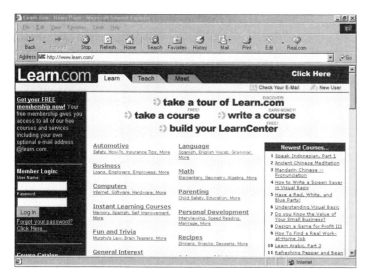

At Learn.com, you can take free online courses, create an online course for others to take, and share ideas and chat with fellow Learn. com members.

A good way to become acquainted with everything Learn.com has to offer is to click the Take a Tour of Learn.com link located at the top of the home page. Try it:

▼ **Try It Yourself**

1. Point your browser to *www.learn.com* and click the Take a Tour of Learn.com link.

2. A small screen pops up in the upper-left side of your monitor. Make the screen larger by clicking the maximize screen icon in the upper-right corner of the screen. Read the introduction and then click the Next link at the bottom of the screen.

3. Continue the tour by reading the contents of each new screen and then clicking the Next link until you get to a screen that provides a link to register as a member of the Learn.com community.

▲

Like the SmartPlanet Web site, the only way to take advantage of everything Learn.com has to offer is by registering as a member. The registration process is quick and easy, and it includes a section that allows you the option of receiving eight different email newsletters on various topics of interest. After you've become a registered member, you can create your very own "LearnCenter." A LearnCenter is a Web-based resource for "storing, presenting, and managing all your training data," according to the Learn.com Web site. "Your LearnCenter can contain courses you write, courses already existing on Learn.com, or virtually any other information you choose."

Indeed, the LearnCenter Web-based system for taking and making online courses is quite impressive and extremely user friendly. What's even better is that creating your very own LearnCenter costs absolutely nothing. In fact, you might even make some money here.

"If you have a clean (G-rated), easy-to-learn topic you'd like to share with others, try your hand at creating a Learn.com course, says the Learn.com staff. "If your course is selected for publication, you can earn up to 30% of advertising revenue generated by your course."

While you're waiting to get rich, you have a wide choice of free and easy-to-learn online classes to choose from at Learn.com. Just click any of the 15 categories listed on the home page or on any of the Newest Courses links in the right sidebar. All the courses at Learn.com are absolutely free, so you really can't lose here. Most of the classes have a five-star user rating, as well as reviews from people who have taken the class.

Staying on a Learning Curve

Another place to go for free online learning, and more, is at *www.learn2.com.*

According to the About Us section of the Learn2.com Web site, if "you need to learn the latest programming language to improve your performance at work or you need some advice on preparing a family budget, Learn2.com is there with well-researched, timely information that is delivered in a way that is convenient, engaging, and fun."

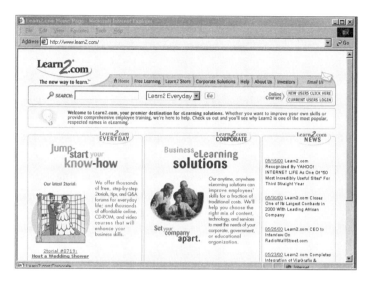

Learn2.com offers "thousands of free step-by-step 2torials, tips, and Q and A forums for everyday life," as well as eLearning solutions for businesses.

Learn2.com claims that its Web site attracts more than 700,000 visitors each month "for information on everything from how to tie a tie to how to write a resume."

Learn2.com has more than 1,200 online courses that can also be purchased on CD-ROM or video. However, if you want to check out some of the many free online courses available, simply click the Free Learning link in the top menu bar, or click the Jump Start Your Know-How link, located at the site's home page. Then go to the Channels section located in the left sidebar.

There's lots to look at here. All the freebies can be accessed through the 12 category links under the Channels heading. There's also a 2torial Top 10 link. Surprisingly, the Tie a Necktie free online tutorial held the top spot, with Shop for Car Insurance and Make a Kite ranking second and third, respectively. Clean Your Bathroom ranked fourth. (How little we know!)

Also listed under the Channels heading is a Survival Guides link with such free guides as the Aches and Pains Survival Guide, the Dollars and Sense Survival Guide, the On-Your-Own Survival Guide, and more.

If you want to check out the fee-based online courses offered by Learn2.com, many of which are oriented toward professional development, go to the Online Courses section on the right side of

From Bookseller to Online University

Stay tuned for even more free online learning, soon to be brought to you by Barnes & Noble. Information about this new Web site, called Barnes & Noble University, can be found at *www. barnesandnoble university.com.*

your screen. For starters, click the Click Here for a Demonstration link. You'll then be asked to download a Learn2.com browser plug-in called StreamMaker®. After downloading the plug-in, you'll be treated to a highly creative and professional multimedia sound, video, and animated tour of everything Learn2.com has to offer.

To view all the fee-based online courses available, also called tutorials, click the Click Here for a Complete Catalog Listing link in the Online Courses section. You'll be taken to the Online Courses, Learning on Demand, On Your Desktop page. The left sidebar has a list of subject categories, including Microsoft Certified, Networking, Databases, Finance, and more.

Some of the other primary features of the Learn2.com Web site are located under its Business eLearning Solutions link, which can be accessed from the home page. You can check out the Learn2University, featuring "hundreds of interactive, self-paced courses that your employees can access from home or work." There is also information about Learn2.com's custom training services and some of the other professional, Web-based-learning–related services offered by Learn2.com.

There's a Big World of Web-Based Learning Out There

This next section could become an entire book in the not-too-distant future. For now, though, here's an alphabetical list of some of the other cyberspace e-learning sites that are currently available to the lifelong learner—that being you, of course.

- **Edupoint**—*www.edupoint.com*
  Tagged as "the Marketplace for Continuing Education," Edupoint.com has a huge database of continuing education programs. To access those classes available at a distance, use the search function located in the Find Continuing Education from 3,000 Learning Providers box. Make sure that you check the Distance Learning check box when you do your search.

- **eHow**—*www.ehow.com*
  Want to learn how to do anything and everything? Go to—
  where else?—eHow. According to the folks at eHow, this
  Web-based service was created "to give people a fast and
  easy way to find out how to do a variety of real-world activities, provide ways to accomplish them, and join a community
  of like-minded people who share a passion for getting things
  done."

- **Element K**—*www.elementk.com*
  Element K claims to be "the most convenient, powerful,
  proven way for today's time-starved people to gain the skills
  they need to succeed." Its "Total Online Corporate
  University" offers courses in information technology, business management skills, and proprietary training. Element K
  currently has more than 450,000 registered users.

- **eMind**—*www.emind.com*
  "Knowledge, Vision, Success" is the tag line for this e-learning Web site that offers professionals online courses in
  accounting, securities, personal development, and information technology. Formerly Yipinet, eMind.com recently
  formed an alliance with OnlineLearning.net, a premier supplier of online courses for academic credit.

- **Free Ed**—*www.free-ed.net*
  According to this Web site, "Free-Ed is committed to providing an online, virtual university where users from around the
  world can study, take courses, and participate in community
  activities at no cost." Check out the links in the Course
  Catalogs box. There are numerous classes and links to information available at this Web site, and you don't have to sign
  up and become a registered member to take any of the
  classes.

- **Free Skills**—*www.freeskills.com*
  As stated on its Web site in the Press Info section,
  FreeSkills.com was created by Visualsoft UK Ltd. It
  describes itself as "a totally free Internet-based training site
  offering a wide range of training courses with no charge

whatsoever to the user. Currently, the site features IT courses ranging from MS Word 97 Essentials, right through to NT 4.0 Systems Support, MS SQL Server, and Novell NetWare design, with new and updated courses being added all the time...."

- **Mind Edge**—*www.mindedge.com*
  MindEdge bills itself as "the Web's premier resource for adult learning, training, and continuing education. Find courses around the corner or around the world." Go to the right sidebar to use this Web site's extensive search function that allows visitors to qualify their search criteria with various types of distance learning courses, price ranges, and starting dates.

- **OnlineLearning.net**—*www.onlinelearning.net*
  According to this Web site, "OnlineLearning.net is the leading online supplier of instructor-led continuing adult education and holds the exclusive worldwide electronic rights to classes developed by the renowned UCLA Extension for online delivery. Accredited courses are offered in Business & Management, Computers & Information Systems, Education, and Writing.

  "OnlineLearning.net offers other instructor-led courses from the University of San Diego, the California CPA Education Foundation, and curriculum materials publisher Houghton Mifflin. All instructor-led courses offered through OnlineLearning.net provide academic or professional credit.

  "OnlineLearning.net also offers its own instructor-led Computer Certification Programs & Courses, including Microsoft Certification, Certified Novell Engineer, A+ Certification, Cisco, and Red Hat Linux courses."

- **World Wide Learn**—*www.worldwidelearn.com*
  Based in Calgary, Alberta, Canada, the World Wide Learn Web site "celebrates online education with a categorized directory of online learning resources and acts as a gateway to courses, tutorials, classes, degrees, and workshops from around the world that are offered entirely online and avail-

able to adult learners worldwide." Check out the long list of links to online courses and learning guides located in the left sidebar.

Wrapping It Up

As you can see, the Web is loaded with sites devoted to online learning. This already vast, rapidly growing, and oftentimes confusing network of knowledge that's available anytime and anywhere needs to be lassoed and tamed before it gets out of hand. At the same time, it's good to know that there are numerous options to choose from. Possibly the best advice is to be careful about what you pay for, to try going with well-known and reputable online learning companies, and to take a look at all the free stuff that's out there before you pay for anything.

Here's what was covered in this final chapter:

- You learned about four Web portals to online learning: HungryMinds.com, SmartPlanet.com, Learn.com, and Learn2.com.

- You learned how to access free online classes at these four Web sites.

- You were introduced to nine more Web sites devoted to providing you with online education that you can access from anywhere at any time as long as you have a computer and an Internet connection.

This concludes this chapter—and the book, except for the appendix that follows. Hopefully you have enjoyed what you read, will find the appendix useful, and have discovered some information that benefits your quest to learn over a lifetime.

Congratulations! You are now the consummate master of an educational universe that can be found only on the World Wide Web.

PART V

Appendixes

APPENDIX A

Web Site Directory

As you already know, the World Wide Web has more than enough information about higher education. To discover higher education Web sites that might interest you, just go to a search engine and type in some keywords. However, search engine results are usually fraught with Web site links that are not related to what you really want to know. Here's an alternative approach to sifting through search engine results: This appendix lists all the important Web sites mentioned in this book, sorted by chapter topic. If you recall a Web site you read about in this book, you don't have to sift through all the pages or use a search engine to find it. Instead, look through this list of sites to find the URL you're looking for and save yourself some time and energy.

Chapter 1: Finding College and University Web Sites and Guidebooks Online

www.ohiou.edu

Ohio University

www.pcwebopedia.com

Online dictionary of Internet and computer-related terms

www.campustours.com

Source for virtual college tours

www.microsoft.com/windows/mediaplayer/en/default.asp

Where to get Windows Media Player

www.apple.com/quicktime/download

Where to get QuickTime

www.real.com/player

Where to get RealPlayer

www.macromedia.com/shockwave/download

Where to get Macromedia Shockwave/Flash

http://browserwatch.internet.com/plug-in.html

All about browser plug-ins

www.embark.com

Major Web portal to higher education sites

www.studyabroad.com

For students who want to study abroad

www.about.com

A site with everything about everything

www.yahoo.com

Major search engine

www.snap.com

Major search engine

http://searchenginewatch.com

Information and links to search engines

www.allaboutcollege.com

Web portal to higher education sites

www.collegenet.com

Web portal to higher education sites

http://collegeprep.okstate.edu

Web portal to higher education sites

www.collegexpress.com

Web portal to higher education sites

www.jayi.com

Fishnet: The College Guide

www.gocollege.com

Web portal to higher education sites

www.nces.ed.gov/ipeds/cool/Search.asp

National Center for Educational Statistics: IPEDS COOL Search

www.collegequest.com

Peterson's College Quest

www.powerstudents.com

Information about higher education

www.collegeboard.org

The College Board, makers of SAT and PSAT tests

www.collegebound.net

The College Bound Network, publishers of *College Bound* magazine

www.edunetwork.com

The Education Network Web portal to higher education sites

www.review.com

Princeton Review standardized test preparation services

www.usnews.com/usnews/edu

U.S. News Online higher education site

www.accesseric.org

Educational Resources Information Center (ERIC)

www.adobe.com/products/acrobat/readstep.html

The site for Adobe Acrobat Reader

www.ed.gov

U.S. Department of Education

www.amazon.com

Amazon.com booksellers and more

www.bn.com

Barnes and Noble booksellers and more

www.quintcareers.com/teen_books.html#college

For finding college guidebooks

www.collegeview.com

Web portal to higher education sites

Chapter 2: Choosing the Right College

www.collegeispossible.org/choosing/calendar.htm

College Is Possible Web portal to higher education sites

www.newvisions.org/colguide.html#types

New Visions for Public Schools, from New York City

www.carnegiefoundation.org

Carnegie Classification of Institutions of Higher Education

www.edunetwork.com

The Education Network Web portal to higher education sites

http://eric-web.tc.columbia.edu/hbcu/index.html

Historically Black Colleges and Universities

www.nadeducation.adventist.org/main.html

Seventh Day Adventist Colleges and Universities

www.ajcunet.edu/

Jesuit Colleges and Universities

www.gospelcom.net/cccu/

Christian Colleges and Universities

www.elca.org/dhes/colleges/college.html

Evangelical Lutheran Church of America Colleges and
Universities

www.hillel.org

Hillel: The Foundation for Jewish Campus Life

www.nccaa.org/
National Catholic College Admission Association

www.sciencewise.com/molis/
Minority On-Line Information Service

http://collegefund.org/main.htm
American Indian College Fund

http://strong.uncg.edu/colleges.html
Listing of residential colleges worldwide

www.usnews.com/usnews/edu/college/cosearch.htm
U.S. News Online's college search function Web page

www.nces.ed.gov
U.S. Department of Education's National Center for Education Statistics

www.nces.ed.gov/ipeds/cool/Search.asp
Integrated Postsecondary Education Data System College Opportunities On-Line

www.epinions.com
Epinions Web site

www.usnews.com/usnews/edu/college/corank.htm
College rankings from *U.S. News* Online

http://4colleges.4anything.com
Links to college ranking sites

www.library.uiuc.edu/edx/rankings.htm
University of Illinois at Urbana-Champaign ranks the rankings

www.embark.com
Web portal to higher education sites

www.review.com
The Princeton Review

www.ecollegebid.org

eCollegeBid allows you to bid on college tuition

www.collegeboard.com/press/cost99/html/991005.html

College Board Web site section about tuition and fees

www.collegeboard.com/toc/html/tocstudents000.html

College Board Web site section about choosing and preparing
for college

www.mapping-your-future.org

Web site related to career planning

www.aacc.nche.edu/allaboutcc/snapshot.htm

American Association of Community Colleges

www.collegenet.com

Web portal to higher education sites

http://collegeprep.okstate.edu/

Advice on how to prepare for college visits

www.collegeboard.com/features/campus/html/framcamp.html

College Board's guide to campus visits

www.usnews.com/usnews/edu/college/find/covisits.htm

U.S. News Online's section on campus visits

www.college-visits.com

College Visits, Inc., Web site

www.niep.com/pages/cp.html

National Institute for Educational Planning

www.collegiatechoice.com

Collegiate Choice Walking Tours Videos

www.nacac.com/exhibit/fair.cfm

National Association for College Admission Counseling

Chapter 3: Communicating with Undergraduates and College-Bound Peers

www.usc.edu

University of Southern California

www.utexas.edu/world/personal

University of Texas at Austin Web section on student personal Web sites

http://www2.lehigh.edu

Lehigh University

www.newsdirectory.com/college/press

Links to college newspaper Web sites

www.review.com

The Princeton Review

www.embark.com

Web portal to higher education sites

www.mapping-your-future.org/services/chatnight.htm

Hosts live college chat sessions

http://collegelife.about.com/education/collegelife/mpboards.htm

About.com's College Life discussion board section

Chapter 4: Applying Online

www.asu.edu/admissions/applyingtoasu

Arizona State University's admissions department

www.uchicago.edu/uchi/admissions/menu.html

University of Chicago's admissions department

www.embark.com/apply

Embark.com's apply to college section

www.embark.com/college/LINKS/search/findschool.stm

Embark.com's college search section

www.review.com

The Princeton Review

www.collegeboard.com/collapps/html/index000.html

The College Board's college application section

www.commonapp.org

The Common Application

www.collegexpress.com

Web portal to higher education sites

www.powerstudents.com

Information about higher education

www.collegexpress.com/admissions/index.html

The College Express admissions section

www.usnews.com/usnews/edu/college/apply/coappfaq.htm

U.S. News Online's FAQ section on college applications

www.achievaprep.com

Achieva guidance counseling service

www.petersons.com

Peterson's Education Supersite

www.jayi.com

Fishnet: The College Guide

Chapter 5: Perfecting Your Essay Online

www.collegeboard.org/frstlook/cae/html/cae_toc.html

Excerpts from the College Board's The College Application Essay book

www.m-w.com/dictionary.htm

Merriam-Webster's Collegiate Dictionary

www.collegeboard.org/collapps/essay/html/indx000.html

College Board's advice on writing the application essay

www.back2college.com/essay1.htm

Application essay advice

www.collegegate.com

Editing service

www.collegexpress.com/admissions/essay.html

Application essay advice

www.usnews.com/usnews/edu/college/coessay.htm

Application essay advice and articles

www.bartleby.com/141/index.html

William Strunk Jr.'s *Elements of Style*

http://andromeda.rutgers.edu/~jlynch/Writing

Grammar and style guide

www.nytimes.com

The New York Times

www.ivyessays.com

Editing service

http://user.mc.net/~moeller/essays/essays.htm

Sample application essays

http://www2.rogue.cc/OWL/College/exbuck.htm

Sample application essays

www.aci-plus.com/tips/tips21.htm

Sample application essays

www.myessay.com

Editing service

Chapter 6: Your Guide to the PSAT, SAT, and ACT Tests

www.pbs.org/wgbh/pages/frontline/shows/sats/

PBS *Frontline*'s "Secrets of the SAT Test"

www.collegeboard.org

The College Board

www.ets.org

Educational Testing Service

www.act.org

ACT test Web site

www.powerprep.com:

SAT and ACT test preparation

www.testprep.com:

SAT test preparation

www.4Tests.com

SAY and ACT test preparation

www.review.com

The Princeton Review test preparation

www.kaptest.com

Kaplan, Inc., test preparation

www.nytimes.com

The New York Times

www.amazon.com

Amazon.com bookseller

www.bn.com

Barnes & Noble bookseller

Chapter 7: Finding and Applying for Financial Aid Online

www.collegeispossible.org/paying/glossary.htm

Glossary of financial aid terms

http://cuinfo.cornell.edu/UAO/finaid.html.

Cornell University financial aid office

www.collegeboard.org/toc/html/tocfinancialaid000.html

The College Board's financial aid section

www.finaid.org

Financial aid Web site

www.ed.gov/offices/OSFAP/Students

U.S. Department of Education financial aid section

www.collegeboard.org/finaid/fastud/html/efc.html

The College Board's EFC calculator

www.ed.gov/prog_info/SFA/StudentGuide/2000-1/need.html

U.S. Department of Education section about the EFC

www.finaid.org/calculators/finaidestimate.phtml

Finaid's EFC calculator

www.ed.gov/prog_info/SFA

Free publications from the U.S. Department of Education

www.ed.gov/prog_info/SFA/StudentGuide/2000-1

Contact information for federal financial aid programs

www.fafsa.ed.gov

FAFSA Web site

www.ed.gov/offices/OSFAP/Students/apply/fexpress.html

To obtain FAFSA software

www.ed.gov/offices/OPE/express.html

To obtain PDF version of FAFSA

www.ed.gov/prog_info/SFA/FAFSA/instr00-1/index.html

Step-by-step instructions for filling out the FAFSA

http://easi.ed.gov

U.S. Department of Education's EASI project

www.uwsp.edu/stuserv/finance/apply/myths.htm

Ten myths about financial aid

www.finaid.org/fafsa/cssprofile.phtml

Information on the difference between the CSS PROFILE and the FAFSA

www.collegeboard.org/finaid/fastud/html/proform.html

To fill out the CSS PROFILE online

http://easi.ed.gov/studentcenter/html/apply/state.html

Listing of state grant and state guaranty agencies

www.finaid.org/otheraid/prepaid.phtml

All about prepaid tuition programs

http://financialaid.uoregon.edu/SC-guide.htm

University of Oregon's information about scholarships

www.fastweb.com

Free scholarship search service online

www.collegeboard.org/fundfinder/html/ssrchtop.html

The College Board's scholarship search service

www.usnews.com/usnews/edu/dollars/scholar/search.htm

U.S. News Online's scholarship search service

www.embark.com

Web portal to higher education

http://search.cashe.com

Sallie Mae Cash for Education

www.salliemae.com

Sallie Mae student loan service

www.scholarships.com

Information about financial aid

www.freescholarships.com

Free scholarships give-away Web site

www.usnews.com/usnews/edu/dollars/ffaid.htm

U.S. News Online's section on student loans

www.finaid.org/loans

Finaid's section on student loans

www.ed.gov/offices/OPE/guaranty.html

State guaranty agencies

www.estudentloan.com

Student loan finder service

www.bankofamerica.com/studentbanking

Bank of America Student Banking Center

http://fry.educationone.com/edonesplash.asp

Bank One student loan service

www.studentloan.com

Citibank's Student Loan Corporation

www.educaid.com

First Union's financial aid and student loan site

www.ed.gov/offices/OSFAP/Students/taxcuts/credits.html

U.S. Department of Education information about tax credits

www.finaid.org/otheraid/tax.phtml

Finaid's section on tax credits

www.ed.gov/offices/OSFAP/Students/repayment/teachers

U.S. Department of Education information on loan forgiveness programs

www.finaid.org/loans/forgiveness.phtml

Finaid's section on loan forgiveness programs

Chapter 8: Shopping for Housing Deals, Student Discounts, and More

www.nces.ed.gov

The National Center for Student Statistics

http://www1.umn.edu/housing/student/index.shtml

University of Minnesota student housing section

www.residentassistant.com

Web site for Resident Assistants

http://ajr.newslink.org

American Journalism Review

www.collegemomadvice.com/getready/whattopack.shtml

What-to-pack advice from the College Mom Advice site

www.studentadvantage.com

Student e-commerce site with discounts

www.edu.com

Student e-commerce site with discounts

www.ibm.com

IBM

www.gradware.com

Computer hardware and software for students

www.studentcredit.com

Student credit card services

www.bigwords.com

Online textbook seller

www.ecampus.com

Online textbook seller

www.efollet.com

Online textbook seller

www.textbooks.com

Online textbook seller

www.varsitybooks.com

Online textbook seller

www.campusbooks.com

Textbook price-comparison service

www.limespot.com

Textbook price-comparison service

www.vivasmart.com

Textbook price-comparison service

www.amtrak.com/student.html

Amtrak for students

www.travelocity.com

Air fares and travel reservations

www.aa.com

American Airlines

www.collegeplus.com

United Airline's program for students

www.counciltravel.com

Student travel services

www.smarterliving.com/student

Student travel discounts

www.railconnection.com

Europass and Eurailpass

www.isecard.com

International Student Exchange Card

www.hostels.com

Information on hostels and hostelling

www.statravel.com

For students traveling abroad

www.eurotrip.com

For students traveling abroad

Chapter 9: Conducting Research Online and Writing Papers

www.powa.org

Paradigm Online Writing Assistant

www.google.com

Search engine

http://owl.english.purdue.edu/

Online Writing Lab at Purdue University

http://owl.english.purdue.edu/Files/132/introduction.html

Writing a research paper workshop

http://departments.colgate.edu/diw/NWCAOWLS.html

Links to online writing labs

www.researchpaper.com

Research paper assistance

www.elibrary.com

Infonautic's electronic library

www.dushkin.com/online/study/dgen2.mhtml

Dushkin-McGraw Hill site about research papers

http://owl.english.purdue.edu/Files/34.html

Information about APA and MLA styles

www.apa.org/books/4210010.html

APA style guide

www.apa.org/apa-style

APA Style Helper software

www.mla.org

MLA style guide

http://webster.commnet.edu/mla.htm

MLA style guide

www.albany.edu/library/internet

University at Albany library

www.refdesk.com

Reference-related site

http://websearch.about.com/internet/websearch/library/weekly/a
a061199.htm

Information about the Invisible Web

http://dmoz.org

Open Directory Project

http://gwis2.circ.gwu.edu/~gprice/direct.htm

Direct Search database

www.thebighub.com

The Big Hub database

www.ipl.org

Internet Public Library

www.library.regents.edu

Regents College library

www.ipl.org/teen/aplus

A+ Research and Writing for High School and College Students

www.ipl.org/teen/aplus/internet.htm

Learning to research on the Web

www.vanguard.edu/faculty/R_Harris/search.htm

List of research links

www.studentadvantage.com

Student Advantage

www.britannica.com

Updated *Encyclopedia Britannica* online

www.loc.gov

The Library of Congress

www.libraryspot.com

The Library Spot

www.bibliomania.com

Full texts of classic fiction online

http://etext.lib.virginia.edu

University of Virginia library

http://leo.stcloudstate.edu/catalogue.html

The Write Place Catalogue

www.plagiarism.org

Antiplagiarism site

www.bartleby.com/99

A Collection of Passages, Phrases, and Proverbs Traced to Their
Sources in Ancient and Modern Literature

www.iss.stthomas.edu/studyguides

Study guides and strategies from the University of St. Thomas

www.iln.net

The Interactive Learning Network

http://personal.cfw.com/~clayford

Curious and useful math

www.biology.arizona.edu

University of Arizona biology site

Chapter 10: Choosing a Major and Discovering Your Career Goals

www.careersandcolleges.com

Help with choosing college majors and career paths

gopher://minerva.acc.virginia.edu/00/pubs/career/handouts/1/6

Bell Atlantic's Choosing and Using Your Major

www.uncwil.edu/stuaff/career/majors.htm

University of North Carolina at Wilmington's (UNCW) Career Services Department

www.collegeview.com/guidance/experts/choosingmajor/index.epl

CollegeView's online guidance office

www.embark.com/college/cm/maj/art/majart.stm

Embark.com's choosing a major section

www.embark.com/college/cm/maj/majint/toc.stm

Embark.com's Inside Scoop on Top Majors

www.psu.edu/dus/md/mdmisper.htm

Penn State's Common Misconceptions About Choosing a Major

www.college.upenn.edu/requirements/factors.html

University of Pennsyvania's Choosing a Major: Factors to Consider

www.quintcareers.com)

Quintessential Careers Web site

www.queendom.com/tests/success.html

Success likelihood test

www.ncsu.edu/careerkey

The Career Key

http://self-directed-search.com

Online self-assessment test

http://stats.bls.gov/ocohome.htm

Occupational Outlook Handbook

http://mooni.fccj.org/~gharr/free.htm

Free career options booklet

Chapter 11: Finding Jobs and Internship Programs Online

www.berkeley.edu

University of California, Berkeley

www.monster.com

Job search site

http://ajr.newslink.org

American Journalism Review

www.epinions.com/educ-FA_Jobs

Epinions on student employment

www.coolworks.com.

Where to find "cool" jobs

http://collegegradjobs.about.com/careers/collegegradjobs/msub-seasonal.htm

About.com's seasonal job search information

www.jobmonkey.com

Job Monkey

www.student.com/subsection/summerjobs

Student.com's summer jobs section

www.internshipprograms.com

For finding internships

www.review.com

The Princeton Review

www.studentadvantage.com

Student Advantage

Chapter 12: Having Fun Online

www.uzone.com

Uzone student culture site

www.studyfree.com

Academic resources for the e-generation

www.student.com

Student culture site

www.newsu.com

Student news

www.sexualrecords.com

World's sexual records

www.napster.com

MP3 site

www.zdnet.com/gamespot

ZDNet Gamespot

www.station.sony.com

Sony Online Entertainment

www.dmoz.org/Games

DMOZ Open Directory's games database

www.roleplaygames.about.com/games/roleplaygames

About.com's role-playing games site

www.funcom.com

Free online games

http://zone.msn.com/default.asp

Microsoft Network Game Zone

www.greekchat.com

Greek organizations chat site

www.greekpages.com
Links to Greek organizations

www.stophazing.org
Anti-hazing site

www.greekcentral.com
Information about Greek organizations

www.freebiestuff.com
Site for freebies

www.100percentfreestuff.com
Site for freebies

www.greek101.com
Shopping for Greek stuff

www.cbs.com/lateshow/topten
David Lettermen's Top Ten

www.cbs.com
CBS Television

www.soapcentral.com
Soap Opera Central

http://www.tvguide.com/soaps
TV Guide's soap opera section

www.abc.go.com/soaps/soaps_home.html
ABC's soap opera section

www.mtv.com
MTV

www.ticketmaster.com
Ticketmaster

www.entertaindom.com
Entertainment site

Chapter 13: Welcome to the Age of the Virtual Campus

www.rit.edu

Rochester Institute of Technology (RIT)

http://distancelearning.rit.edu

RIT's distance learning program

www.ed.gov.com

U.S. Department of Education

www.chea.org

Council for Higher Education Accreditation

http://distancelearn.about.com/education/distancelearn/msubac-cred.htm

Information about accreditation from About.com

http://online.uophx.edu

University of Phoenix distance learning program

http://distancelearn.about.com/education/distancelearn/mbody.htm

About.com's distance learning section

www.edpath.com

Guide to complete higher education distance learning degree and certificate programs

www.ed-x.com

The Distance Learning Channel

www.R1edu.org

Distance learning programs at 28 major universities

www.petersons.com/dlearn

Peterson's Lifelong Learning Channel

http://dir.yahoo.com/Education/Distance_Learning/Colleges_and_Universities

Yahoo!'s distance learning databases

www.hungryminds.com

Hungry Minds

www.collegeboard.org/ap/index.html

College Board's pages on Advanced Placement

www.apex.netu.com

Apex Learning

Chapter 14: Are You Cut Out for Distance Learning?

http://distancelearn.about.com/education/distancelearn/msubstudents.htm

About.com's distance learning student resources section

http://nces.ed.gov/pubs2000/2000013.pdf

National Center for Education Statistics report on distance postsecondary distance education

www.chronicle.com/distance

Chronicle of Higher Education's distance learning section

http://illinois.online.uillinois.edu/model/StudentProfile.htm

Illinois Online Network

www.softbook.com

Softbook eBooks

www.access-board.gov/RULES/508nprm.htm

Access Board's Standards for Electronic and Information Technology

www.cast.org/bobby

Center for Applied Statistics

www.academyonline.com/access_matters/access_0799.htm

Academy Online's section on Web access

www.w3.org/TR/1999/WAI-WEBCONTENT-19990505

W3C's Web content accessibility guidelines

Chapter 15: A Smorgasbord of Online Learning

www.hungryminds.com

Hungry Minds' online courses

www.lguide.com

Comparison shop for online courses

www.smartplanet.com

Smart Planet's online courses

www.learn.com

Free online courses

www.learn2.com

Learn2.com's online courses

www.barnesandnobleuniversity.com

Barnes & Noble University

www.edupoint.com

Edupoint's continuing education portal

www.ehow.com

Free online courses

www.emind.com

Emind's online courses

www.free-ed.net

Free online courses

www.freeskills.com

Free online courses

www.mindedge.com

Mind Edge's online courses

www.onlinelearning.net

Online Learning's online courses

www.worldwidelearn.com

World Wide Learn's online courses

APPENDIX B

Glossary

A

accreditation   A process in which an educational institution is recognized as a viable place to learn. Standards are established by various accrediting agencies composed of educational experts. If an institution meets the standards set down by the agency, it is acknowledged with accreditation status.

adult learner   A college or university student who is over the age of 24. These students typically hold down full-time jobs or have family responsibilities in addition to educational desires.

Advanced Placement (AP)   According to the College Board, who develops and administers the Advanced Placement program, "AP gives you the chance to try college-level work in high school, and to gain valuable skills and study habits for college. If you get a 'qualifying' grade on the AP exam, there are thousands of colleges worldwide that will give credit or advanced placement for your efforts."

American College Test (ACT)   A standardized test that is about 5 minutes shorter than the three-hour SAT test. The ACT has four sections: English, math, reading, and science reasoning. You can take the ACT five times over a period of one year. Each section of the ACT is given a separate score on a scale of 1 to 36. You'll also be given an average composite score of all four sections. The current average composite score is approximately 20.5.

American Psychological Association (APA)   One of two major research-paper writing styles. In relation to research papers, APA style conforms to specific rules for quoting and citing sources and references in a term paper, including the proper format for citing electronic sources. The emphasis in APA style is usually on the author's last name and date of publication. *See also* MLA.

application essay   An important piece of your overall application to a college or university. The application essay can give admissions officers a more personalized perspective of an applicant. Additionally, the essay is an obvious reflection of an applicant's writing ability, and is sometimes seen as an indirect reflection of a student's brainpower.

assessment tests   Tests that can help you figure out the kind of career you might want to consider pursuing or that expose the kinds of skills you have. Many of these assessment tests are available online for free. Such tests, from a pure vanity standpoint, are fun to take, but they can also spur some interesting thoughts concerning your future.

asynchronous learning/teaching   A method of instruction in which the process of learning and the process of teaching do not occur simultaneously or in conjunction with each other. A good example of asynchronous learning/teaching is a videotaped lecture that a student brings home and views at his or her own convenience. *See also* synchronous learning/teaching.

B

Beta tester   A person who agrees to test preliminary versions (Beta versions) of software and also reports any problems with the software to the manufacturer.

Bobby   Created by the Center for Applied Statistics, an educational not-for-profit organization, Bobby is a Web-based tool that analyzes Web pages for their accessibility to people with disabilities.

C

cable modem   A modem that operates through a cable television line.

Carnegie Classifications   A system developed by The Carnegie Foundation in 1970 "to provide more meaningful and homogeneous categories" for classifying colleges and universities. Currently, there are nine general classifications and ten classifications within a "specialized institutions" category.

chat room   A place on the Web where two or more Internet users can engage in a live conversation that is typed in from their respective computer keyboards.

co-op   An on-site work experience related to your field of study or career interest. A co-op differs from an internship in that an internship is usually a one-time assignment, whereas a co-op involves repeated assignments.

college   An education institution that primarily awards bachelor's degrees, some master's degrees, and possibly some associate's degrees.

college fair   The higher education version of a corporation trade show. College fairs are held in convention centers around the country throughout the year. These fairs are sponsored by the National Association for College Admission Counseling (NACAC) and are endorsed by the National Association of Secondary School Principals (NASSP).

Common Application   The recommended form used by 209 selective, independent colleges and universities for admission to their undergraduate programs.

community college   A primarily two-year institution that awards associate's degrees.

Continuing Education Units (CEUs)   CEUs offer formal documentation, recognized by major institutions in the United States, that you've completed a class.

CSS Financial Aid PROFILE   A financial aid application service administered by the College Scholarship Service, which is the financial aid division of the College Board. The CSS Profile is used as the basis for awarding nonfederal financial aid dollars.

D

Digital Subscriber Line (DSL)   A high-speed data transmission line that works using telephone wires.

discussion board   A place online where visitors can openly exchange messages and ideas. Also referred to as a bulletin board, discussion forum, or group and message board, a discussion board usually consists of threaded messages.

domain name   *See* URL.

E

Early Action (EA)   An admission process in which a student is permitted to apply to institutions of preference and receive a decision in advance of the normal response date. The student is not committed to enroll at the institution or to make a deposit before May 1. (Note that the EA process includes practices known as *early notification* and *early evaluation*.)

Early Decision (ED)   An admission process in which a commitment is made by a student to the institution that, if admitted, he or she will enroll. Although the student may apply to other colleges, he or she may have only one ED application pending at a time. If accepted by the college to which he or she has applied ED, the student is required to withdraw all other applications and make a non-refundable deposit by a date well before May 1.

eBooks   A technology that enables you to download books, magazines, and more into a hand-held device with a monitor about the size of a textbook.

.edu   The URL suffix for college and university sites worldwide.

Elements of Style, The   A popular book on grammar and writing style written by William Strunk, Jr., back in 1918 and still used widely today.

essay   According to Webster's Collegiate Dictionary, an essay is "an analytic or interpretative literary composition usually dealing with its subject from a limited or personal point of view."

Expected Family Contribution (EFC)   A term you'll encounter when searching for financial aid. According to the College Board, the EFC "is the amount the college will expect you and your family to pay—in other words, your share of the total college costs. The EFC is determined based on an analysis of a family's income and assets."

F

Federal Methodology (FM)   One way of calculating your EFC. FM is used for federal or state government financial aid programs. *See also* IM.

Federal Supplemental Educational Opportunity Grant (FSEOG) Another financial need-based grant that does not have to be repaid. According to the Department of Education, FSEOG is for undergraduate students with "exceptional" financial need—in other words, students with the lowest EFCs. The grant also gives priority to students who receive Federal Pell Grants. FSEOG awards are between $100 and $4,000.

Federal Work-Study (FWS) A form of federal financial aid. These programs help students find jobs, usually consisting of community-service work or jobs related to the student's field of study. Pay is at least minimum wage and could be higher depending on a student's skills or the type of work involved. The amount you earn can't exceed the total of your FWS award.

financial aid An umbrella term for any of the multitude of ways a student can acquire the money to pay for a college education. Forms of financial aid include loans, grants, scholarships, and the work-study program.

Free Application for Federal Student Aid (FAFSA) The U.S. Department of Education's form you fill out to qualify for various federal financial aid programs, including the Pell Grant.

G

grant A form of financial aid given by the government that you don't have to repay. There are two major categories of grants: federal and state.

Greek organizations An important part of campus life for many students. These fraternity and sorority organizations offer a wide variety of social, educational, and community-service oriented activities.

H

hazing The right-of-passage rituals frequently associated with pledging a fraternity or sorority. Hazing has taken some vicious turns in recent years, and many colleges and universities forbid these activities.

Holland's Personality Life-Styles   Six personality styles that are the basis of a test created by career-theory expert Dr. John Holland. The highest score you get is considered your personality type. The theory is that people who work in places that are congruent to their personality type will more than likely be successful and happy in their careers.

Hope Scholarship Credit   One of two federal tax credit systems available for students. Under the Hope Scholarship, you can receive a maximum tax credit of $1,500. *See also* Lifetime Learning Credit.

hostelling   The act of traveling and staying in hostels. This mode of travel is often called "backpacking" in many parts of the world and is perhaps best described as "traveling cheaply with an adventurous spirit." Hostels usually offer dormitory-style accommodations with large shared rooms and bunk beds, a common bathroom, and maybe a self-serve kitchen area.

I–K

Institutional Methodology (IM)   One way of calculating your EFC. IM is used primarily for school or private financial aid programs (and is used in conjunction with another form, called the CSS Financial Aid Profile). *See also* FM.

International Student ID Card (ISIC)   A student identification card endorsed by the United Nations and recognized worldwide. The acronym is usually pronounced "eye-zic," and it will get you international discounts on airfares, accommodations, travel insurance, and much more.

internship   An on-site work experience directly related to either your major field of study or your career interest.

Invisible Web   Online databases that are not usually accessible through a search engine. The search engine spiders and crawlers that find and index Web sites are unable to find these databases.

L

Lifetime Learning Credit   One of two federal tax credit systems available for students. Under the Lifetime Learning Credit, you can receive a maximum tax credit of $1,000. *See also* Hope Scholarship Credit.

loan   One of the major forms of financial aid available to students. There are many types of loans available, including federal-backed student or parent loans, private loans, college-based loans, special loans that can be forgiven under particular circumstances, and more.

M–N

Macromedia Shockwave/Flash   A video, audio, and animation browser plug-in developed by Macromedia, Inc.

Modern Language Association (MLA)   One of two major research-paper writing styles. MLA style conforms to very specific rules for quoting and citing sources and references in a term paper. The emphasis in MLA style is on the title of a work. *See also* APA.

Myers-Briggs Type Indicator (MBTI)   A popular personality-assessment test used today by many employers. Scores from the MBTI identify an individual as one of 16 possible personality types and can be interpreted to reveal learning, leadership, and managerial styles.

O

Occupational Outlook Handbook   A nationally recognized source of career information, designed to provide valuable assistance to individuals making decisions about their future work lives.

online distance learning   A method of learning in which the Web and all its capabilities are used to offer classes through an Internet connection. Students can enroll in classes and earn credit in an anytime, anywhere environment without ever setting foot inside a bricks-and-mortar classroom.

OWL (Online Writing Lab)   A college or university Web site that provides numerous resources to help students become better writers and researchers.

P

paper mill   One of many sites littered across the Web that sells complete term papers. Some students, who may be strapped for time because of other responsibilities, or who are just plain irresponsible, buy these finished term papers and turn them in as their own work.

Pell Grant   A financial-need based federal grant that does not have to be repaid. The maximum award for the 1999–2000 award year was $3,125.

Perkins Loan   The U.S. Department of Education says "a Federal Perkins Loan is a low-interest (5 percent) loan for both undergraduate and graduate students with exceptional financial need. Your school is your lender. The loan is made with government funds with a share contributed by the school. You must repay this loan to your school." Currently, you can borrow up to $4,000 per year of undergraduate study.

plagiarize   To steal and pass off someone else's ideas or words as your own.

plug-in   An application that gives an Internet browser more capabilities, such as playing various audio and video file formats.

PLUS Loan   A low-interest educational loan for parents who have a good credit rating. The interest should be no more than 9 percent, and rates can fluctuate each year of repayment. PLUS loans are known to have more flexible standards of credit worthiness than nonfederal loans. Loans are based on your cost of attendance less the total amount of financial aid you receive.

Portable Document Format (PDF)   A file format developed by Adobe Systems. PDF preserves all the fonts, formatting, colors, and graphics of any source document, regardless of the application and platform used to create it. PDF files are compact and can be shared, viewed, navigated, and printed exactly as intended by anyone with a free Adobe Acrobat Reader. You can download the Acrobat reader from *www.adobe.com/products/acrobat/readstep. html*.

portal   A Web site that provides access, or a doorway, to other Web sites. Portals usually offer a large selection of other resources and services such as online shopping, free email, newsletters and e-zine subscription services, online discussion boards, and compendiums of information about various topics of interest.

Preliminary Scholastic Aptitude Test/National Merit Scholarship Qualifying Test (PSAT/NMSQT)   The test that prepares you for the more important SAT test. Taking the PSAT also makes you eligible for the National Merit Scholarship. The PSAT test is 80 minutes in length and consists of two verbal, two math, and one writing skills sections. Scores are reported on a 20-to-80 scale with average scores near 50.

Q

Quick Time Virtual Reality (QTVR)   A panoramic picture format that is increasing in popularity on the Web. You can view a QTVR image only if you have the Quick Time software installed on your computer.

QuickTime   An audio and video browser plug-in developed by Apple Macintosh that is also available to PC users.

R

RealPlayer   An audio and video browser plug-in developed by real.com.

regional accreditation   Accreditation by an agency recognized by the Department of Education (DE) and the Council for Higher Education Accreditation (CHEA).

research universities I   Institutions of higher education that offer a full range of baccalaureate programs and give a high priority to research.

resident assistant (RA)   A student housing monitor and guidance counselor, as well as an administrative aide and liaison between the student residents and the student-housing department.

Role Playing Game (RPG)   A popular online game in which users create their own characters to inhabit various three-dimensional virtual worlds that are created by the makers of the games. You purchase the games on CD-ROM and then go to the game-maker's Web site to play and compete against multiple players simultaneously.

rush   The process of pledging to join a fraternity or sorority.

S

SAT II   A series of subject-oriented tests, ranging from writing and world history to Modern Hebrew and Chinese. Not all colleges require the SAT II. Each SAT II subject test is one hour long, and you cannot take more than three subject tests at one time. You can take the SAT II six times over a period of one year. All SAT II subject tests, except for the English language proficiency subject test, are scored on a scale of 200–800.

scholarship   A form of financial aid, usually given by companies, organizations, or private individuals, that you don't have to repay. Kinds of scholarships include academic scholarships, athletic scholarships, free scholarships, private scholarships, National Merit Scholarships, and more.

Scholastic Aptitude Test (SAT)   Also called the SAT I. This test is three hours in length and consists of seven sections: three verbal, three math, and one experimental. The experimental section is either math or verbal and is used for research purposes, so it's not tallied into your score. (You won't know which section is experimental when you take the test.) You can take the SAT seven times over a period of one year. You'll receive a score for the verbal section and a score for the math section with each scored on a scale of 200–800. The national average is about 500 in each section for a combined total of 1000. Schools that are relatively difficult to get into usually require higher-than-average scores.

Stafford Loan   A federal financial aid program. According to the U.S. Department of Education, "Direct and FFEL Stafford Loans are the Department's major form of self-help aid. Direct Stafford Loans are available through the William D. Ford Federal Direct Loan (Direct Loan) Program; FFEL Stafford Loans are available through the Federal Family Education Loan

(FFEL) Program. The terms and conditions of a Direct Stafford or a FFEL Stafford are similar. The major differences between the two are the source of the loan funds, some aspects of the application process, and the available repayment plans. Under the Direct Loan Program, the funds for your loan are lent to you directly by the U.S. government. Under the FFEL Program, the funds for your loan are lent to you from a bank, credit union, or other lender that participates in the FFEL Program." Qualified dependent students can borrow up to $2,625 during their first academic year. Qualified independent students can borrow up to $6,625 during their first academic year.

state grant agencies   One place to look for state financial aid. State grant agencies provide information and applications for financial aid specific to the individual state. *See also* state guaranty agencies.

state guaranty agencies   Local state agencies that handle the administration of student loans under the Federal Family Education Loan (FFEL) program. *See also* state grant agencies.

Student Aid Report (SAR)   A precise look at the information you provided on your FAFSA. The SAR includes your calculated EFC, which is used in determining the amount of money you and your family can afford to contribute toward the cost of your higher education.

synchronous learning/teaching   A method of instruction in which the process of learning and the process of teaching occur simultaneously, in real time. In addition to the traditional classroom instructional approach, an example of synchronous learning/teaching is an online chat room in which there are text-based, real-time communications between students and teachers. *See also* asynchronous learning/teaching.

T

theme-oriented dormitory   University housing in which students with similar interests and studies live together in the same building or on the same floor. Another version of this idea is substance-free student housing arrangements, wherein residents sign pledges not to take drugs or drink alcohol.

threaded messages   In online discourse, a series of posted messages in reply to a particular topic or topics.

Title IV   A classification set in place by the Higher Education Act of 1965 which establishes a school's eligibility to participate in federal student financial assistance programs administered by the U.S. Department of Education. Schools that are eligible under Title IV have various institution codes that designate different federal financial assistance programs available at various campuses.

Top Level Domain (TLD)   The suffix at the end of a URL. For universities and colleges around the world, the TLD is *.edu* (dot ee dee you).

trade/vocational college   An education institution that confers degrees in specific areas such as business, agriculture, liberal arts, law, education, engineering and technology, health science, military science and theology.

traditional student   A college or university student who is in the age group 18 to 23. These students generally take a full load of college-credit classes each semester they are enrolled in college. Traditional students can take advantage of online distance learning, although they usually don't as much as their adult learner counterparts.

transferability   The ability to transfer college credits, from one university to another, which can be applied toward a particular degree program. Not all institutions accept credits earned at other institutions; policies vary from institution to institution.

U–V

uniform resource locator (URL)   A Web site's global address. This is what you type into your browser's address bar to go to a Web site's home page.

university   An education institution that awards bachelor's, master's, and doctoral degrees.

W–Y

Webcam   A digital camera hooked up to a computer that hosts a Web page. Webcams allow viewers to see live images over the Internet. Note that many of the Webcams you find in Web sites may not be operational, or may show very choppy video images.

Windows Media Player   The Microsoft Windows browser plug-in used for playing audio and video files.

Workforce Investment Act   Signed by President Clinton in 1998, this act includes Section 508 of the Rehabilitation Act Amendments. Section 508 requires the Architectural and Transportation Barriers Compliance Board—the U.S. government agency known as the Access Board—to set standards for federal agencies to ensure that federal employees with disabilities have "comparable" access to and use of information and data to non-disabled federal employees.

World Wide Web Consortium (W3C)   A highly regarded and internationally renowned member-supported consortium, including both software vendors and a variety of consumers, whose goal is to establish international standards for the World Wide Web.

Z

zShops   An Amazon.com feature. When you buy from zShops, you buy from a private seller or company instead of buying directly from Amazon.com, which may or may not save you money. zShops are similar to Web auctions except that, in a zShop, prices are fixed (you can't bid a price on an item).

INDEX

Tell Us What You Think!

As the reader of this book, *you* are our most important critic and commentator. We value your opinion and want to know what we're doing right, what we could do better, what areas you'd like to see us publish in, and any other words of wisdom you're willing to pass our way.

You can email or write me directly to let me know what you did or didn't like about this book—as well as what we can do to make our books stronger.

Please note that I cannot help you with technical problems related to the topic of this book, and that due to the high volume of mail I receive, I might not be able to reply to every message.

When you write, please be sure to include this book's title and author as well as your name and phone or fax number. I will carefully review your comments and share them with the author and editors who worked on the book.

Email: *internet_sams@mcp.com*

Mail: Mark Taber
              Associate Publisher
              Sams Publishing
              201 West 103rd Street
              Indianapolis, IN 46290 USA

SAMS
Teach Yourself
Today

Mark Orwoll

SAMS
Teach Yourself
Today

e-Travel

Planning Vacations, Finding Bargains,
and Booking Reservations Online

AIRPLANE TICKETS   RESTAURANTS
HOTELS   RES
CAR RENTALS
CRUISES   & SOM
DESTINATION
DISCOUNTS $ PL   RVATIONS

Sams Teach Yourself
e-Travel Today

Planning Vacations, Finding Bargains,
and Booking Reservations Online

Mark Orwoll
ISBN: 0-672-31822-9
$17.99 US/$26.95 CAN